Daniel

A Commentary

By Chris White

D1571809

Edited by:
Leah Matthews
Copyright 2013 CWM Publishing
ISBN: 978-0-9912329-0-1

To my amazing wife and best friend Connie, for her steadfast love and support. You are a gift from God.

Table of Contents

Introduction

The Book of Daniel is one of the most important books in the Bible. It contains a great deal of practical information, as well as a wealth of technical details about future events.

It also helps us to trust in the preservation of scripture, as this book's historical claims have been validated through recent archeological finds, as well as recent linguistic discoveries.

It also contains many prophecies that should astound anyone who considers the implications that this book, written so long ago, was able to accurately predict the future.

For example the first 36 verses of chapter 11 describe future events so accurately that critics have had to claim that the Book of Daniel was written after the event it describes. They do this in order to defend their view that predictive prophecy is impossible, a position that is very difficult to maintain in this case because copies of the Book of Daniel have been found among the Dead Sea Scrolls, making it a very improbable notion that this book was written after the events described.

But it also is probably the single most important book in the Old Testament with regard to prophecies that have <u>yet</u> to be fulfilled. Of these prophecies none are more important to Daniel himself than the prophecies concerning the man we call the Antichrist and the period of time just preceding, and just after his so-called "abomination of desolation."

If one wants to fully understand the subject of the Antichrist, and the Last Days, they must become extremely familiar with the intricacies of this great book.

Though this book offers us so much information, it comes at a cost. The Book of Daniel is also one of the more difficult to understand in all of scripture when it comes to prophecy. It is my conviction however that the exact same face value, or literal hermeneutic, that we apply to any other portion of scripture should be applied to this book as well, and that doing so will demystify the more difficult sections that have historically been so controversial.

I think that any commentator of the Book of Daniel should be up-front with their biases because strongly held presuppositions have too often shaped the interpretation of this book in the past.

My main biases are as follows: I am firmly "premillennial" which means I believe that there is a literal 1000-year period that will occur after Jesus returns to Earth (Rev 20: 1-15). I am also "dispensational," meaning that I believe that God's many promises to the Jews will come to pass in the future, and that He is not done with them (Romans 11: 25-32). I also believe wholeheartedly in the inspiration and infallibility of scripture in its original languages.

I take great pains to discover the long-held beliefs and traditions of the church and rarely stray from them. That being said, there are a number of occasions in this book that I depart from some of these traditional interpretations. When I do this, I do so with great fear and trepidation. I am not one to take a different position on something simply because it is different. If I ever do this I hope you will agree that I at least have a sound argument for doing so, and even if you disagree, you should be able to see that the reason I departed was because of the hermeneutic that we probably share. In other words, I try to let hermeneutics trump tradition if they are ever in conflict.

So let us begin our study of Daniel, and I pray that the Holy Spirit guide me, the writer, and you, the reader, to teach us more about this book.

Chapter 1

Daniel Finds Favor in Babylon

Dan 1:1 In the third year of the reign of Jehoiakim king of Judah, Nebuchadnezzar king of Babylon came to Jerusalem and besieged it.
Dan 1:2 And the Lord gave Jehoiakim king of Judah into his hand, with some of the articles of the house of God, which he carried into the land of Shinar to the house of his god; and he brought the articles into the treasure house of his god.

This is a picture of Babylon who has just defeated Judah and is taking away spoils from Jerusalem, including many of the holy items that were in the temple.

Nebuchadnezzar king of Babylon came to Jerusalem and besieged it.

I think understanding the context will help us better understand the Book of Daniel, and get the most of this study, so I will take some time to describe it.

There were two main powers in the area at this time. Egypt, which had been a political power for a long time, in fact, it was probably one of the earliest political powers in the world, and the Neo-Babylonian kingdom, which was somewhat newer, but nevertheless very strong. It is Nebuchadnezzar, king of Neo-Babylonia who we see defeating Israel here.

These two powers, Egypt and Babylon, were fighting amongst each other as well. And at the same time Babylon was trying to expand its Empire.

Babylon had previously taken the northern parts of Israel captive at this time, and so Judah was all that was left of Israel, and was naturally very scared of Babylon. Because of this fear Judah made some political arrangements with Egypt to protect them against Babylon. This arrangement was against the explicit warnings of God through the prophets. God wanted Israel to trust in Him and turn from their sin, not look for protection from their enemies.

Just before this time, Egypt marched to Babylon planning on defeating their only rival for power in the area. The battle's name was the Battle of Carchemish, which we know about from a tablet called the "Nebuchadnezzar Chronicle" currently housed in the British Museum.

The Babylonians proved too strong for Egypt, and the Egyptian army took flight. Nebuchadnezzar, who at that time is only a general, not yet the king, though he is a prince and heir to his father's throne, pursues Pharaoh Neco's fleeing Egyptian army and wipes them out, making the Neo-Babylonian Empire the only game in town, so to speak.

Historians are not sure if it was on Nebuchadnezzar's way down to Egypt or on his way back from pursuing Neco's army that he besieged Israel, but besiege it he did in 605 BC.

This could be for a number of reasons: it could have been simply for the spoils that they would get from sacking Jerusalem, but it could also have been a kind of punishment because of Judah's political arrangement with the Egyptians. Either way it was now clear that such a seige would not bring repercussions from the Egyptians.

This is the first time Babylon besieged Judah. The Neo-Babylonians will do this two more times, which will ultimately end in Jerusalem's utter destruction.

And the Lord gave Jehoiakim king of Judah into his hand

This suggests that this attack, though terrible, was part of God's plan.

10

The prophets would warn Judah during this time, after they were initially defeated, telling them not to rebel against the Babylonian rule, that it was part of God's plan.

But they rebelled against Nebuchadnezzar, which ended up causing the last two sieges as well as Jerusalem's utter destruction.

With some of the articles of the house of God

We will hear more about these items later in the book. Apparently Nebuchadnezzar put them away not to be used, perhaps in a type of museum, but one of his descendants, Belshazzar, will take them out for use at the last Neo-Babylonian party in history.

In addition to these, the Babylonians also take another kind of treasure back to Babylon with them, that is the people of Israel, including the author of this book, Daniel.

Dan 1:3 Then the king instructed Ashpenaz, the master of his eunuchs, to bring some of the children of Israel and some of the king's descendants and some of the nobles.

King's descendants and some of the nobles

A prophecy is actually being fulfilled in this verse.

Hezekiah was warned by Isaiah that some of his descendants would be dragged off to Babylon and made Eunuchs (Isaiah 39:7.) This was because of Hezekiah's having looked to Egypt to save him and Judah as opposed to God, as well as many other things. The mentioning of the **king's descendants** being carried off here is certainly part of that fulfillment.

Dan 1:4 young men in whom there was no blemish, but good-looking, gifted in all wisdom, possessing knowledge and quick to understand, who had ability to serve in the king's palace, and whom they might teach the language and literature of the Chaldeans.

Dan 1:5 And the king appointed for them a daily provision of the king's delicacies and of the wine which he drank, and three years of training for them, so that at the end of that time they might serve before the king.

Nebuchadnezzar's tactic here is probably a wise one from the world's standpoint. He is taking children who will help, as it says: **serve in the king's palace.** This is a lot like Genghis Khan or similar leaders that really valued talent and looked for it in the people that they conquered.

The idea of taking the young people was probably because they would be easier to indoctrinate into the Babylonian ways, as well as being less likely to rebel.

Dan 1:6 Now from among those of the sons of Judah were Daniel, Hananiah, Mishael, and Azariah.
Dan 1:7 To them the chief of the eunuchs gave names: he gave Daniel the name Belteshazzar; to Hananiah, Shadrach; to Mishael, Meshach; and to Azariah, Abed-Nego.

It could be said that they had to change these names because their other names were Jewish, and had specific references to Yahweh in them.

For example, the name Daniel has "El" in it, which is God in Hebrew. It means "God is my judge."

Hananiah, had "Yah" in it, another name for God, and so on.

Whatever the reason was, they changed their names. Each of their new names has something to do with a Babylonian god.

Dan 1:8 But Daniel purposed in his heart that he would not defile himself with the portion of the king's delicacies, nor with the wine which he drank; therefore he requested of the chief of the eunuchs that he might not defile himself.

So what was he not **defiling himself** with here? Daniel gives a spiritual reason why he didn't want to do this to the chief eunuch. He didn't make excuses and say something like "I have health problems." This right off the bat begins to show us something of Daniel's character: he was bold about his faith.

The reason he didn't want to eat the food provided was almost certainly because the food was not kosher. Under the Mosaic law, they not only had to refrain from eating certain types of meats, but even meats that were allowed had to be killed in a certain way. Even if the meat provided was kosher, it was probably sacrificed to idols, which was a common Babylonian practice. All of these were the defilements that Daniel was trying to avoid.

I think one of the greatest lines in this whole chapter is that Daniel **purposed in his heart** not to do this.

This is the idea of repentance, or changing your mind. Choosing in your heart not to be defiled with sin is how one protects oneself from sin.

This was probably a dangerous thing for Daniel to do because he could have been branded as uncooperative. He was refusing the king's menu, and Nebuchadnezzar wasn't a guy you said no to.

Daniel was being bold here, but at least one of the reasons that he could be so bold and make this request is because of the next verse.

Dan 1:9 Now God had brought Daniel into the favor and goodwill of the chief of the eunuchs.

Daniel, like Joseph before him, was given favor with his captors, and they saw something in him that they liked. The text tells us that the reason for that was supernatural; that is that **God had brought Daniel into their favor**.

Daniel and Joseph have a lot in common. They're the only two 'big' characters in the Bible in which nothing bad is spoken of about them.

13

They both interpreted dreams to the king, which gave them favor with the king, and ultimately great government jobs in which they managed huge sections of their respective empires.

They were both people who lived through incredibly difficult circumstances but stayed faithful to God and knew He was with them.

Dan 1:10 And the chief of the eunuchs said to Daniel, "I fear my lord the king, who has appointed your food and drink. For why should he see your faces looking worse than the young men who are your age? Then you would endanger my head before the king."

The eunuch is afraid to do as Daniel asks because he doesn't want to be punished by Nebuchadnezzar if they don't turn out to be as healthy as Daniel thinks that they will be.

This eunuch was right to be afraid of Nebuchadnezzar. From what we know about Nebuchadnezzar, he was a very ruthless guy.

He would burn people alive. He would turn people's houses into "ash heaps."

He threatened to kill every single adviser he had because they wouldn't tell him the correct interpretation of his dream! In short, he's a guy that you don't want to mess with or your head would be rolling in no time at all.

So I can sympathize a bit with the eunuch's concerns here.

Dan 1:11 So Daniel said to the steward whom the chief of the eunuchs had set over Daniel, Hananiah, Mishael, and Azariah,
Dan 1:12 "Please test your servants for ten days, and let them give us vegetables to eat and water to drink.
Dan 1:13 Then let our appearance be examined before you, and the appearance of the young men who eat the portion of the king's delicacies; and as you see fit, so deal with your servants."

Dan 1:14 So he consented with them in this matter, and tested them ten days.
Dan 1:15 And at the end of ten days their features appeared better and fatter in flesh than all the young men who ate the portion of the king's delicacies.
Dan 1:16 Thus the steward took away their portion of delicacies and the wine that they were to drink, and gave them vegetables.

It's pretty self-evident what happened there. Daniel convinced the eunuch to give them a shot for ten days, and at the end of the ten days Daniel and his friends were indeed healthier than the others and the mission was a success.

Thus the steward took away their portion of delicacies

I used to think that the other captives were probably mad at Daniel for this, because the **delicacies** were taken away. But I don't think it was like that at all. The reason is because the other captives in this three-year program were most likely Jews taken at the same time as Daniel, though we cannot be certain of that.

If that is the case, however, then this was probably a great victory; they were now able to essentially eat a kosher diet in Babylon and not defile themselves.

Dan 1:17 As for these four young men, God gave them knowledge and skill in all literature and wisdom; and Daniel had understanding in all visions and dreams.

I think what is being spoken of here is not necessarily their book learning that they got from this program, though that is true. But here it says that **God gave them knowledge** and skill in all learning.

It could simply mean that God helped them with their academic studies, but because it also says that God gave Daniel understanding **in visions and dreams**, I believe that this verse is speaking of a supernatural gift that God had given Daniel and his three friends.

It's interesting how God blesses His people here.

In Daniel's life He gave him gifts of interpreting these dreams, which would ultimately be an extremely significant part of Daniel's ministry to the king. Nebuchadnezzar realizes that Daniel's God is bigger than his god because of this ability that God gave Daniel.

I think that this illustrates the talents and abilities that God gives each of us have a purpose and that we should use our talents in ways that glorify God.

**Dan 1:18 Now at the end of the days, when the king had said that they should be brought in, the chief of the eunuchs brought them in before Nebuchadnezzar.
Dan 1:19 Then the king interviewed them, and among them all none was found like Daniel, Hananiah, Mishael, and Azariah; therefore they served before the king.
Dan 1:20 And in all matters of wisdom and understanding about which the king examined them, he found them ten times better than all the magicians and astrologers who were in all his realm.**

So we find that God's helping them with their studies and giving those spiritual gifts had won them favor with the king in a big way. This idea that Nebuchadnezzar **interviewed them** is interesting because the word there actually denotes an intense interrogation.

There was a kind of test where you would go before Nebuchadnezzar and he would grill you with the questions or other tests.

It says they were **found ten times better**. The phrase there literally means "10 hands", and it doesn't necessarily mean 10 times better. It just is used to denote many times more than, not necessarily or specifically 10.

The magicians and astrologers

This appears to be two different job descriptions.

Like many other nations of the day, like Egypt, Babylon had a lot of occult practitioners as regular members of the king's entourage.

Dan 1:21 Thus Daniel continued until the first year of King Cyrus.

King Cyrus was the name of the king who conquered Babylon many years later.

Daniel lived to be 85 or 90 years old, but this verse isn't necessarily talking about when Daniel died. After citing the various meanings for the word "**continued**" and interacting with other arguments, Stephen Miller of the New American Commentary writes:

> "Apparently the writer's point was that Daniel lived throughout the entire Neo-Babylonian period (the exile) and continued into the reign of Cyrus (when the Jews were released from captivity), thus outliving his Babylonian masters."[1]

Chapter 1   Daniel

Chapter 2

Nebuchadnezzar Has a Disturbing Dream

Dan 2:1 Now in the second year of Nebuchadnezzar's reign, Nebuchadnezzar had dreams; and his spirit was *so* troubled that his sleep left him.

Second year of Nebuchadnezzar's reign

We see this was early on in Nebuchadnezzar's kingdom; in fact Nebuchadnezzar at this time, was a new king of an almost brand-new empire.

Nebuchadnezzar's dad, Nabopolassar, was the first king of the so-called Neo-Babylonian Empire.

Before that the area was ruled by the Assyrians. Nabopolassar defeated the Assyrians and destroyed Nineveh, the Assyrian capital city.

Nebuchadnezzar had dreams

Some people take the plural **dreams** to mean that these dreams were occurring over a longer period.

Stephen Miller in the *New American Commentary* takes a slightly different approach saying:

> "Had dreams" probably should be understood to indicate that the king was in a state of dreaming rather than that he dreamed several dreams, for the text only reports one.

And his spirit was *so* troubled that his sleep left him.

19

Ancient peoples believed that dreams were messages from the gods, and Nebuchadnezzar apparently feared that the strange revelation contained some kind of message for him.

It's hard to say what troubled him about them, but it could be that he understood that the statue that he saw represented his kingdom and he wondered if it was an omen of its destruction, or it could be that he knew nothing of its interpretation but just knew that it was important.

Nebuchadnezzar might have even known this dream was from God. We see later it indeed was from God, and God has a way of making sure we know that a dream from him was not a normal dream.

Dan 2:2 Then the king gave the command to call the magicians, the astrologers, the sorcerers, and the Chaldeans to tell the king his dreams. So they came and stood before the king.
Dan 2:3 And the king said to them, "I have had a dream, and my spirit is anxious to know the dream."

The magicians, the astrologers, the sorcerers, and the Chaldeans

So he calls the people together that he thought might be able to help him interpret this dream. They were all occultists of one form or another. These types of occult advisors are also seen in Genesis with Pharaoh as well. This was apparently a common group of people to have at the Kings service in those days.

To tell the king his dreams

Miller points out that archeologists have found dream interpretation books from the time period in the region.

It is likely, based on the initial reaction of these guys, that they planned on using the methods laid out in books like Miller references to interpret his dream.

But as we will see, Nebuchadnezzar has decided this dream is far too important to be given the usual treatment, and he has come up with a plan to make sure that he finds out what it really means.

Dan 2:4 Then the Chaldeans spoke to the king in Aramaic, "O king, live forever! Tell your servants the dream, and we will give the interpretation."
Dan 2:5 The king answered and said to the Chaldeans, "My decision is firm: if you do not make known the dream to me, and its interpretation, you shall be cut in pieces, and your houses shall be made an ash heap.
Dan 2:6 However, if you tell the dream and its interpretation, you shall receive from me gifts, rewards, and great honor. Therefore tell me the dream and its interpretation."
Dan 2:7 They answered again and said, "Let the king tell his servants the dream, and we will give its interpretation."
Dan 2:8 The king answered and said, "I know for certain that you would gain time, because you see that my decision is firm:
Dan 2:9 if you do not make known the dream to me, there is only one decree for you! For you have agreed to speak lying and corrupt words before me till the time has changed. Therefore tell me the dream, and I shall know that you can give me its interpretation."
Dan 2:10 The Chaldeans answered the king, and said, "There is not a man on earth who can tell the king's matter; therefore no king, lord, or ruler has ever asked such things of any magician, astrologer, or Chaldean.
Dan 2:11 It is a difficult thing that the king requests, and there is no other who can tell it to the king except the gods, whose dwelling is not with flesh."

Then the Chaldeans spoke to the king in Aramaic, "O king, live forever!"

The mention of the word **Aramaic** here doesn't mean that these guys all of a sudden started speaking a different language. The use of this word here is probably a parenthetical notation placed in the text to mark the change in the written language, because at this very point in the text until the end of chapter 7, the language is not Hebrew but Aramaic.

Some people postulate that the reason it is in Aramaic from here until chapter 7 is because it deals with gentile history, and Aramaic was the gentile language of the time.

Tell your servants the dream, and we will give the interpretation

At first these advisors weren't blinking an eye about this. Interpreting dreams is actually pretty easy, because when you're speaking in symbols it is impossible to say you have the wrong interpretation.

Make known the dream to me, and its interpretation

It's possible that Nebuchadnezzar grew up watching these guys interpret his father's dreams, and that he had his doubts about their methods. It also could be, as one commentator said, a kind of "professional development program." In other words Nebuchadnezzar was using this as an opportunity to weed out the dead weight on his staff.

The Chaldeans

In this verse we have the first mention of **Chaldeans** as a class of soothsayers to the king. Critics cite the use of this word as a mistake that only a second century B.C. writer would make. Critics suppose that in Daniel's day, the term **Chaldean** was *only* used as a racial designation, describing what the Chaldeans thought was the "master race" who ruled Nebuchadnezzar's superpower empire.

> "But linguistic research has demonstrated that the Babylonian word for an astrologer-priest, and their word for their supposed master race, were homonyms, both having the sound **Chaldean** (*kas-du* in Babylonian), but

each retaining their own meaning. This is the same way that the English sound *tu* can mean *to*, *two*, or *too*.

Daniel's understanding of this is clear from the text, because he *also* uses the term **Chaldean** in its racial sense (Dan 3:8 and 5:30)." – David Guzik

In other words, recent science has once again silenced the mouths of the critical scholars regarding the Book of Daniel.

Dan 2:5 The king answered and said to the Chaldeans, "My decision is firm: if you do not make known the dream to me, and its interpretation, you shall be cut in pieces, and your houses shall be made an ash heap.

My decision is firm:

I don't see Nebuchadnezzar saying this with anger, instead I seem him saying it because he has made a logical decision about how to get the correct interpretation of this dream.

You shall be cut in pieces

This means they would be dismembered, a kind of torture, as well as execution.

Your houses shall be made an ash heap

This means that their family was also going to be affected, if not killed.

These were no idle threats by Nebuchadnezzar, whose harsh treatment of King Zedekiah (2 Kgs 25:7), two Jewish rebels named Ahab and Zedekiah (not King Zedekiah; Jer 29:22), and Daniel's three friends (chap. 3) prove that he would have no qualms about carrying out this cruel threat upon his counselors.[2]

Dan 2:7 They answered again and said, "Let the king tell his servants the dream, and we will give its interpretation."

Dan 2:8 The king answered and said, "I know for certain that you would gain time, because you see that my decision is firm:
Dan 2:9 if you do not make known the dream to me, *there is only* one decree for you! For you have agreed to speak lying and corrupt words before me till the time has changed. Therefore tell me the dream, and I shall know that you can give me its interpretation."

It's possible that their second response angered the king because he perceived that his counselors, after hearing his plans, were trying to **gain time**, or worse, planning on deceiving him in some way.

Dan 2:10 The Chaldeans answered the king, and said, "There is not a man on earth who can tell the king's matter; therefore no king, lord, or ruler has *ever* asked such things of any magician, astrologer, or Chaldean.

This was a bad move for these guys. Telling Nebuchadnezzar that no other king would do this or ask such a thing was like saying, "you're a bad king for asking this," even though in truth, it was a brilliant, but ruthless plan.

David Guzik puts it this way:

> "The strategy of the wise men was to convince the king that he was unreasonable, not that they were incompetent."

These men's lives ended a few moments later, but we also read that it was because of them saying this foolish thing to the king that the decree went out to kill <u>all</u> the wise men of Babylon.

Dan 2:12 For this reason the king was angry and very furious, and gave the command to destroy all the wise men of Babylon.
Dan 2:13 So the decree went out, and they began killing the wise men; and they sought Daniel and his companions, to kill them.

So in other words, when these close advisors to the king were called in it was only their lives that were on the line at that point. But because they offended the king with their response, Nebuchadnezzar decided that **all the wise men of Babylon** should all be done away with.

Dan 2:11 It is a difficult thing that the king requests, and there is no other who can tell it to the king except the gods, whose dwelling is not with flesh."

Except the gods, whose dwelling is not with flesh:

> "As far as these pagan magicians, astrologers, and wise men knew, this was true. They did not know what we know so plainly in Jesus - that He is *Immanuel, God with us* (Mat: 1:23)" – David Guzik

Dan 2:13 So the decree went out, and they began killing the wise *men;* and they sought Daniel and his companions, to kill *them.*
Dan 2:14 Then with counsel and wisdom Daniel answered Arioch, the captain of the king's guard, who had gone out to kill the wise *men* of Babylon;
Dan 2:15 he answered and said to Arioch the king's captain, "Why is the decree from the king so urgent?" Then Arioch made the decision known to Daniel.

Arioch, the captain of the king's guard

The chief executioner.

With counsel and wisdom

This means Daniel answered Arioch in good taste or in an accepted manner.

Why is the decree from the king so urgent?

Some translations have it as harsh instead of **urgent**. Both would be true. Based on the timeline this was probably very early in the morning, so it was obvious to Daniel that it was urgent, but it was clearly very harsh as well.

Dan 2:16 So Daniel went in and asked the king to give him time, that he might tell the king the interpretation.
Dan 2:17 Then Daniel went to his house, and made the decision known to Hananiah, Mishael, and Azariah, his companions,
Dan 2:18 that they might seek mercies from the God of heaven concerning this secret, so that Daniel and his companions might not perish with the rest of the wise *men* of Babylon.
Dan 2:19 Then the secret was revealed to Daniel in a night vision. So Daniel blessed the God of heaven.

This is a great picture of faith and prayer. These four friends were probably very young here, and their life was on the line. Daniel goes to them and essentially says, "Guys, we have to pray."

There was some precedent here because they would have known from their study of the scriptures of Joseph and that interpretations of dreams belong to God (Genesis 40:8), but they would have never heard that God could also tell the dream. They only knew that nothing was too hard for God (Genesis 18:14).

Night vision

There is not too much agreement among commentators as to the exact meaning of this phrase.

> "Most likely they continued in prayer until God revealed the dream. A vision may be received when awake (cf. 9:20–23) or asleep (cf. 7:1), and it is difficult to imagine that the young men had gone to sleep with an imminent death penalty hanging over their heads." – Miller

In other words it was a vision that happened to occur at night in Miller's view. It is not out of the question however that Daniel could have gone to sleep before they got an answer, perhaps trusting in faith for a sleeping revelation.

Dan 2:20 Daniel answered and said: "Blessed be the name of God forever and ever, For wisdom and might are His.
Dan 2:21 And He changes the times and the seasons; He removes kings and raises up kings; He gives wisdom to the wise And knowledge to those who have understanding.
Dan 2:22 He reveals deep and secret things; He knows what *is* in the darkness, And light dwells with Him.
Dan 2:23 "I thank You and praise You, O God of my fathers; You have given me wisdom and might, And have now made known to me what we asked of You, For You have made known to us the king's demand."

Blessed be the name of God forever and ever

Daniel's first reaction to receiving the answer to his prayer is praise and worship. This is the same pattern all through scripture and should be ours today as well.

Dan 2:24 Therefore Daniel went to Arioch, whom the king had appointed to destroy the wise *men* of Babylon. He went and said thus to him: "Do not destroy the wise *men* of Babylon; take me before the king, and I will tell the king the interpretation."
Dan 2:25 Then Arioch quickly brought Daniel before the king, and said thus to him, "I have found a man of the captives of Judah, who will make known to the king the interpretation."

Commentators tend to give Arioch a hard time here because of him saying, "**I have found,**" when he had nothing to do with it. It is true that he was trying to make himself look good here, but we also should note that he was also unnecessarily putting his neck on the line here. He trusted that Daniel had the right answer for some reason. There would have been no way for him to know. There must have been something about the experience at the prayer meeting that made it obvious to everyone, including Arioch.

Dan 2:26 The king answered and said to Daniel, whose name *was* Belteshazzar, "Are you able to make known to me the dream which I have seen, and its interpretation?"
Dan 2:27 Daniel answered in the presence of the king, and said, "The secret which the king has demanded, the wise *men,* the astrologers, the magicians, and the soothsayers cannot declare to the king.
Dan 2:28 But there is a God in heaven who reveals secrets, and He has made known to King Nebuchadnezzar what will be in the latter days. Your dream, and the visions of your head upon your bed, were these:

But there is a God in heaven

Daniel used this most amazing opportunity to glorify God.

Has made known to King Nebuchadnezzar what will be in the latter days

Daniel does not take credit for this. This humility is in contrast to Arioch trying to take credit.

Joseph in Egypt had a similar response when God revealed the dream interpretation to him:

> And Pharaoh said to Joseph, "I have had a dream, and *there is* no one who can interpret it. But I have heard it said of you *that* you can understand a dream, to interpret it." So Joseph answered Pharaoh, saying, "*It is* not in me; God will give Pharaoh an answer of peace." - Gen 41:15-16

Dan 2:29 As for you, O king, thoughts came *to* your *mind while* on your bed, *about* what would come to pass after this; and He who reveals secrets has made known to you what will be.

Daniel goes one step further: He tells Nebuchadnezzar what he was thinking before he had the dream, which was **what would come to pass after this**. Nebuchadnezzar was thinking big thoughts, maybe related to his kingdom, maybe a bigger picture,

28

we don't know. But God further glorifies himself here by showing that He indeed is as Psalm 139 says:

> You know my sitting down and my rising up; You understand my thought afar off. You comprehend my path and my lying down, And are acquainted with all my ways. - Psa 139:2-3

Dan 2:30 But as for me, this secret has not been revealed to me because I have more wisdom than anyone living, but for *our* sakes who make known the interpretation to the king, and that you may know the thoughts of your heart.

I think Daniel was a great witness to Nebuchadnezzar. Even though at this time the King was ruthless, a case can be made that Nebuchadnezzar gets saved later in his life, he even writes a chapter in the Bible, which is basically the equivalent of his testimony.

And if indeed he was saved it can no doubt be chalked up to Daniel's faithful witness to him. Every time God presented an occasion for Daniel to witness to Nebuchadnezzar throughout this book, Daniel always made sure Nebuchadnezzar knew it was his God Yahweh that did the miracles that he had witnessed.

Dan 2:31 "You, O king, were watching; and behold, a great image! This great image, whose splendor was excellent, stood before you; and its form was awesome.
Dan 2:32 This image's head was of fine gold, its chest and arms of silver, its belly and thighs of bronze,
Dan 2:33 its legs of iron, its feet partly of iron and partly of clay."

The first part of Nebuchadnezzar's dream involved a statue which was made of 5 different materials. The head made of gold, the chest and arms of silver, its belly and thighs of bronze, its legs of iron, its feet partly of iron and partly of clay.

Stephen R. Miller says the following of the phrase "**its form *was* awesome**."

> " In verse 31:The word ("awesome") is from a root word meaning "to fear." Nebuchadnezzar was frightened by the statue; this certainly is understandable, for the huge image would have stood like a dazzling colossus before the king."

So we see that Nebuchadnezzar's dream was of a giant statue. We are not told exactly how big the statue was in his dream, but the image Nebuchadnezzar built in the next chapter, (which he forced everyone to worship) may have been patterned after this one, and that structure was ninety feet tall.

Dan 2:34 You watched while a stone was cut out without hands, which struck the image on its feet of iron and clay, and broke them in pieces.

There are two things in this verse that are worth noting before we begin reading Daniel's interpretation of this dream.

The first is that the stone that Nebuchadnezzar watched being cut out was without hands. We will see in verse 44 that this means that this rock is not of human origin, but rather it is from God and distinct from the other elements in this dream in that regard.

The second thing worth noting is that the rock strikes the statue on its feet, not its toes. I will argue later that the feet and toes are described as one cohesive unit, they are still a part of the last empire, that of the legs of iron, but that both the feet and toes together represent a latter part of that kingdom which I think is supported in part because of this verse. I will expand on this in a few moments.

Dan 2:35 Then the iron, the clay, the bronze, the silver, and the gold were crushed together, and became like chaff from the summer threshing floors; the wind carried them away so that no trace of them was found. And the stone that struck

the image became a great mountain and filled the whole earth.

This is the last verse before Daniel begins his interpretation of this dream. It basically describes the statue's utter destruction as a result of the rock hitting its feet.

It is also of extreme significance as we will see that this rock began very small, and then **became** a mountain and filled the whole earth, it was not a mountain when it initially struck the statue. But over some amount of time, not discussed here, it grows to fill the whole earth.

Dan 2:36 "This is the dream. Now we will tell the interpretation of it before the king.

Daniel declares that he has accomplished phase one of Nebuchadnezzar's request, he told him what the dream was. He then declares his intention to begin phase two, that is telling the interpretation of the dream.

Oftentimes when there is a symbolic prophecy in the Bible, like in the book Revelation, there is an interpretation given of that symbolism in the Bible. In the book of Revelation an angel would tell us the meaning of John's vision about the woman riding the beast, for example. Also, later on in the book of Daniel we see angels giving literal interpretations of Daniel's symbolic visions.

We must make sure that our interpretations of these symbolic visions are consistent with what scripture tells us the interpretation of the vision is. It seems like a simple thing, but it is a sometimes overlooked hermeneutical principal.

Daniel Interprets Nebuchadnezzar's Dream

Dan 2:37 You, O king, are a king of kings. For the God of heaven has given you a kingdom, power, strength, and glory;

Daniel boldly speaks of the sovereignty of God here, telling Nebuchadnezzar that his kingdom was really given to him by Daniel's God. This was not a necessary part of the interpretation of the dream. Daniel takes a risk here in telling the most powerful man on earth that he was really only a servant of Yahweh.

Daniel may have seen this extraordinary circumstance as a perfect way to witness to the king. It is one of many instances in this particular story that Daniel makes sure to let everyone know that the miracles they see are because of God, not Him. We will see later that this seems to have had the effect that Daniel intended because we see Nebuchadnezzar bowing down and offering sacrifices to Yahweh at the end of this chapter.

Dan 2:38 and wherever the children of men dwell, or the beasts of the field and the birds of the heaven, He has given them into your hand, and has made you ruler over them all—you are this head of gold."

The first part of this verse is defining the extent of the dominion God had given to Nebuchadnezzar, which is expressed as total, that is all of the known world and everything in it. This is important because I think it shows in part that the following empires will also have a similar dominion, such as that of Babylon; that is, in order for a kingdom to qualify to be one of these parts of this statue, it must be a world-ruling empire.

You *are* this head of gold.
Here we begin to see that the statue's various materials represent kings or kingdoms. This is the only instance in this interpretation where Daniel refers to a person, that is to a king instead of a kingdom. For instance, in the very next verse it says:

Dan 2:39 But after you shall arise another kingdom inferior to yours; then another, a third kingdom of bronze, which shall rule over all the earth.

It becomes very clear as we progress in Daniel's interpretation that kingdoms are meant here and not necessarily kings, though in some cases it may apply to use them synonymously like in the case of Nebuchadnezzar, and even then we can see in verse 39, which says, "But **after you** shall arise **another kingdom."** that Daniel intended to refer to Nebuchadnezzar's kingdom even when he says "you".

Stephen Miller, in the New American Commentary, writes concerning this next kingdom in verse 39:

> "2:39a Daniel disclosed that another "kingdom" would rise after the Babylonian Empire. History is plain that the next great power to appear on the world scene was the Medo-Persian Empire led by the dynamic Cyrus the Great. This empire is symbolized by the silver chest and arms of the great statue...Medo-Persian dominance continued for approximately 208 years (539–331 B.C.)"

The Medes and Persians ruled together as one empire. This is even alluded to in other places in Daniel.

> "For example, in Dan 8:20 the two-horned ram (symbolizing one kingdom) represents "the kings of Media and Persia," and in chap. 6 the author referred to the "laws of the Medes and Persians" (cf. vv. 8, 15), indicating that Darius ruled by the laws of the Medo-Persian Empire, not a separate Median kingdom."

Daniel was an old man when Babylon was conquered by Cyrus the Great. The night of its conquest is detailed in Chapter 5, with the feast of Belshazzar and the writing on the wall. Daniel's gifts were noticed by the Medo-Persians as well, and he went on to serve them for the few years before his death.

Cyrus was also notable because it was him that allowed the exiled captive Jews to return to Israel.
There is almost no disagreement among conservative scholars that the Medo-Persian Empire is in view here.

A third kingdom of bronze, which shall rule over all the earth.

This third kingdom of Bronze is that of Greece. Alexander the Great conquered the known world, including the Medo-Persian Empire.

This we know not just from secular history, but also because when the angel interprets a vision Daniel has in Chapter 8 of a goat defeating a ram with two horns, it says the following:

> The ram which you saw, having the two horns—*they are* the kings of Media and Persia. And the male goat *is* the kingdom of Greece. The large horn that *is* between its eyes *is* the first king. - Dan 8:20-21

So not only do we know this from history, we have confirmation of the Bible's viewpoint from the very same book. Again there is almost no disagreement among conservative scholars about the interpretation of the third bronze section of this statue being Greece.

Dan 2:40 And the fourth kingdom shall be as strong as iron, inasmuch as iron breaks in pieces and shatters everything; and like iron that crushes, *that kingdom* will break in pieces and crush all the others.

Again we have near universal agreement among conservative scholars as to the identity of the legs of iron - The Roman Empire.

Before going into the next part about the feet and toes where there are significant differences in belief among conservative scholars, I want to briefly explain the reason I keep saying "agreement among conservative scholars" and not simply "scholars" when referring to the interpretation of these kingdoms.

The reason is that those who believe that prophecy is impossible as a part of their world view cannot see any of this chapter as predictive prophecy, and they do have a different interpretation of these kingdoms as a result. But I won't be detailing their view here. If you would like to learn more about it, I would recommend the book I have been referencing, that is Stephen Miller's *Daniel* from the New American Commentary. He interacts with this view at length.

To make a long story short, since Rome was nothing more than an insignificant village at the time Daniel wrote this, even by their liberal dating, they obviously can't have the legs of iron being Rome. So by some funny business, they squeeze Greece into this final empire instead of Rome.

But for those of us that can believe that God can see the past, present and future, we are free to stand in awe at the accuracy in which God foretells the future. So let's move on to the really challenging section of this prophecy.

Dan 2:41 Whereas you saw the feet and toes, partly of potter's clay and partly of iron, the kingdom shall be divided; yet the strength of the iron shall be in it, just as you saw the iron mixed with ceramic clay.
Dan 2:42 And *as* the toes of the feet *were* partly of iron and partly of clay, *so* the kingdom shall be partly strong and partly fragile.
Dan 2:43 As you saw iron mixed with ceramic clay, they will mingle with the seed of men; but they will not adhere to one another, just as iron does not mix with clay.

This is where there tends to be some disagreement among even conservative scholars.

But before I get into that, let me talk about where everyone tends to agree. That is that these feet and toes are somehow a part of the Roman Empire. In other words, the feet and toes mixed with iron and clay, while different, are not a part of a new kingdom but still a part of the legs of iron of the Roman Empire, just a chronologically later part; the end of the Roman Empire, if you will. Everyone tends to agree on that, but with many variations.

Here are some of the main conservative views people have about the feet and toes:

1. That the feet and toes represent the final period of the Roman Empire being divided, weak, trying to cleave its divided empire together but failing.

2. The feet and toes represent the final kingdom of the Antichrist in the last days. There are many variations of both of these views, some of which we will talk about in depth as we progress.

3. That the feet and toes represent a nephilim hybrid kingdom in the last days. We will talk about that in depth a little later as well.

I used to hold to the 2nd view, that the feet and toes were representing an end times kingdom, and that there would be a need to revive the Roman Empire.

I still believe that there will be an end times kingdom of the Antichrist, but for reasons I will demonstrate here, I am now firmly convinced that the Antichrist's kingdom is not in view in this chapter. Furthermore, I hold that the belief that Daniel 2 and Daniel 7 are talking of the same events could be one of the more dangerous views held by conservative scholars today, because this view could allow the Antichrist to come onto the world scene almost entirely unnoticed, and even embraced as the Messiah by some.

I will talk much more in depth about this as we continue our verse-by-verse study in Daniel especially in chapter 7 and 11.

I would also agree with Miller, who holds the opposing view to me, that in addition to your view on Daniel 2 and 7, your view about the rock that destroys this statue is the key to any person's interpretation of this passage, and I would ask you to withhold your judgment on this matter until we get to those verses.

For now, let's continue this verse-by-verse study, and be very critical of everything I am about to say, because although I am convinced of this interpretation, you need to remember that this will be a minority viewpoint on this passage, and you should be wary anytime someone is teaching something in the Bible that is not widely held.

The kingdom shall be divided

A very important part of this is that the last kingdom at some point will be divided.
Since both views I think rightly presume that the feet and toes represent a chronologically later point of Rome, we can safely say that this is saying that Rome will be divided toward the end of its existence, whether you believe that its end was in the past or will be in the future.

Here we have a few problems for the revived Roman Empire (RRE) view.

The first is that you have an unambiguous fulfillment of this passage in the history of the fall of Rome. We know that Rome was divided into several parts, eventually settling into just two parts, that is the east and west empires. We will see that the other elements of the feet and toes prophecy fit like a glove to the events of that period as well.

And the second major problem here for the RRE view is that forcing this prophecy to the end times means that you have to hold the view that the Antichrist has a divided weak kingdom in the end times.

The descriptions of the Antichrist's kingdom in the Bible do not give the impression that it will be weak or divided , but rather that he will have absolute power, and that those who do not worship him will be killed. This does not sound like a weak or divided kingdom.

I will now go into some more depth on the first point, that the divided and partly strong-partly weak kingdom describes perfectly the end of Rome in the ancient past.

If you look up the phrase "The Crisis of the Third Century," you will learn of about a one hundred year or so time period in

Roman History where they almost lost everything. It was the first time in Rome's history that they started to show weakness. All the years of their dominance and absolute iron fisted - or should I say iron legged - rule was starting to slow down during this time.

In 285 Diocletian split the empire into four parts called the tetrarchy, but it didn't last. It briefly was united again under Constantine, but it quickly split again after his death into three divisions. It was total chaos, everyone claiming to be emperor for a few years.

Eventually, when all the dust settled, there were only two divisions of Rome, that is the eastern half and western half, and that is how it would stay until Rome fizzled out of existence. Rome would never again rise to the prominence it once had after this point, and it will grow less and less powerful until it is a shadow of its former self, constantly sacked by invading barbarians, penniless and powerless.

The exact date of Rome's fall varies because of the "death by a thousand cuts" nature of its decline, but most historians put its fall at about 480 AD. A mere 100 years after the division of east and west was solidified.

I'm trying to establish that the end of Rome is characterized by weakness and division, and as we noted before, the one thing that both sides of the argument about the feet and toes made of iron and clay agree on is that the passage is saying that the end of the Roman Empire will be characterized by weakness and division.

The only difference is that some say the end of the Roman Empire is in the past, and some say we need to "revive" a Roman Empire first, and then watch its end be characterized by weakness and division.

The toes of the feet *were* partly of iron and partly of clay

In this verse it seems to suggest that only **the toes** were of this
mixed clay and iron composition, but we know from verse 33,
where it only refers to **its feet** and not the toes being of this
composition, that the author is referring to the feet and toes as
one unit. This is further demonstrated in verse 34 in which the
statue is said to be struck on its feet only, whereas one would
think that the toes would be mentioned here if there was an
important distinction.

In other words, idiomatically the final empire consists of **only**
two parts, the legs of iron being the first, and the feet and toes of
iron and clay being the second. And the words "feet" and "toes"
can be used independently and interchangeably to refer to the
final stage of the final kingdom.

The kingdom shall be partly strong and partly fragile.

Again this is a terrific description of the last 300 or so years of
the Roman Empire, there were times during this period, a period
often called "the decline of the Roman Empire" in which Rome
was **partly strong** in some ways, but **partly fragile** in others.

We have seen already to an extent, and will see again in the next
verse, that it is grammatically necessary to see that the clay and
iron are representative of the divisions of the empire, in this case,
the east and the west empires. So in order for this interpretation
to be a perfect match, we would need to see a clear description in
history of one of these divisions being much weaker than the
other.

The so called "final split" of the Roman Empire occurred at a
time when it was becoming clear that the western empire was
going to be a lot more dangerous place to live than the east. This
is when Constantine moved the capital from Rome to
Constantinople. Eventually Rome would be sacked by Alaric in
410 while Constantinople would not be sacked until the Middle
Ages.

Here are a few quotes about the weakness of the Western Empire
compared to the Eastern.

"The East, always wealthier, was not so destitute, especially as Emperors like Constantine the Great and Constantius II had invested heavily in the eastern economy. As a result, the Eastern Empire could afford large numbers of professional soldiers and augment them with mercenaries, while the Western Roman Empire could not afford this to the same extent. Even in major defeats, the East could, certainly not without difficulties, buy off its enemies with a ransom."

"The political, economic and military control of the Eastern Empire's resources remained safe in Constantinople….. In contrast, the Western Empire was more fragmented. Its capital was transferred to Ravenna in 402 largely for defensive reasons."

"The Western Empire's resources were much limited, and the lack of available manpower forced the government to rely ever more on confederate barbarian troops operating under their own commanders, where the Western Empire would often have difficulties paying. In certain cases deals were struck with the leaders of barbaric mercenaries rewarding them with land, which led to the Empire's decline as less land meant there would be even less taxes to support the military…..As the central power weakened, the State gradually lost control of its borders and provinces, as well as control over the Mediterranean Sea. "

The divided parts of this kingdom were noticeably different in strength. As I mentioned, the eastern empire would survive in some capacity for hundreds of years after the west had long disappeared.

Dan 2:43: As you saw iron mixed with ceramic clay, they will mingle with the seed of men; but they will not adhere to one another, just as iron does not mix with clay.

There is a lot of confusion about this verse, which I think is due to the English translation of the Aramaic. Remember this section of Daniel is written in Aramaic and not Hebrew.

It should first be noted that other translations such as the ESV render the underlying Aramaic phrase this way:

> "As you saw the iron mixed with soft clay, so they will **mix with one another in marriage**, but they will not hold together, just as iron does not mix with clay. (ESV)"

So instead of **mingle with the seed of men** they **mix with one another in marriage.**

So the question is: Is the ESV capturing the intent of the Aramaic here?

Let's first take this word translated as "mingle":

It is the Aramaic word "Arab" (ar-av) which corresponds to the Hebrew "Arab". In other words, this word, if you look it up, will be in Aramaic, and its only use is right here in Daniel, because Aramaic is very rare. However, most Aramaic words correspond directly to Ancient Hebrew words, and that is the case here. In fact, they are even pronounced the same.

The Hebrew word "Arab" means: to pledge, exchange, mortgage, engage, occupy, undertake for, give pledges, be or become surety, take on pledge, give in pledge. [3]

For example in Genesis 43:9, when Judah was begging his father to let him take Benjamin to Egypt as per Joseph's request, he says that he will become surety for Benjamin. The word "surety" is where we get the word "mingle".

> I myself will be **surety** for him; from my hand you shall require him. If I do not bring him back to you and set him before you, then let me bear the blame forever. - Gen 43:9

Another example of its use is in 2 Kings 18:23 where the word "pledge" is the word translated "mingle" in our passage

> Now therefore, I urge you, give a **pledge** to my master the king of Assyria, and I will give you two thousand horses—if you are able on your part to put riders on them! - 2Ki 18:23

But the same word for "mingle" also can mean "to mix together". And in fact, of the two times it is used that way in the Bible, it is speaking of the intermarriage of Jewish and pagan tribes.

> For they have taken of their daughters for themselves, and for their sons: so that the holy **seed** have **mingled** themselves with the people of those lands: yea, the hand of the princes and rulers hath been chief in this trespass. - Ezr 9:2

Here we have a very similar phrase to the one in our verse. I think this shows some precedent that the translators of the KJV believed that mingling seed was referring to intermarriage with two groups.

> But they **mingled** with the Gentiles And learned their works- Psa 106:35

So I think you can see that the ESV here has a pretty decent rendering of this phrase when it says: they will **mix with one another in marriage.**

But even if that is true, we still have to determine who **they** are, and who they are trying to intermarry with, and perhaps more importantly, what is it referring to.

So we need to find out who **they** are in this verse. And I will suggest the simple method of sentence structure and basic grammar to find out who **they** are.

If we look just before this in verse 41, we see that Daniel says that the feet and toes of clay and iron are representing a divided kingdom. The next three verses repeatedly refer to these two divisions of the kingdom as iron and clay.

Grammatically there is no other possible plural subject other than the separate, divided parts of the kingdom represented by the iron and clay. This is confirmed in verse 44, when it says "in the days of these kings," making it clear that the plural subject that was in view in verse 43 must be referring to the kings of the divided kingdom in verse 41.

So what this verse is saying is that the divided parts of the empire will pledge their offspring to one another in an attempt to become strong again, but it will not work.

Now it would be one thing if I had to go looking for some obscure fulfillment of this in Roman history, but the strength of this interpretation is the unambiguous fulfillment of it in the history of Rome, which I think you will see gives the interpretations a great deal more credibility.

Now in order for this to be true, we can't just go picking any arranged marriages of emperors in Ancient Rome. Almost every senator, general, prefect or any other person with imperial ambitions had arranged marriages to secure their legitimacy to the throne. I'm only slightly exaggerating when I say that you can't read a single page in the entire history of Rome without reading about an arranged political marriage.

But we are looking for a very specific type of political marriage here. It has to be toward the very end of Rome's existence because it is regarding the feet and toes, it has to be between the eastern and western empires, the two kings of the divided kingdom need to pledge their offspring to one another, and for the specific purpose of trying to unify Rome and keep it from demise. This should narrow it down quite a bit.
There are two instances where this exact thing happened at the end of the Roman Empire.

The first is in 467, only about 9 years before the last Roman emperor. This is a time when the Vandals were posing a major threat to Rome and while Leo was reigning strongly in the east. There had not been an emperor in the west for a few years because a man named Ricimer, who had been ruling behind the scenes by manipulating puppet emperors for many years, had not appointed another puppet emperor and was hoping no one would care or that people would just accept him as the default emperor.

Well this became a problem in the eastern empire because of the threat of the Vandals and the imminent war that they were going to have to have with them.

So Leo decided to choose an emperor of the west for the west. He chose a guy named Anthemius and sent him to the west with a big army so that Ricimer would have to get with the new program.

Here is the marriage connection: The emperor of the east, Leo, gave his daughter, Leontia, to Anthemius' son, Marcian, to legitimize the reign of his new appointee to the west, essentially saying, "Ok, east and west, we are all one big happy family now. So let's go fight the Vandals or we are all in big trouble."

In addition, Anthemius also gave his only daughter, Alypia, to Ricimer, which also made Anthemius, who was a Greek-speaking foreigner to the west, acceptable to the Latin-speaking Romans, of which Ricimer had become kind of a ring leader.

This plan actually might have worked, too, but the battle with the Vandals went very badly, and Anthemius would soon be killed, and they would all be right back at the place that they started.

Which brings us to the second attempt of cleaving the east and the west together with marriages. This time it occurs in 474, just two years before the last Roman Emperor, with Julious Nepos. There are actually a lot of people that argue that Nepos was the last Roman Emperor, choosing not to count the child Romulus Augustulus who "ruled" for about a year after Nepos was exiled.

This time Leo married off his niece to Nepos. The surname Nepos actually means nephew. Because he took the surname nephew as his title, referring to his now-nephew status to Leo in the east, it should show us the importance of that marriage in the attempt to unify the east and the west. But it was too late for Rome. There were too many problems. And just like this verse in Daniel says, these two divisions of the final kingdom **do not adhere to one another** and the fall of the western Roman Empire is put somewhere around this time at 476-480.

But they will not adhere to one another.

I want to briefly speak about the nephilim interpretation of this verse and point out that whatever this is, it will not adhere or cleave together. That is to say, it won't work. There are many that say this verse is proof of a future nephilim hybrid program in the end times. But even if you were to assume that the word **they** is speaking of angels, you would have to conclude that it doesn't work - there would be no hybrids made in this interpretation as they simply **do not adhere** together..

Dan 2:44 And in the days of these kings the God of heaven will set up a kingdom which shall never be destroyed; and the kingdom shall not be left to other people; it shall break in pieces and consume all these kingdoms, and it shall stand forever.
Dan 2:45 Inasmuch as you saw that the stone was cut out of the mountain without hands, and that it broke in pieces the iron, the bronze, the clay, the silver, and the gold—the great God has made known to the king what will come to pass after this. The dream is certain, and its interpretation is sure."

Ok so here we are at the most crucial part, the identification of this stone. Let's briefly recall what happened with this stone in Nebuchadnezzar's dream in verses 34-35:

> You watched while a stone was cut out without hands, which struck the image on its feet of iron and clay, and broke them in pieces. Then the iron, the clay, the bronze, the silver, and the gold were crushed together, and

45

> became like chaff from the summer threshing floors; the
> wind carried them away so that no trace of them was
> found. And the stone that struck the image became a
> great mountain and filled the whole earth. - Dan 2:34-35

So this stone strikes the statue on the feet, and it eventually
grows to fill the whole earth.

A kingdom

This stone is a kingdom, a kingdom that God will institute during
the Roman Empire that will eventually grow to encompass the
entire world. This is agreed upon by many scholars, even Miller
who holds to a "Revived Roman Empire" view.

There are some that would say that this has to be speaking of
Jesus because of Eph 2:20 which says He is a cornerstone, but
that would offend the explicit teaching in this verse that this rock
is a kingdom in the same way that the others were a kingdom.

This rock is representative of what is known all throughout the
Bible as the "Kingdom of God." I will show you a few verses to
demonstrate two points:

1. That Jesus Christ begins the Kingdom of God in his day
   (during the Roman Empire).

2. That the Kingdom of God is supposed to start small and
   then grow large. (Typified by starting with the apostles
   and spreading to all those who will ever be saved.)

1.) That Jesus Christ begins the Kingdom of God in his day:

> And saying, "The time is fulfilled, and the kingdom of
> God is at hand. Repent, and believe in the gospel." - Mar
> 1:15

> But if I cast out demons by the Spirit of God, surely the
> kingdom of God has come upon you.- Mat 12:28

Now at one point the Pharisees asked Jesus when the kingdom of God was coming, so he answered, "The kingdom of God is not coming with signs to be observed, nor will they say, 'Look, here it is!' or 'There!' For indeed, the kingdom of God is in your midst." - Luk 17:20-21

It should be here noted that there seems to be a present and future sense of the kingdom of God, in the sense that the ultimate fulfillment of the kingdom of God is not here or in this world but rather in the future. But I believe it can be shown with certainty that Jesus considered the Kingdom of God, to have been established with Him on earth during his teaching ministry.

2.) That the Kingdom of God is supposed to start small and then grow large.

Another parable He put forth to them, saying: "The kingdom of heaven is like a mustard seed, which a man took and sowed in his field, which indeed is the least of all the seeds; but when it is grown it is greater than the herbs and becomes a tree, so that the birds of the air come and nest in its branches." Another parable He spoke to them: "The kingdom of heaven is like leaven, which a woman took and hid in three measures of meal till it was all leavened." - Mat 13:31-33

These two parables are describing the small and then growing large aspect of the Kingdom of God.

So this is in a sense a prophecy for all ancient peoples as to a general time the Messiah would come; that is, the Kingdom of God would be established sometime during the Roman Empire. This may be one reason that messianic expectations were so high in Jesus' day.

Shall never be destroyed; and the kingdom shall not be left to other people;

Here it contrasts God's kingdom with the usual fate of the kingdoms of man. It won't have a successor, nor an end, it won't be divided among generals or anyone else.

It shall break in pieces and consume all these kingdoms, and it shall stand forever.

I would suggest that this verse is expressing the different nature of God's Kingdom to man's, and it includes all the previous kingdoms here to further drive home that point. That is, when God's Kingdom is fully and eternally established, there will be no more manifestations of man's kingdoms.

The great God has made known to the king what will come to pass after this. The dream is certain, and its interpretation is sure."

Daniel again makes sure that Nebuchadnezzar, who is probably showing signs of his utter amazement at this point, knows that it was Yahweh who deserves the glory for this feat.
He also adds that the dream and interpretation are certain and sure. This is what will happen, and that God wants Nebuchadnezzar to know it.

Dan 2:46 Then King Nebuchadnezzar fell on his face, prostrate before Daniel, and commanded that they should present an offering and incense to him.
Dan 2:47 The king answered Daniel, and said, "Truly your God *is* the God of gods, the Lord of kings, and a revealer of secrets, since you could reveal this secret."

It appears from verse 46 that the offerings were made to Daniel himself as if he were a god. But then in verse 47, it seems to suggest that Nebuchadnezzar was giving this worship to Daniel's God, which makes more sense as it seems unlikely given the great pains that Daniel went through to make sure that it was not him but God, that Daniel would accept such a sacrifice.

While this was probably the equivalent of planting a seed in Nebuchadnezzar's heart that Yahweh was God of all and worthy of submission, his worship of Yahweh here is not to be looked at as his conversion, as we will see in the next chapter that this is a short lived piety.

Dan 2:48 Then the king promoted Daniel and gave him many great gifts; and he made him ruler over the whole province of Babylon, and chief administrator over all the wise *men* of Babylon.
Dan 2:49 Also Daniel petitioned the king, and he set Shadrach, Meshach, and Abed-Nego over the affairs of the province of Babylon; but Daniel *sat* in the gate of the king.

David Guzik summarized these verses this way:

> "Daniel not only had his life spared, but he was promoted to high office - and he made sure his friends were also promoted. It was fitting that Daniel's friends got to share in his advancement, because they accomplished much of the victory through their prayers."

Chapter 2   Daniel

Chapter 3

Daniel's Friends Are Tested

Dan 3:1 Nebuchadnezzar the king made an image of gold, whose height was sixty cubits and its width six cubits. He set it up in the plain of Dura, in the province of Babylon.

We don't really know when this happened, other than it was after Daniel's companions were promoted to their positions of authority, which occurred after Daniel interpreted Nebuchadnezzar's dream. We know this because we see that the other wise men make reference to their promotion in verse 12, and seem to be jealous of it.

Nebuchadnezzar the king made an image

I have always assumed that this big statue was a likeness of Nebuchadnezzar himself, but I'm not so sure it was. In no place does the text say that it was made to look like Nebuchadnezzar, instead it always uses the phrase: "the image which King Nebuchadnezzar had set up." This or a similar phrase is said eight times in this chapter. That is the only connection to Nebuchadnezzar it has; that is, that it was "set up" by him.

It also seems to directly refute the idea that it was a statue of Nebuchadnezzar himself in verse 14 which says Nebuchadnezzar spoke, saying to them, "*Is it* true, Shadrach, Meshach, and Abed-Nego, *that* you do not **serve my gods** or worship the gold image which I have set up?"

The idea is further refuted by noting that the Babylonians did not seem to have a concept of the divine King.[4]

It seems here that what was being asked of them was to serve his gods. The image that he set up was apparently for this purpose. There is no indication that there was any other way for them to "serve his gods" other than the worshipping of the image he set up.

Also in verse 28, when Nebuchadnezzar ends up giving them praise for not giving in to his commandment (this is post furnace) it suggests that it was about the worship of a god.

> Nebuchadnezzar spoke, saying, "Blessed be the God of Shadrach, Meshach, and Abed-Nego, who sent His Angel and delivered His servants who trusted in Him, and they have frustrated the king's word, and yielded their bodies, that they should not serve nor worship any god except their own God! - Dan 3:28

As we will see this was a test of loyalty, given only to the state employees, and it was considered a loyalty to the gods of Babylon. It was a test that, we will see, was probably designed specifically to expose these three Jewish men or Jews in general, as they could not, as good Jewish men, bow down to a false god without disobeying the covenant. It is clear from the verses we have already read that Nebuchadnezzar considered the worship and service of **his gods** to be the point of this particular test. Again there is no indication in the Bible or in the historical record that Nebuchadnezzar considered himself to be a god, or solicited worship of himself.

Whose height *was* sixty cubits *and* its width six cubits

One thing that folks argue about is this monument's size, and these measurements work out to a very tall and thin object. Think of two tractor trailers stacked end to end and you have the sense of it. It was basically a big obelisk. The relevant point is that the proportions are wrong if this is of a man. Those that insist this is of Nebuchadnezzar will say that there was a big platform and that the height of a podium should be taken into account.

Gold

If this statue was made of pure gold it would be a lot of gold. Most scholars think it was overlaid with gold, perhaps with a wooden frame and sheets of gold laid on top. Such an idea has precedent in the scripture (Ex 27:1-2, 39:38, 30:3)

Dan 3:2 And King Nebuchadnezzar sent word to gather together the satraps, the administrators, the governors, the counselors, the treasurers, the judges, the magistrates, and all the officials of the provinces, to come to the dedication of the image which King Nebuchadnezzar had set up.
Dan 3:3 So the satraps, the administrators, the governors, the counselors, the treasurers, the judges, the magistrates, and all the officials of the provinces gathered together for the dedication of the image that King Nebuchadnezzar had set up; and they stood before the image that Nebuchadnezzar had set up.

I could go through each of these titles of people and describe their duties, but it should suffice to say that all these people were Nebuchadnezzar's government employees. (The administrators, the governors, the counselors, the treasurers, the judges, the magistrates, and all the officials of the provinces.)

This was not every citizen in Babylon, this was only for those that were employees of the state.

The plain of Dura, in the province of Babylon.

This was probably about 15 or 20 miles outside the city. So it may explain why this event could have been an unexpected surprise for these officials, which would seem to be necessary if it was indeed a test of their loyalty to the Babylonian god(s). It is also close enough, that is it was in the province of Babylon, so that Nebuchadnezzar's decree for them all to leave the city and come to this place would have been able to be done relatively quickly.

This is also one possible argument as to the reason Daniel was not here during this story.

53

Some scholars point out that the last verse of the chapter before this, Dan 2:49, is meant to explain his absence:

> Moreover, at Daniel's request the king appointed
> Shadrach, Meshach and Abednego administrators
> over the province of Babylon, while Daniel himself
> remained at the royal court - Dan 2:49

In other words they say that this verse is intended by Daniel to explain his absence from the next event; that is, since he was to remain at the royal court it would mean that he was still in the city taking care of official business in the absence of the king who had gone to the plain of Dura.

Other explanations for Daniel's absence may be that since he was such a high official in the government, perhaps he was on official duty in a foreign land, or perhaps he did catch wind of this plan and found an excuse not to go. The latter being the most unlikely of the three, given Daniel's character.

**Dan 3:4 Then a herald cried aloud: "To you it is
commanded, O peoples, nations, and languages,
Dan 3:5 that at the time you hear the sound of the horn,
flute, harp, lyre, and psaltery, in symphony with all kinds
of music, you shall fall down and worship the gold image
that King Nebuchadnezzar has set up;**

So here we see that all these people were gathered together and then someone explains why they are all there, and what the plan was.

A herald

This was a documented way for communication in the ancient near east.

Peoples, nations, and languages

This shows the Babylonian government was a multinational one, though the herald probably spoke to them all in Aramaic which was the "lingua franca" of the day.

In the next verse he more clearly explains this situation to them.

Dan 3:6 and whoever does not fall down and worship shall be cast immediately into the midst of a burning fiery furnace."

It appears that there was a furnace built within view of the statue. Such furnaces have been discovered by archeologists in Babylon. They were huge, often built on the side of hills so one could walk up to the top of it and throw things down in it. They had another door on the side at ground level as well. They even know that these furnaces were used for executions in those times.

There was probably a temptation to fall down. They may have made excuses like: "well maybe we can just act like we are worshiping but in our heart..."

We are told by the Lord that though we should make every effort to flee and avoid situations like this, if we are ever caught in a situation where we are required to choose to deny Christ or die, we are called to die. The Lord was very serious about this aspect of our discipleship. We are expected to count the cost that our following Him may require our lives, and I believe we are also told to expect such a scenario in the end times in which Christians will be massively persecuted before the rapture.

Dan 3:7 So at that time, when all the people heard the sound of the horn, flute, harp, and lyre, in symphony with all kinds of music, all the people, nations, and languages fell down and worshiped the gold image which King Nebuchadnezzar had set up.

I'm not sure what the significance of the music is, and the naming of each instrument. It may be just a good historical account of the events, or it may have some significance. If it does, I don't know it.

Dan 3:8 Therefore at that time certain Chaldeans came forward and accused the Jews.

This word here "Chaldeans" is in other translations called "astrologers". In chapter 1 I mentioned some of the issues with this word and how it could be used both as an ethnic Babylonian person, or a specific job in the occult administration, namely an astrologer. Basically these were the people that Daniel was put in charge of in chapter 2 by Nebuchadnezzar.

These guys were probably jealous of Daniel and his friends' promotion, or perhaps they resented being governed by Jews, or both, and they might have put the king up to this whole idea in order to get rid of these Jewish men.

There is circumstantial evidence for this, for example in Daniel 6 this is exactly what happened. These occultist that Daniel was in charge of learned enough about Daniel and his God to come up with a scheme which they convinced Darius of which was similar to this one, in that the only people that could ever be found guilty of it would be the Jews.

The same is true for this situation. It is not surprising that everyone on the plain of Dura bowed down that day, not just because of the furnace situation, but because in a polytheistic society there was nothing wrong with bowing to other gods that you may or may not know -- the more gods you worshipped the more bases you covered so to speak. There were certainly no people other than the Jews who would consider dying rather than worshipping another god. It would seem that whoever came up with this scheme had to have the Jews in mind, and this seems to be confirmed in the next few verses.

**Dan 3:9 They spoke and said to King Nebuchadnezzar, "O king, live forever!
Dan 3:10 You, O king, have made a decree that everyone who hears the sound of the horn, flute, harp, lyre, and psaltery, in symphony with all kinds of music, shall fall down and worship the gold image;
Dan 3:11 and whoever does not fall down and worship shall be cast into the midst of a burning fiery furnace.
Dan 3:12 There are certain Jews whom you have set over the affairs of the province of Babylon: Shadrach,**

Meshach, and Abed-Nego; these men, O king, have not paid due regard to you. They do not serve your gods or worship the gold image which you have set up."

First these men remind the king of his oath to kill anyone who didn't do this. This may be because they knew Nebuchadnezzar liked these guys, which was another reason they probably resented them, and so they may have thought he might not be inclined to kill them.

There are a few things that give us a reason to suspect these men as having planned this entire thing as in the case of Daniel 6, or at least planned how to take advantage of this situation.

They mention that these men are **Jews** in verse 12. They also mention that Nebuchadnezzar appointed them to high positions. They remembered this event, and cited the job promotion, the very thing that Daniel 6 tells us was the reason they plotted a similar event to kill Daniel; that is, jealous ambition.

Dan 3:13 Then Nebuchadnezzar, in rage and fury, gave the command to bring Shadrach, Meshach, and Abed-Nego. So they brought these men before the king.
Dan 3:14 Nebuchadnezzar spoke, saying to them, "Is it true, Shadrach, Meshach, and Abed-Nego, that you do not serve my gods or worship the gold image which I have set up?
Dan 3:15 Now if you are ready at the time you hear the sound of the horn, flute, harp, lyre, and psaltery, in symphony with all kinds of music, and you fall down and worship the image which I have made, good! But if you do not worship, you shall be cast immediately into the midst of a burning fiery furnace. And who is the god who will deliver you from my hands?"

So they brought them before the king. This is all probably taking place in the plain of Dura. It may be a distinct place where the king was, perhaps a royal tent or some other structure.

It appears that the king is making an exception for these three men, because verse 6 says that whoever did not worship would be **immediately** cast into the furnace. It also seems as though he is making sure to confirm this with them as opposed to take it on hearsay which means that Nebuchadnezzar did not himself see them refuse to bow. This possible special treatment may have been because he remembered them and was impressed by their work, which I tend to think is the case based on an upcoming verse. But he certainly is not happy about it regardless of this. Verse 4 uses the words **rage and fury** to describe his disposition at this point.

"And who *is* the god who will deliver you from my hands?"

When Nebuchadnezzar says this It may be an indication that he was aware their God was Yahweh. It would be very improbable, no matter how many people he saw a day, that he would have not remembered these guys, at least by now when reminders of who they were had been offered. I am sure that the subject of Yahweh had come up often in connection to the Jews and even specifically Daniel and these guys. So Nebuchadnezzar may be specifically saying to them, look guys even your God can't help you with what I am about to do to you. Nebuchadnezzar obviously didn't know much about Yahweh at this point, or it could be as many say that he was being intentionally blasphemous at this point.

David Guzik says the following:

> "This was an even greater test for Shadrach, Meshach, and Abed-Nego. It is one thing to make a stand for God; it is a greater thing to stick to your stand when pointedly asked, "Is it true?" Peter could follow Jesus after His arrest, but he wilted and denied Jesus when asked, "Is it true?""

Dan 3:16 Shadrach, Meshach, and Abed-Nego answered and said to the king, "O Nebuchadnezzar, we have no need to answer you in this matter."

Stephen Miller says of their answer:

"No apology was to be given for their stand. This was
not a "proud reply" as Lacocque thinks; it was a
"firm" reply. Their minds were made up."

So they look around at Nebuchadnezzar's ragtime band, all the
musicians probably looking at them as they played, and they said
to the court, "You don't need to do all this, we can go ahead and
give you our answer." And they give one of the best answers of
all time.

**Dan 3:17 If that is the case, our God whom we serve is
able to deliver us from the burning fiery furnace, and He
will deliver us from your hand, O king.
Dan 3:18 But if not, let it be known to you, O king, that
we do not serve your gods, nor will we worship the gold
image which you have set up."**

If that be the case:

> "Our God is able to deliver us from the burning fiery
> furnace; either to prevent their being cast into it, or to
> preserve them unhurt in it, and to bring them safe out
> of it: instances of his power in other cases, such as
> the passage of the Israelites through the Red sea safe,
> when their enemies were drowned, with others,
> confirmed their faith in this:

> "And he will deliver us out of thine hand, O king;
> they might have a well grounded hope and persuasion
> of deliverance, arising partly from former instances
> of the divine power and goodness in such like cases;
> and partly from the consideration of the glory of God,
> which would be greatly conspicuous herein; and
> chiefly because of the king's defiance of God, and
> blasphemy against him [What God can save you],
> which they had reason to believe would be taken
> notice of; for it does not appear that they had any
> foresight of certain deliverance, or any secret
> intimation of it to them, or a full assurance of it, as is

evident by what follows." - Gills Exposition of the entire Bible

"They did not doubt God's ability but neither did they presume to know God's will. In this they agreed with Job: Though He slay me, yet will I trust Him (Job 13:15). They recognized that God's plan might be different than their desires. I have my own desires and dreams and I pray that God fulfills them. But if He doesn't, I can't turn my back on Him." -David Guzik

We know from several passages in the Bible and from history that it is sometimes God's desire for believers to be martyred. We even see in Revelation 6: 9-11 that God waits to judge the world specifically until more martyrs are killed. God has His purposes for this. This is also why He tells us not to think of what we will say as our last words but that He will say them for us. It is one of the most powerful testimonies possible for a child of God.

This "**But if not**" is a stinging rebuke to the Word of Faith movement. The idea that any lack of answered prayer is because of your lack of faith rather than the will of God. These men are listed in the so called "hall of faith" in the book of Hebrews, but you can see that they were decidedly unsure if God was going to save them or not. They realized that sometimes it is God's will not to answer their prayers. They would be considered to have a lack of faith by the modern Word of Faith movement because they weren't claiming this deliverance.

This is similar to Paul with his thorn in the flesh, or Jesus in the garden praying for the cup to pass if possible. They all said, in effect, "not my will but yours be done."

Dan 3:19 Then Nebuchadnezzar was full of fury, and the expression on his face changed toward Shadrach, Meshach, and Abed-Nego. He spoke and commanded that they heat the furnace seven times more than it was usually heated.

Ok, now they really angered the king! The **expression on his face changed** and he was **full** of fury. He orders something in his anger here that he will come to regret, that is heating up the furnace past its normal operating temperature.

Miller quotes another scholar about the phrase **"Seven times hotter"**

> "Baldwin points out that "seven times" is a proverbial expression and cites Prov 24:16 and 26:16 as examples.60 Hartman calls this "an idiomatic way of saying 'as hot as possible,'"61 and he seems to be correct. Thus the expression signifies that the furnace was heated to maximum intensity."

Dan 3:20 And he commanded certain mighty men of valor who were in his army to bind Shadrach, Meshach, and Abed-Nego, and cast them into the burning fiery furnace.
Dan 3:21 Then these men were bound in their coats, their trousers, their turbans, and their other garments, and were cast into the midst of the burning fiery furnace.
Dan 3:22 Therefore, because the king's command was urgent, and the furnace exceedingly hot, the flame of the fire killed those men who took up Shadrach, Meshach, and Abed-Nego.
Dan 3:23 And these three men, Shadrach, Meshach, and Abed-Nego, fell down bound into the midst of the burning fiery furnace.

The king's command was urgent

Nebuchadnezzar had an anger problem here, and he was "full" of fury, and what is happening here is people following orders which are probably a little hasty, but it doesn't sound like the time or place to tell the king that he should rethink his orders. It was probably best to walk on eggshells around the king at this point given his disposition, unless you had a death wish.

I have often wondered how this fire killed the men that opened the furnace. I think the answer is almost certainly the phenomenon known as "backdraft." Here is the definition of this:

> "A backdraft is an explosive event at a fire resulting from rapid re-introduction of oxygen to combustion in an oxygen-starved environment, for example, the breaking of a window or opening of a door to an enclosed space."[5]

So when they opened the door of this now superheated furnace it reintroduced oxygen and took out some of Nebuchadnezzar's best men.

God Delivers His Servants

Dan 3:24 Then King Nebuchadnezzar was astonished; and he rose in haste and spoke, saying to his counselors, "Did we not cast three men bound into the midst of the fire?" They answered and said to the king, "True, O king."

So Nebuchadnezzar is getting confirmation of this, because he is noticing something.

Dan 3:25 "Look!" he answered, "I see four men loose, walking in the midst of the fire; and they are not hurt, and the form of the fourth is like the Son of God."

This is almost certainly a "Christophany," an appearance of Jesus Christ in the Old Testament. And there are a lot of good lessons to be learned from it. The idea that in the time of fiery trial in your life Jesus will be there with you.

It is a temptation when trials come to get angry with God and move away from Him, but if we decide to use the trial as a reason to draw even closer to God, He will be nearer than ever before. I often think of that famous footsteps poem where God carries you in your times of trouble. When you are at your worst, God is at His best, but we must not run away from Him in troubles but to Him. It has been said that sometimes God does not want to yank you out of trials; He wants to go through them with you, and use them to break the things that bind you as we see these men also only had their bindings loosed from the fire and nothing else.

The translation of **Son of God**, as to what Nebuchadnezzar said he saw in the fire with them, is probably a bad translation according to many of the language scholars I have read, though I know there are disagreements about that.

I agree with those that say this phrase is probably referring to a member of the "Divine Council" or so-called "Sons of God." The Babylonian religion had a huge emphasis on the so-called Divine Council. Much of their mythology dealt with what we would call the Sons of God or high ranking angels from Genesis 6. There are a large number of parallels between their stories and the stories in the Bible. Michael Hesier even points out that a certain number of the Sons of God in their mythology became confined to the underworld while another number remained in heaven, though the reason for this is not stated in their mythology. Their version of the Sons of God were also involved in a mixing of angels and human beings and creating unnatural offspring which resulted in a flood being sent.

Basically the Babylonians had a sort of shady understanding of the truth, but the bad part is that in their culture they worshipped the created beings rather than the creator.

Dan 3:26 Then Nebuchadnezzar went near the mouth of the burning fiery furnace and spoke, saying, "Shadrach, Meshach, and Abed-Nego, servants of the Most High God, come out, and come here." Then Shadrach, Meshach, and Abed-Nego came from the midst of the fire.
Dan 3:27 And the satraps, administrators, governors, and the king's counselors gathered together, and they saw these men on whose bodies the fire had no power; the hair of their head was not singed nor were their garments affected, and the smell of fire was not on them.

Servants of the Most High God

Even before they are out of the furnace, Nebuchadnezzar recognizes that these men serve the **Most High God.**

The three Hebrews experienced literally the promise, "When you walk through the fire, you will not be burned; the flames will not set you ablaze" (Isa 43:2).

Dan 3:28 Nebuchadnezzar spoke, saying, "Blessed be the God of Shadrach, Meshach, and Abed-Nego, who sent His Angel and delivered His servants who trusted in Him, and they have frustrated the king's word, and yielded their bodies, that they should not serve nor worship any god except their own God!

Nebuchadnezzar is giving them praise for their conviction to disobey him here. He recognized that this was about their refusal to worship any God but Yahweh and that he was trying to get them to do what he now knows Yahweh is not okay with at all.

Dan 3:29 Therefore I make a decree that any people, nation, or language which speaks anything amiss against the God of Shadrach, Meshach, and Abed-Nego shall be cut in pieces, and their houses shall be made an ash heap; because there is no other God who can deliver like this."

Nebuchadnezzar here makes it illegal to slight Yahweh, and such an offence would be upon the penalty of what seems to be Nebuchadnezzar's favorite punishment, that is being cut into pieces and making their houses an ash heap.

This could have been done by Nebuchadnezzar out of fear, as he recognized he had blasphemed this powerful God who obviously did exist and was serious, and this was perhaps his attempt to appease Him.

This and the next line make me think that Nebuchadnezzar was onto these guys who were trying to plot against the Jewish employees - I think a good boss knows about the office politics to some degree. This decree about not talking bad about the Jewish God may have been a way to prevent something similar from happening again.

64

He does to Shadrach, Meshach, and Abed-Nego in the next verse the very thing that seemed to anger the occultist the most - he promotes them.

Dan 3:30 Then the king promoted Shadrach, Meshach, and Abed-Nego in the province of Babylon.

It should be noted that there was found a tablet that appears to confirm the names of these men as employees of Babylon, as well as two other Babylonian employees that are mentioned in the Bible.

> Nabuzeriddinam=Nebuzaradan (2 Kgs 25:8, 11; Jer 39:9–11, 13; 40:1, etc.) and Nergalsharusur (Neriglissar)=Nergal-Sharezer (Jer 39:3, 13).[6]

Chapter 4

Dan 4:1 Nebuchadnezzar the king, To all peoples, nations, and languages that dwell in all the earth: Peace be multiplied to you.

Nebuchadnezzar the king:

This is a unique chapter for several reasons, one of those reasons being that It was written by a gentile king. Daniel includes this epistle from Nebuchadnezzar in his collection of prophecies and highlights of his life that we call the Book of Daniel.

To all peoples, nations, and languages that dwell in all the earth

This letter of Nebuchadnezzar is addressed to the whole world, probably intended for distribution throughout the kingdom. Many proclamations of the kings of Babylon and Assyria were similarly addressed.

This letter was probably written in Aramaic as that was the official language of the kingdom, and as we have already mentioned several times in this study this portion of Daniel is one of the few places in the Bible where the original language of the text is Aramaic.

Dan 4:2 I thought it good to declare the signs and wonders that the Most High God has worked for me.

To declare the signs and wonders that the Most High God has worked for me

This is basically Nebuchadnezzar's testimony about his salvation, if indeed he was saved.

I thought it good

Here we see his motivations for declaring his testimony to the world: he **thought it good**. This is a good lesson for us too. It is good to tell people what God has done for you, Doing so is a way of evangelism, and in some situations and for some people it is the most effective way for you to tell people about God.

I also would like to think that these are the words of a man who has been changed and now desires the same for those he has influence on; his passion is to tell people about the God that saved him.

Many of you might have felt similar to this when you were saved.

Dan 4:3 How great are His signs, And how mighty His wonders! His kingdom is an everlasting kingdom, And His dominion is from generation to generation.

Nebuchadnezzar starts and ends this epistle with a doxology. He praises God for his miracles and the fact that God's kingdom, unlike his own or any other kingdom among man, is an everlasting kingdom.

Nebuchadnezzar Dreams of a Tree

Dan 4:4 I, Nebuchadnezzar, was at rest in my house, and flourishing in my palace.

I think this mention of prosperity here is significant to the story of Nebuchadnezzar's testimony in that it may be drawing attention to the hardness of one's heart in the midst of prosperity.

In what follows we will see that God goes to extreme measures to humble Nebuchadnezzar. I have a hunch that this attention-getter was proportional to the amount of Nebuchadnezzar's pride and prosperity, which was very high.

One lesson we might take from this is that we should never consider anyone unsaveable, especially those in leadership who we are encouraged by God to pray for. I suspect there would be a lot more conversions of world leaders if there were a lot more Daniels in the world, who we will see even more clearly in Chapter 6 was serious about his prayer life.

Dan 4:5 I saw a dream which made me afraid, and the thoughts on my bed and the visions of my head troubled me.
Dan 4:6 Therefore I issued a decree to bring in all the wise men of Babylon before me, that they might make known to me the interpretation of the dream.
Dan 4:7 Then the magicians, the astrologers, the Chaldeans, and the soothsayers came in, and I told them the dream; but they did not make known to me its interpretation.
Dan 4:8 But at last Daniel came before me (his name is Belteshazzar, according to the name of my god; in him is the Spirit of the Holy God), and I told the dream before him, saying:
Dan 4:9 "Belteshazzar, chief of the magicians, because I know that the Spirit of the Holy God is in you, and no secret troubles you, explain to me the visions of my dream that I have seen, and its interpretation.

We have here a very similar situation as we saw in Chapter 2. Nebuchadnezzar has a dream which he feels is very significant, so he calls in his advisors for its interpretation.

As in Chapter 2 I will note that God seems to use the local strongly held belief in the importance of dreams as a vehicle in which to speak to Nebuchadnezzar.

What I mean is that there is no doubt that he and other kings of the ancient world often had dreams that were of no significance, yet they were probably interpreted for the kings by similar dream advisors all the same. Here though, as was the case in Chapter 2, Nebuchadnezzar is **troubled**, which I take to mean that he understood that this dream was special in some way. We know from the text that indeed it was God who had sent him this dream and that his feelings about it being significant were indeed correct.

I wonder if God still does this today with people in places of tremendous power. That is if He sends them ominous warnings in their dreams. We know that God still works with people through dreams (Acts 2:17). I wouldn't at all be surprised if world leaders today were also warned of their destruction unless they repent like Nebuchadnezzar was here as we will see.

Though these two instances (Dan 2 & 7) are similar, there are some differences. For example it seems that though the advisors were not able, or some would argue were unwilling, to interpret this dream, Nebuchadnezzar does not get upset with them like in Chapter 2 or at least we are not told he did.

I would note that it should be remembered that at the end of Chapter 2 Daniel was put in charge of these guys and was presumably training them to do their jobs. So this shouldn't represent an exact duplicate of the former instances because these guys were supposedly now using the Daniel method of dream interpretation, though it becomes clear in the book that many of them resented Daniel and therefore didn't listen to what he had to say, especially if what he had to say was for them to repent and turn to Yahweh worship.

Only after they fail is Daniel called in. We are nowhere told why Daniel was not there at first, but it can be safely assumed that those he was chief over were expected to be able to do this without him.

Nebuchadnezzar, after referring to Daniel by his Hebrew name, which would appear to indicate a change in Nebuchadnezzar, he then explains that he is referring to the one known as Belteshazzar.

Dan 4:10 These were the visions of my head while on my bed: I was looking, and behold, A tree in the midst of the earth, And its height was great.

Dan 4:11 **The tree grew and became strong; Its height reached to the heavens, And it could be seen to the ends of all the earth.**
Dan 4:12 **Its leaves were lovely, Its fruit abundant, And in it was food for all. The beasts of the field found shade under it, The birds of the heavens dwelt in its branches, And all flesh was fed from it.**
Dan 4:13 **"I saw in the visions of my head while on my bed, and there was a watcher, a holy one, coming down from heaven.**
Dan 4:14 **He cried aloud and said thus: 'Chop down the tree and cut off its branches, Strip off its leaves and scatter its fruit. Let the beasts get out from under it, And the birds from its branches.**
Dan 4:15 **Nevertheless leave the stump and roots in the earth, Bound with a band of iron and bronze, In the tender grass of the field. Let it be wet with the dew of heaven, And let him graze with the beasts On the grass of the earth.**
Dan 4:16 **Let his heart be changed from that of a man, Let him be given the heart of a beast, And let seven times pass over him.**
Dan 4:17 **'This decision is by the decree of the watchers, And the sentence by the word of the holy ones, In order that the living may know That the Most High rules in the kingdom of men, Gives it to whomever He will, And sets over it the lowest of men.'**
Dan 4:18 **"This dream I, King Nebuchadnezzar, have seen. Now you, Belteshazzar, declare its interpretation, since all the wise men of my kingdom are not able to make known to me the interpretation; but you are able, for the Spirit of the Holy God is in you."**

So there you have it: The dream God gave to Nebuchadnezzar. A very big and fruitful tree was ordered to be cut down by the decree of a watcher in order to glorify God. A period of time was set where the man's heart would be changed to that of a beast including eating grass and it will be done "'**In order that the living may know That the Most High rules in the kingdom of**

men, Gives it to whomever He will, And sets over it the lowest of men.'"

This idea of the watcher is interesting. The term according to Stephen Miller is:

> "literally "one who is awake" and occurs only in this chapter (vv. 13, 17, 23) in the Bible, although in the Genesis Apocryphon from Qumran it is used as a term for an angel.[19] Montgomery adds, "We have here the earliest mention of the Wakeful Ones, generally known in our translations as the Watchers, who play so important a role in Enoch, Jubilees, the XII Testaments, etc." [20] The idea is that this heavenly being is awake and keeping watch over the activities of the human race.[21]" (Miller, 1994-08-31, p. 133)

We usually think of this term "Watcher" as only referring to fallen angels but it is clear here as well as places like Ezek 1:18 that unfallen or holy watchers are to be included.

This decision *is* by the decree of the watchers, And the sentence by the word of the holy ones

The idea that the watchers are here decreeing judgment of Nebuchadnezzar is very interesting because the giving out of judgment is the primary job of the so-called "Divine Council" which are basically synonymous with these **un**-fallen or holy **watchers**. We see that they did not however always judge righteously, for example in Psalm 82.

> A Psalm of Asaph. God stands in the congregation of the mighty; He judges among the gods. How long will you judge unjustly, And show partiality to the wicked? Selah Defend the poor and fatherless; Do justice to the afflicted and needy. Deliver the poor and needy; Free them from the hand of the wicked. They do not know, nor do they understand; They walk about in darkness; All the foundations of the earth are unstable. I said, "You are gods, And all of you are children of the Most High. But you shall die

like men, And fall like one of the princes." Arise, O
God, judge the earth; For You shall inherit all
nations.- Psa 82:1-8

God divided the nations to the sons of God or "Divine Council"
after Babel.

> Remember the days of old, consider the years of
> many generations; ask your father, and he will show
> you; your elders, and they will tell you. 8 When the
> Most High gave to the nations their inheritance, when
> He separated the sons of men, He fixed the bounds of
> the peoples according to the number of the SONS OF
> GOD. 9 For the LORD's portion is His people, Jacob
> His allotted heritage. - Deut 32:7

In 2 Chronicles we have an insight into a council meeting in
which God has made a decree about the king, but he includes the
angels in the decision-making process, on how exactly it will be
done.

> Then Micaiah said, "Therefore hear the word of the
> LORD: I saw the LORD sitting on His throne, and **all
> the host of heaven standing on His right hand and
> His left**. 19 And the LORD said, '**Who will persuade
> Ahab king of Israel to go up, that he may fall at
> Ramoth Gilead?**' So one spoke in this manner, and
> another spoke in that manner. 20 Then a **spirit** came
> forward and stood before the LORD, and said, 'I will
> persuade him.' The LORD said to him, 'In what way?'
> 21 "So he said, 'I will go out and be a **lying spirit** in the
> mouth of all his prophets.' And the Lord said, 'You shall
> persuade him and also prevail; go out and do so.' 22
> Therefore look! The LORD has put a **lying spirit** in the
> mouth of these prophets of yours, and the LORD has
> declared disaster against you." - II CHRONICLES 18:18

It is not unusual that Nebuchadnezzar would know of watchers
who decreed fates.
As mentioned previously these beings were very well understood
in Babylonian and Assyrian mythology. Although they had a

kind of paganized view of them, they understood that the watchers had a function of decreeing fates.

Nebuchadnezzar knew what a "watcher" was and that they had the authority to determine how he was humbled.

For more on the Divine Council of the Bible see Dr. Michael Heiser's work on the subject at his website **www.thedivinecouncil.com**.

Daniel Interprets Nebuchadnezzar's Dream

Dan 4:19 Then Daniel, whose name was Belteshazzar, was astonished for a time, and his thoughts troubled him. So the king spoke, and said, "Belteshazzar, do not let the dream or its interpretation trouble you." Belteshazzar answered and said, "My lord, may the dream concern those who hate you, and its interpretation concern your enemies!

This gives some credence to some commentators' views that this dream was easy to interpret and that even his trained advisors knew the interpretation but were afraid to tell the king.

Daniel himself doesn't even speak and is very worried until Nebuchadnezzar reassures him, and then he tells him what it means, and even then Daniel gives a caveat that he wishes that the dream applied to Nebuchadnezzar's enemies.

So here is the interpretation of the dream:

Dan 4:20 "The tree that you saw, which grew and became strong, whose height reached to the heavens and which could be seen by all the earth,
Dan 4:21 whose leaves were lovely and its fruit abundant, in which was food for all, under which the beasts of the field dwelt, and in whose branches the birds of the heaven had their home—

**Dan 4:22 it is you, O king, who have grown and become
strong; for your greatness has grown and reaches to the
heavens, and your dominion to the end of the earth.**

So this first part is clear: The fruitful tree is Nebuchadnezzar and
his flourishing kingdom.

**Dan 4:23 "And inasmuch as the king saw a watcher, a
holy one, coming down from heaven and saying, 'Chop
down the tree and destroy it, but leave its stump and roots
in the earth, bound with a band of iron and bronze in the
tender grass of the field; let it be wet with the dew of
heaven, and let him graze with the beasts of the field, till
seven times pass over him';
Dan 4:24 this is the interpretation, O king, and this is the
decree of the Most High, which has come upon my lord
the king:
Dan 4:25 They shall drive you from men, your dwelling
shall be with the beasts of the field, and they shall make
you eat grass like oxen. They shall wet you with the dew of
heaven, and seven times shall pass over you, till you know
that the Most High rules in the kingdom of men, and gives
it to whomever He chooses.**

As we will see this came to pass in a very literal way. David
Guzik makes the point that Nebuchadnezzar probably had no
clue as to how literal it would be. He really would be turned
mentally into an animal.

It would seem that any commentator on this passage is
contractually obliged to mention that something like what is
being described here is a real medical condition. Guzik writes:

> "The form of insanity in which men think of
> themselves as animals and imitate the behavior of an
> animal has been observed. Some call it generally
> insania zoanthropica [Clinical lycanthropy] and more
> specifically in Nebuchadnezzar's case, boanthropy,
> the delusion that one is an ox.

ii. Walvoord quotes a Dr. Raymond Harrison of Britain, who in 1946 had a patient suffering from boanthropy, just as Nebuchadnezzar suffered. [including eating grass outside the asylum]"

Clinical lycanthropy is an interesting condition. In reading briefly on it I noted that there is neurological activity that is showing a genuine change in perception of a person's body shape, etc.

But there also appears to be in some cases occasional lucidity or coming back to normal for a brief spell, where the person can describe the feelings they are having. This lucidity, in Nebuchadnezzar's case, may have been an opportunity for him to repent, which we will now see was the ultimate goal of this judgment.

Dan 4:26 "And inasmuch as they gave the command to leave the stump and roots of the tree, your kingdom shall be assured to you, after you come to know that Heaven rules.

After you come to know that Heaven rules.

This realization is what all of us must come to. The difference is that Nebuchadnezzar had further to fall than some of us in order to realize that God, not us, is the king of our lives and everything else.

Testifying to Jews, and also to Greeks, repentance toward God and faith toward our Lord Jesus Christ. - Act 20:21

Repentance toward God is a part of our need — we are all in rebellion against God (Rom 3:10-19). We need to change our minds about that rebellion, to lay it down, admit that He is God, and we and our ways and our plans must take a back seat to His.

Even Nebuchadnezzar had a belief that Yahweh was greater than other gods before this occasion (Dan 2:47) but he did not yet humble himself to Him. This process is God benevolently bringing Nebuchadnezzar to a place of humility for his own good.

Dan 4:27 Therefore, O king, let my advice be acceptable to you; break off your sins by being righteous, and your iniquities by showing mercy to the poor. Perhaps there may be a lengthening of your prosperity."

Daniel's beautiful council to his king and perhaps friend: "Please stop sinning — perhaps we can lengthen the days before this happens." Notice that Daniel does not suggest it can be altogether avoided. Perhaps he knows that the decree has been made and the decision is final. In other words God knows that it will take a very big act for Nebuchadnezzar to change his mind and Daniel agrees with that. Daniel only suggests that the time before the inevitable humbling can be lengthened.

And because it was a full year later that this happened, as we will see, we can reasonably assume that there was in fact a lengthening of time given. That is to say that Nebuchadnezzar might have taken Daniel's advice here to a degree.

Dan 4:28 All this came upon King Nebuchadnezzar.
Dan 4:29 At the end of the twelve months he was walking about the royal palace of Babylon.
Dan 4:30 The king spoke, saying, "Is not this great Babylon, that I have built for a royal dwelling by my mighty power and for the honor of my majesty?"

He is looking at the kingdom and attributes its greatness to himself. This is despite having the more than enough testimony from Daniel who in a miraculous way in Chapter 2 showed Nebuchadnezzar that his kingdom was given to him by Yahweh, and that is the only reason it is his to rule or that it is prosperous.

Remember this is the king recounting his testimony. These words of pride might have been bitter to him now as he recounts the story, especially knowing what happens next.

Dan 4:31 While the word was still in the king's mouth, a voice fell from heaven: "King Nebuchadnezzar, to you it is spoken: the kingdom has departed from you!
Dan 4:32 And they shall drive you from men, and your dwelling shall be with the beasts of the field. They shall make you eat grass like oxen; and seven times shall pass over you, until you know that the Most High rules in the kingdom of men, and gives it to whomever He chooses."
Dan 4:33 That very hour the word was fulfilled concerning Nebuchadnezzar; he was driven from men and ate grass like oxen; his body was wet with the dew of heaven till his hair had grown like eagles' feathers and his nails like birds' claws.

A voice fell from heaven: "King Nebuchadnezzar, to you it is spoken: the kingdom has departed from you!"

So part of Nebuchadnezzar's testimony is this voice that made sure he remembered the previous dream and the reason that this was going to happen to him, namely , so that he will **know that the Most High rules in the kingdom of men, and gives it to whomever He chooses.**

Many commentators note that there is a period of Nebuchadnezzar's reign in which there is no record of any of his decrees or any other official business; they have essentially an argument from silence of this event's historicity.

Dan 4:34 And at the end of the time I, Nebuchadnezzar, lifted my eyes to heaven, and my understanding returned to me; and I blessed the Most High and praised and honored Him who lives forever: For His dominion is an everlasting dominion, And His kingdom is from generation to generation.
Dan 4:35 All the inhabitants of the earth are reputed as nothing; He does according to His will in the army of heaven And among the inhabitants of the earth. No one can restrain His hand Or say to Him, "What have You done?"

Dan 4:36 At the same time my reason returned to me, and for the glory of my kingdom, my honor and splendor returned to me. My counselors and nobles resorted to me, I was restored to my kingdom, and excellent majesty was added to me.
Dan 4:37 Now I, Nebuchadnezzar, praise and extol and honor the King of heaven, all of whose works are truth, and His ways justice. And those who walk in pride He is able to put down.

At last, in a moment of clarity Nebuchadnezzar repents.

> "Now the account reverts to first person, and Nebuchadnezzar continues his personal testimony. At the end of the seven years, the king raised his eyes toward heaven, an act of submission, surrender, and acknowledgment of his need for the Most High God. Yahweh had proven he was truly the sovereign Lord and could humble the greatest king on earth. God observed Nebuchadnezzar's simple gesture of humility and repentance and graciously restored his "sanity" ("knowledge, power of knowing"). Then the king "praised" God as sovereign ("the Most High") and "honored" and "glorified" him as the eternal One ("him who lives forever")" (Miller, 1994-08-31, p. 143).

Dan 4:35 All the inhabitants of the earth are reputed as nothing; He does according to His will in the army of heaven And among the inhabitants of the earth. No one can restrain His hand Or say to Him, "What have You done?"

He recognizes in these statements the very thing he needed to which according to verse 32 was **that the Most High rules in the kingdom of men, and gives it to whomever He chooses.**

God is God and we are not. We owe him our lives on that basis alone. Just as Job learned, God can do what He pleases and we should trust Him. We can rest knowing that this God with total control is a good God. Jesus tells us to look to Him and His personality for the character of God (John 14: 7-11).

Now I, Nebuchadnezzar, praise and extol and honor the King of heaven, all of whose works *are* truth, and His ways justice. And those who walk in pride He is able to put down.

This is really the last we hear of Nebuchadnezzar except for Daniel's recap and validation of the events of this chapter.

This is when he is brought before Belshazzar during this drunken party to explain the writing on the wall to them. He says:

> O king, the Most High God gave Nebuchadnezzar your father a kingdom and majesty, glory and honor. And because of the majesty that He gave him, all peoples, nations, and languages trembled and feared before him. Whomever he wished, he executed; whomever he wished, he kept alive; whomever he wished, he set up; and whomever he wished, he put down. But when his heart was lifted up, and his spirit was hardened in pride, he was deposed from his kingly throne, and they took his glory from him. Then he was driven from the sons of men, his heart was made like the beasts, and his dwelling was with the wild donkeys. They fed him with grass like oxen, and his body was wet with the dew of heaven, till he knew that the Most High God rules in the kingdom of men, and appoints over it whomever He chooses. "But you his son, Belshazzar, have not humbled your heart, although you knew all this. And you have lifted yourself up against the Lord of heaven. They have brought the vessels of His house before you, and you and your lords, your wives and your concubines, have drunk wine from them. And you have praised the gods of silver and gold, bronze and iron, wood and stone, which do not see or hear or know; and the God who holds your breath in His hand and owns all your ways, you have not glorified. - Dan 5:18-23

So I think we can take Daniel's word for it here that Nebuchadnezzar didn't end up all that bad; in fact, he might even have been saved. I think in a way this section of scripture details the evangelism of Nebuchadnezzar from the first moment that Daniel and his friends impressed him with their knowledge, to the dream interpretation, to the fiery furnace, and finally to this humbling of Nebuchadnezzar. It shows us that we ought not to give up on the people we are praying for, especially those in power.

It shows us that we all need to repent and realize God's kingship of our lives and submit to him. And know that he will bring things in your life to get you to do that because he loves you and doesn't desire anyone to perish.

Chapter 5

Belshazzar Sees Handwriting on a Wall

Dan 5:1 Belshazzar the king made a great feast for a thousand of his lords, and drank wine in the presence of the thousand.

Belshazzar the king

We open up this chapter with a new King of Babylon. Nebuchadnezzar is gone and we are here introduced for the first time to Belshazzar.

Up until the early 1880's critics of the Bible would point out that the archeological records available at that time showed no evidence for a king named Belshazzar. And even worse, the records that they did have said that the last king of Babylon was Nabonidus, not Belshazzar. That all changed when archeologists discovered the so-called Nabonidus cylinder which is now in the British Museum. This as well as subsequent finds now show that while Nabonidus was indeed the last king of Babylon, he had a son named Belshazzar whom he co-ruled with. Nabonidus however spent most of his reign on religious journeys in the wilderness and was generally hated for it, so Belshazzar his son was left to rule the kingdom.

This chapter occurs only a few years after Nebuchadnezzar's death, but even in that short time there were a number of different kings with very short reigns between the two times.

Guzik gives a rundown of the events:
- Nebuchadnezzar dies after a 43-year reign

- His son, Evil-Merodach (described in 2Kings2 5:27-30 and Jer 52:31-34) rules for only two years when he is assassinated by his brother-in-law Neriglassar, because his rule was arbitrary and licentious
- Neriglassar (mentioned as Nergalsharezer in Jer 39:3, 13) rules for four years until he dies a natural death
- His son, Laborosoarchod, only a child and of diminished mental capacity, rules for only nine months when he is beaten to death by a gang of conspirators
- The conspirators appoint Nabonidus, one of their gang, to be king. He rules until Cyrus the Persian conquers Babylon

So we join Belshazzar who was the son and co-ruler of Nabonidus on the night that Babylon would fall. Outside the city gates was a huge Persian army who was camped outside the city waiting for the city to surrender. But the city was well stocked and well watered and was believed to be impenetrable, so in that sense they were not worried.

Despite the strength of the city however, Babylon was in no position be merry, as a huge Persian army had defeated them in battle just days before, a battle in which Nabonidus apparently back from a pilgrimage was leading and fled during the course of, and all that held back the Medo-Persian empire from becoming the new ruler of the world was the city of Babylon.

Made a great feast for a thousand of his lords, and drank wine in the presence of the thousand.

The Greek historians Herodotus and Xenophon both attest to there being a feast in progress the night that Babylon was conquered.

The reason for having this feast is debated. Some commentators suggest it was to demonstrate Belshazzar's confidence in the city walls and their security from the army outside the gates.

Others suggest it may be that since his father, the first ruler, had fled in the battle days before Belshazzar had declared himself to be the first ruler, this was a coronation ceremony.

Herodotus suggests that this was an annual Babylonian feast that just happens to fall on an inopportune day.

The reason for the feast is not all that important. What is important is what Belshazzar does next.

Dan 5:2 While he tasted the wine, Belshazzar gave the command to bring the gold and silver vessels which his father Nebuchadnezzar had taken from the temple which had been in Jerusalem, that the king and his lords, his wives, and his concubines might drink from them.
Dan 5:3 Then they brought the gold vessels that had been taken from the temple of the house of God which had been in Jerusalem; and the king and his lords, his wives, and his concubines drank from them.
Dan 5:4 They drank wine, and praised the gods of gold and silver, bronze and iron, wood and stone.

While he tasted the wine

Some suggest that this phrase basically means that when Belshazzar got drunk he ordered these items to be brought in.

Nebuchadnezzar had taken from the temple which *had been* in Jerusalem

These were the items that Nebuchadnezzar had taken from the temple in Jerusalem when he conquered it back when Daniel was brought to Babylon as a young boy. These were considered very holy items by God. God had specific roles for many of these items and He was serious about them.

Nebuchadnezzar kept these items in a museum of sorts. Belshazzar's sacrilege here is confusing to scholars as it is something that few superstitious people, which the Babylonians were, would do regardless of what god they worshipped, that is to use a sacred item in a common way like this. But it gets

85

weirder—he does this while praising other gods, presumably his gods.

And praised the gods of gold and silver, bronze and iron, wood and stone.

It doesn't mean the god of wood or silver but rather, from Daniel's viewpoint, the gods who were nothing more that wood or stone or metal; in other words, gods that were not really gods at all.

I think that this demonstrates a very specific contempt for Yahweh by Belshazzar. I think that information about Yahweh was big news in Babylon both before and after Nebuchadnezzar's conversion in the last chapter (if indeed he was truly converted). After all there was no shortage of unbelievable stories and miracles about these Jews that claimed their God was the only true God—miracles like people going into a furnace in front of all the nobles and not being burned.

We will see later that Daniel tells us that Belshazzar knew everything that happened to Nebuchadnezzar and about how and why Yahweh humbled him. Nebuchadnezzar made sure everyone knew it when he published a tract that went out to the entire world glorifying Yahweh. Yet for some reason Belshazzar was going all in here with this super blasphemy.

It could also have been related to the religious tensions that his father had been causing. His father Nabonidus was wildly unpopular because of his religious reforms. As I mentioned Nabonidus spent most of his time away from Babylon in pursuit of his religious beliefs. He was devoted the moon god Sin, which was not the main god of the Babylonian's, and he removed idols from temples and a number of other things that angered the people and especially the priesthood in Babylon.

So this may have been Belshazzar's attempt, with his father now killed or captured outside the gates, to praise the gods of Babylon to the exclusion of others, though this is by no means certain from the text.

It could have been a defiance of Yahweh or the followers of Yahweh who said that Nebuchadnezzar's kingdom would end, or it could be, as some suggest, a way to demonstrate that he was not afraid of the surrounding armies, though it is not clear how this specific act would demonstrate that.

What we can be sure of is that this is an unprecedented and specific attack on Yahweh by Belshazzar. And I'm sure by what happens next that he knew he was gambling here. I'm sure there were a few nobles in the room that swallowed hard when they heard this drunken king give orders to go get the temple materials. They knew that Yahweh was not to be messed with;, they had seen him do amazing things.

And He is about to something else quite amazing.

Dan 5:5 In the same hour the fingers of a man's hand appeared and wrote opposite the lampstand on the plaster of the wall of the king's palace; and the king saw the part of the hand that wrote.
Dan 5:6 Then the king's countenance changed, and his thoughts troubled him, so that the joints of his hips were loosened and his knees knocked against each other.

I think the king's reaction to this supernatural event demonstrates more than a guilty conscience. I think he knew he was taking a risk with this stunt — that's why he only did it when he was drunk. I think there was tension in the room already when they were committing this sacrilegious act on holy items, but not just any holy items, the ones that were Yahweh's whom I'm sure many in the room remembered and even saw with their own eyes the great things Yahweh was capable of.

After all the writing could have been anything; perhaps it was saying something favorable. But because he knew he was in the process of doing evil **his thoughts troubled him, so that the joints of his hips were loosened and his knees knocked against each other.** That's a pretty uncontrolled fear. I mean really, that's like totally losing it, and in front of all your friends no less. It is likely that he thought that his offense of God would result in his death, and he was correct.

Archeologists have discovered a large room in Babylon in the king's court that is very likely to be this very room. It is big enough, it has plaster walls as verse 5 says and it is in the right place.

> "Archeologist Robert Koldewey, who found the Ishtar gate and other great finds in Babylon, said: "It is so clearly marked out for this purpose [as a throne-room] that no reasonable doubt can be felt as to its having been used as their principal audience chamber. If anyone should desire to localize the scene of Belshazzar's eventful banquet, he can surely place it with complete accuracy in this immense room."[7]

Dan 5:7 The king cried aloud to bring in the astrologers, the Chaldeans, and the soothsayers. The king spoke, saying to the wise men of Babylon, "Whoever reads this writing, and tells me its interpretation, shall be clothed with purple and have a chain of gold around his neck; and he shall be the third ruler in the kingdom."
Dan 5:8 Now all the king's wise men came, but they could not read the writing, or make known to the king its interpretation.
Dan 5:9 Then King Belshazzar was greatly troubled, his countenance was changed, and his lords were astonished.

The king cried aloud to bring in the astrologers.

Apparently the King was screaming for his astrologers here.

Then King Belshazzar was greatly troubled, his countenance was changed, and his lords were astonished.
So when his guys couldn't read this writing, he really gets worried. The king feels that this writing is somehow about his fate. The thing is, his intuition is dead on, the same way that when Nebuchadnezzar had his dreams he knew that they were very different and very important, even though before Daniel showed up he didn't yet know what they meant.

Dan 5:10 The queen, because of the words of the king and his lords, came to the banquet hall. The queen spoke, saying, "O king, live forever! Do not let your thoughts trouble you, nor let your countenance change.
Dan 5:11 There is a man in your kingdom in whom is the Spirit of the Holy God. And in the days of your father, light and understanding and wisdom, like the wisdom of the gods, were found in him; and King Nebuchadnezzar your father—your father the king—made him chief of the magicians, astrologers, Chaldeans, and soothsayers.
Dan 5:12 Inasmuch as an excellent spirit, knowledge, understanding, interpreting dreams, solving riddles, and explaining enigmas were found in this Daniel, whom the king named Belteshazzar, now let Daniel be called, and he will give the interpretation."

The queen

This is probably referring to the "Queen Mother" wither the wife of Nebuchadnezzar or of Nabonidus not the wife of Belshazzar.[8]

This queen whoever she was seems to be someone who genuinely respects Daniel and his God when she says things like **"whom *is* the Spirit of the Holy God. And in the days of your father, light and understanding and wisdom, like the wisdom of the gods"**, were found in him. I think that there were probably more people like this in the kingdom of Babylon, people who were moved and impacted by God's ministry through Daniel and his friends. I wish that people would look to us as Christians in the workplace like this. If something terrible happens or some questions arise about God that people would think of you: Let's go ask Chris, he is a Christian.

We should all be salt and light to the world and we should make it our goal and ministry to do so.

Made him chief of the magicians

Daniel was currently not chief of the magicians in Belshazzar's reign, and based on her having to remind Belshazzar about him he probably had not been in the short reigns of his relatives either.

Either Daniel stepped down by choice (retired) or he was fired by the new kings. Based on the blasphemy of Belshazzar I think we can assume that Nebuchadnezzar's reverence of Yahweh was not shared by his successors which would surely result in firing the head of the magicians who was a Yahweh worshipper. Remember there were about three or four rulers before this who ruled for only a couple years each. There were a lot of assassinations and dirty dealings as was common in regime changes.

So Daniel, now an old man, is brought before this wicked King.

Dan 5:13 Then Daniel was brought in before the king. The king spoke, and said to Daniel, "Are you that Daniel who is one of the captives from Judah, whom my father the king brought from Judah?
Dan 5:14 I have heard of you, that the Spirit of God is in you, and that light and understanding and excellent wisdom are found in you.
Dan 5:15 Now the wise men, the astrologers, have been brought in before me, that they should read this writing and make known to me its interpretation, but they could not give the interpretation of the thing.
Dan 5:16 And I have heard of you, that you can give interpretations and explain enigmas. Now if you can read the writing and make known to me its interpretation, you shall be clothed with purple and have a chain of gold around your neck, and shall be the third ruler in the kingdom."

That Daniel who is one of the captives from Judah, whom my father the king brought from Judah?

It's not clear why he mentions that Daniel was a Jew, but Daniel who was a Jew being the guy who could read the writing, might have confirmed his suspicion that this was all about the Jewish God Yahweh and his sacrilegious acts he just committed. Or it's possible he was just trying to establish Daniel's identity more clearly.

When Belshazzar tells Daniel that he had **heard** of him, he repeats what the queen said. This hearing of Daniel is therefore to be understood as I *have just now* heard of you from the queen mother, not that he had before this time heard these things of Daniel.

Belshazzar offers Daniel to be the **third ruler** in the kingdom. Even before the archeological evidence confirming that Belshazzar was the second ruler to his often absentee father Nabonidus was found, this offer of the third ruler should have let early commentators know that Belshazzar was a coregent, and the best he could offer was the third position.

This also argues against the idea that this party was a coronation party, because it suggests that Belshazzar still considered his father to be the first ruler of Babylon.

So what will Daniel say to this offer of being the third ruler?

Daniel Interprets the Handwriting on the Wall

Dan 5:17 Then Daniel answered, and said before the king, "Let your gifts be for yourself, and give your rewards to another; yet I will read the writing to the king, and make known to him the interpretation."

Daniel rejects this offer. It's tempting to see this as Daniel being rude here, based on the reprimand of the king that follows, but it is not necessary. Perhaps Daniel, as was his custom, was making sure the King knew that the gift God had given him could not be bought, and this rejection of gifts and title was a humble rejection as opposed to a haughty one.

I will read the writing to the king, and make known to him the interpretation.

Daniel announces that he will interpret this writing but before he does he has something to say.

Dan 5:18 O king, the Most High God gave Nebuchadnezzar your father a kingdom and majesty, glory and honor.
Dan 5:19 And because of the majesty that He gave him, all peoples, nations, and languages trembled and feared before him. Whomever he wished, he executed; whomever he wished, he kept alive; whomever he wished, he set up; and whomever he wished, he put down.
Dan 5:20 But when his heart was lifted up, and his spirit was hardened in pride, he was deposed from his kingly throne, and they took his glory from him.
Dan 5:21 Then he was driven from the sons of men, his heart was made like the beasts, and his dwelling was with the wild donkeys. They fed him with grass like oxen, and his body was wet with the dew of heaven, till he knew that the Most High God rules in the kingdom of men, and appoints over it whomever He chooses.
Dan 5:22 "But you his son, Belshazzar, have not humbled your heart, although you knew all this.
Dan 5:23 And you have lifted yourself up against the Lord of heaven. They have brought the vessels of His house before you, and you and your lords, your wives and your concubines, have drunk wine from them. And you have praised the gods of silver and gold, bronze and iron, wood and stone, which do not see or hear or know; and the God who holds your breath in His hand and owns all your ways, you have not glorified.
Dan 5:24 Then the fingers of the hand were sent from Him, and this writing was written.

Daniel was very bold in his rebuke of Belshazzar, mentioning Nebuchadnezzar who knew that Yahweh had given him his kingdom and recounting the story of Chapter 4 which ultimately brought him to that realization, and contrasting him with Belshazzar, who despite having seen **all this** with his own eyes Belshazzar chose to deliberately blaspheme this God he had seen work.

And you have lifted yourself up against the Lord of heaven.

This phrase shows that Belshazzar was specifically and knowingly challenging Yahweh.

Daniel also notes his drinking wine with the temple objects while praising false gods which I am certain gave Daniel a type of righteous indignation.

He even emphasizes the folly of worshipping these false gods by referring to the gods of Babylon as **the gods of silver and gold, bronze and iron, wood and stone, which do not see or hear or know.** He contrasts their worthlessness with **the God who _holds_ your breath in His hand and owns all your ways.**

Pointing out the folly of the religion of Babylon here in front of everyone was no doubt a bold move, but Daniel could read the writing on the wall so to speak. He knew that Belshazzar's number was up. Both of those phrases originate from the next few verses, by the way. This was yet another evangelism opportunity for Daniel who seemed to make the most of these types of situations.

Dan 5:25 "And this is the inscription that was written: MENE, MENE, TEKEL, UPHARSIN.
Dan 5:26 This is the interpretation of each word. MENE: God has numbered your kingdom, and finished it;
Dan 5:27 TEKEL: You have been weighed in the balances, and found wanting;
Dan 5:28 PERES: Your kingdom has been divided, and given to the Medes and Persians."
Dan 5:29 Then Belshazzar gave the command, and they clothed Daniel with purple and put a chain of gold around his neck, and made a proclamation concerning him that he should be the third ruler in the kingdom.

There were four words written on the wall in front of this lampstand. They were Aramaic words so it is not as though the other folks couldn't read the words, but they didn't know what they meant; they required an interpretation in that sense.

Mene which means "numbered" was written twice, this is possibly for emphasis, and Daniel says it means that: **God has numbered your kingdom, and finished it.**

The two-fold **numbered and finished it** perhaps accounts for the doubled mene. It was not just numbered, but that number was up, and it was all over. This would have had some extra weight given the circumstances outside the city walls.

TEKEL: You have been weighed in the balances, and found wanting;

Tekel means weighed. This demonstrates that this judgment was coming upon him as a result of his lack of weight in some regard.

Dan 5:28 PERES: Your kingdom has been divided, and given to the Medes and Persians."

Peres means divided. Daniel says not only that this means that his kingdom would be dissolved but it would be given to the armies outside the gates. Interestingly, as many of you know, there are no vowels in Hebrew. The same is true in Aramaic. And this word for divided also is the word for Persians.

By Daniel saying his kingdom would be given to the **Medes and Persians** is yet another place in this book where Daniel validates the idea that the Medes and Persians co-ruled the known world after Babylon fell.

Belshazzar would have known that if his kingdom was to be given to them Medes and Persians it would mean that he was as good as dead, and indeed that's how the next verse begins.

They clothed Daniel with purple and *put* a chain of gold around his neck, and made a proclamation concerning him that he should be the third ruler in the kingdom.

I don't know what this is about. The text gives us no reason to think this was mocking Daniel in any way as some suggest. I think it was a way of trying to appease Daniel's God who he realized he had wronged in hopes of keeping what he said from happening. Or it could simply be that he gave it to him because he promised it to him, which would imply that he believed he had given the correct interpretation. In any case this would not have meant very much to anyone, all things considered.

Dan 5:30 That very night Belshazzar, king of the Chaldeans, was slain.
Dan 5:31 And Darius the Mede received the kingdom, being about sixty-two years old.

There is a lot of information about this event in secular history, but Daniel gives it only two verses here.

How did the armies get through the gates? Miller quotes some ancient historians:

> The outer walls were approximately twenty-five feet in width and rose to a height of at least forty feet. These fortifications were too difficult to challenge, and so according to Herodotus and Xenophon, the Medo-Persian army diverted water from the Euphrates River (which ran under the walls of Babylon) into a marsh. With the level of the water lowered, the soldiers were able to wade the river under the walls and enter the city.[100] (Miller, 1994-08-31, p. 167)

But even after they go through the first wall they still had to get though the main gates, but on this night the gates were left open. Some believe that it was a part of a conspiracy. Cyrus had been telling the people of Babylon that he should be king over them, and he already had conquered everything outside the gates. This is believed to have been an inside job.

God in the book of Isaiah says it was Him that left the gates open for Cyrus.

Cyrus was named specifically by God in the book of Isaiah hundreds of years before this. it is recorded that he was shown the scripture that we are about to read, and I can only guess this is one reason that we see him so willing to supply the Jews with the freedom and materials to rebuild their city.

> Who says of Cyrus, 'He is My shepherd, And he shall perform all My pleasure, Saying to Jerusalem, "You shall be built," And to the temple, "Your foundation shall be laid." "Thus says the LORD to His anointed, To Cyrus, whose right hand I have held— To subdue nations before him And loose the armor of kings, To open before him the double doors, So that the gates will not be shut: 'I will go before you And make the crooked places straight; I will break in pieces the gates of bronze And cut the bars of iron. I will give you the treasures of darkness And hidden riches of secret places, That you may know that I, the LORD, Who call you by your name, Am the God of Israel. For Jacob My servant's sake, And Israel My elect, I have even called you by your name; I have named you, though you have not known Me. I am the LORD, and there is no other; There is no God besides Me. I will gird you, though you have not known Me, That they may know from the rising of the sun to its setting That there is none besides Me. I am the LORD, and there is no other; I form the light and create darkness, I make peace and create calamity; I, the LORD, do all these things.' - Isa 44:28-45:7

I love that! That is such a great passage where God glorifies Himself, and it even exemplifies one of the themes in the last few chapters, which is that God is God and does what He wishes, and He raises up who He wants and abases who He wants. He is God, we are not and heaven rules.

Chapter 6

Daniel is Thrown into a Lions' Den

Dan 6:1 It pleased Darius to set over the kingdom one hundred and twenty satraps, to be over the whole kingdom;

So we are now discussing not only a new king here, but a brand new empire as well, that of the Medes and Persians. These two groups jointly ruled the known world after the conquest of Babylon by Cyrus which was discussed in the last chapter.

Darius was appointed as ruler of Babylon which was a very important city in the new empire, though it was not the capital of the Persian Empire.

There is some dispute as to the whether **Darius** is a title for Cyrus or if Darius was the Median co-king with Cyrus. For more on this see the discussion in Daniel 9:1.

One hundred and twenty satraps, to be over the whole kingdom;

Here it notes that the number of satraps was 120. A satrapie, as they are called in history, was something that the Medes came up with to rule an area with a series of governors, but it was put into wide use by Cyrus the Great during this time period, and continued to be an important part of the Medo-Persian government.

Dan 6:2 and over these, three governors, of whom Daniel *was* one, that the satraps might give account to them, so that the king would suffer no loss.

Over the 120 satraps were appointed three governors to watch over the satraps. The reason for this was that they might report the activities of the satraps to the king so that the king would **suffer no loss**.

This appears to mean monetary loss, that is that they were to watch out for corruption and stealing among the satraps and to report any funny business.

The text does not say why Daniel was chosen for this job, but we can imagine that the qualifications of such a job, that is honestly and trustworthiness, would have caused more than a few fingers to point toward Daniel.

One commentator suggests that the incident of the writing on the wall would have certainly been told to the authorities, not to mention that Daniel in the last chapter was essentially the ruler of the kingdom after Belshazzar was killed, even though it was only for a night. I can only imagine that an explanation of such an odd coronation would have needed to be recounted to the new king at some point.

Dan 6:3 Then this Daniel distinguished himself above the governors and satraps, because an excellent spirit *was* in him; and the king gave thought to setting him over the whole realm.

There was something about Daniel that caused the king to give thought to setting him above the whole realm. It says it is because an **excellent spirit** was found in him. We see the exact same thing done for the exact same reason with Joseph in Gen 41: 37-40:

> So the advice was good in the eyes of Pharaoh and in the eyes of all his servants. Pharaoh said to his servants, "Can we find *such a one* as this, <u>a man in whom *is* the Spirit of God?"</u> Pharaoh said to Joseph, "Inasmuch as God has shown you all this, *there is* no one as discerning and wise as you. You shall be over my house, and all my people shall be ruled according

to your word; only in regard to the throne will I be greater than you." -Gen 41:37-40

Dan 6:4 So the governors and satraps sought to find *some* charge against Daniel concerning the kingdom; but they could find no charge or fault, because he *was* faithful; nor was there any error or fault found in him.

Remember from the previous verse that the King had not done this yet; he had just given thought to doing it. This may mean that he announced his plans to set Daniel up in this position at a future time. He may have even said something like "unless someone can bring a charge against him" which may be why these men decided to do this. But that is reading into the text. What we can know is that there was sufficient time between Darius' giving thought to appoint Daniel over them all and the following events to allow them to cook up this scheme.

And it may imply that they were corrupt, that is because Daniel's initial job was to prevent corruption, and if you are wanting to be corrupt it is bad for business to have a righteous man in charge of watching and reporting your conduct.

Although their hatred of Daniel could have been for a number of reasons, not the least of which could have been jealousy of such a high position. We also know that hatred of his God Yahweh was something that was also a source of dislike of Daniel. I think the text also gives us room later on to suggest anti-Semitism as a cause.

David Guzik makes an analogy to an election. When a person is nominated for an important position of rulership, his life is justifiably under intense scrutiny by the press. If the person in question had been in public service for a long time his career would be under the microscope. Daniel had been in public office for a long time, ever since he was a young man, and he is now in his eighties or so.

> "Sometimes today a candidate or nominee for office will be set under this kind of scrutiny - imagine looking as hard as you could at a public servant who

had been in office some 50 years and finding *nothing wrong*. No fraudulent expense accounts. No intern scandals. No questionable business deals. No gifts from lobbyists. No accusations from his staff.

Simply, there were no skeletons in Daniel's closet. His enemies examined his life and found nothing to attack - they had to make up something."

Dan 6:5 Then these men said, "We shall not find any charge against this Daniel unless we find *it* against him concerning the law of his God."

Stephen Miller in the New American Commentary makes several good points here:

" They hoped that there might be something in Daniel's religious beliefs ("the law of his God") that might disqualify him from serving in Darius's court. Daniel was a strict monotheist, and therefore they planned to ensnare him by forcing him to refuse to worship other gods. Thus Daniel's choice would be to obey "the law of his God" or the law of man ("the laws of the Medes and Persians"

I would add to this that they decide, as we will see, that his prayer life was the best way to attack him, which stands to reason, as it was his habit to pray three times a day. Anyone that worked with Daniel, as these men certainly did, would know that he had to take a break periodically to go pray to his God. I'm sure it was the first thing that came to their mind when trying to figure out a way to make his devotion to God a snare to him.

Dan 6:6 So these governors and satraps thronged before the king, and said thus to him: "King Darius, live forever! Dan 6:7 All the governors of the kingdom, the administrators and satraps, the counselors and advisors, have consulted together to establish a royal statute and to make a firm decree, that whoever petitions any god or man for thirty days, except you, O king, shall be cast into the den of lions.

**Dan 6:8 Now, O king, establish the decree and sign the writing, so that it cannot be changed, according to the law of the Medes and Persians, which does not alter."
Dan 6:9 Therefore King Darius signed the written decree.**

All the governors of the kingdom, the administrators and satraps, the counselors and advisors

Here we see a lie from the conspirators. We know they did not actually poll **all** the people, certainly not the most prominent and influential one, that is Daniel.

Verse 6 says they **thronged** the king—they were there in numbers presenting this request as if it was the will of the people, when it was really just a plot against a coworker.

That whoever petitions any god or man for thirty days, except you, O king

This was a religious petitioning or prayer. Some would petition directly to God; others, depending on their religion, would petition through a priest to their God. This should probably be best understood as Darius being a mediator for prayers to gods during this time, not that he himself would be petitioned for things as if he was God.

The angle was probably one of political value to a new king in an area of such religious devotion.

Now, O king, establish the decree and sign the writing, so that it cannot be changed, according to the law of the Medes and Persians

The Medo-Persian law had a stipulation that it could not be changed or repealed too quickly. It could have been a protection against making decisions in haste, which didn't work in this case, or as Guzik suggests it was because of the high view of the king as his mediator between the gods that would make a lot of quick repeals seem to be damaging to this image of the kings of the day.

Deodars of Sicily (XVII, 30), in fact, reports the case of a man put to death under Darius III (336–330) even though he was known to be perfectly innocent because of this loophole.

In any case, we will see it is this loophole that the conspirators will exploit to try to be rid of Daniel.

Dan 6:10 Now when Daniel knew that the writing was signed, he went home. And in his upper room, with his windows open toward Jerusalem, he knelt down on his knees three times that day, and prayed and gave thanks before his God, as was his custom since early days.

So we are told that Daniel does this after he hears of this ridiculous plot. But it also tells us it was his custom to pray in this manner. Therefore we know that Daniel wasn't being defiant here with a public prayer as if to draw attention to his refusal to obey; he simply did not refrain from doing what he always had done.

His windows were probably always open toward Jerusalem during his prayer because of 1 Kings 8: 35-36 which says:

> When the heavens are shut up and there is no rain because they have sinned against You, when they pray toward this place and confess Your name, and turn from their sin because You afflict them, then hear in heaven, and forgive the sin of Your servants, Your people Israel, that You may teach them the good way in which they should walk; and send rain on Your land which You have given to Your people as an inheritance. - 1Ki 8:35-36

One of the main points I would like to make about this is that Daniel was a man of prayer. I think this insight into Daniel's life and custom in verse 10 might explain the rest of the book of Daniel up to this point.

Ask yourself the question: how different would your life be if you thanked God and prayed three times a day like clockwork. I know it would be tempting to turn it into a burden or a work, but imagine you did it out of the purest convictions. I would submit that kings would get saved and you would see God do great things in your day as Daniel saw in his.

We still worship and serve the same God that will preserve people though fire and stop the mouths of lions, the God who gives great visions and raises kings and deposes them. We have access to the throne. In fact since we have been adopted as sons through the propitiation of Christ we can <u>boldly</u> approach the" Throne of Grace" (Heb 4:16).

Dan 6:11 Then these men assembled and found Daniel praying and making supplication before his God.

So these guys knew where to look. They got a number of people together to see this now-illegal act of Daniel. I wonder if Daniel gave them a dirty look from inside the window.

Dan 6:12 And they went before the king, and spoke concerning the king's decree: "Have you not signed a decree that every man who petitions any god or man within thirty days, except you, O king, shall be cast into the den of lions?" The king answered and said, "The thing *is* true, according to the law of the Medes and Persians, which does not alter."

This verse is interesting, as it reveals that they knew that the king would not want to execute Daniel for praying to his God if he had a choice. It is obvious that the King already really liked Daniel, and he must have known that Daniel was faithful to his God and that was at least one of the reasons for the "excellent spirit" found in him. I don't think the king had initially considered that Daniel's prayers would be made illegal by his now-binding decree, and these guys were counting on that.

Dan 6:13 So they answered and said before the king, "That Daniel, who is one of the captives from Judah, does not show due regard for you, O king, or for the decree that you have signed, but makes his petition three times a day."

Dan 6:14 And the king, when he heard *these* words, was greatly displeased with himself, and set *his* heart on Daniel to deliver him; and he labored till the going down of the sun to deliver him.

Here the king pays absolutely no attention to their suggestion that Daniel did this because he wasn't showing regard for the king or his law. The king immediately was displeased with himself, not Daniel. He saw right through these treacherous conspirators.

It is interesting that once again the fact that Daniel was a Jew was brought up by those plotting against him, even though it doesn't seem to have any significance. One could make a case that part of the conspirators' hatred of Daniel was anti-Semitic.

Set *his* heart on Daniel to deliver him; and he labored till the going down of the sun to deliver him

Darius, realizing he had been duped, set out to find a legal loophole to deliver Daniel, but because the execution had to be carried out the same day he had limited time to do so. In the next verse the conspirators approach him:

Dan 6:15 Then these men approached the king, and said to the king, "Know, O king, that *it is* the law of the Medes and Persians that no decree or statute which the king establishes may be changed."

They approached him and reminded him of his obligation to carry out this law.

It amazes me to think that these men thought they would get away with this. They set this whole scheme up knowing that Darius would not want Daniel to be killed. One wonders if they knew he would see right though it as he did, because if he did it surely would not achieve the end of getting them promoted, and as we will see could even be a lot worse for them.

Dan 6:16 So the king gave the command, and they brought Daniel and cast *him* into the den of lions. *But* the

king spoke, saying to Daniel, "Your God, whom you serve continually, He will deliver you."

So the king does it—he gives the order to cast Daniel into the den of lions.

We see this touching scene of Darius telling Daniel that he hopes that Daniel's God will deliver him, which is now their last hope.

There are many reasons that we could speculate as to what would give Darius such confidence in Daniel's God. Perhaps it was the stories that were known of Daniel's God in Babylon, both from Daniel himself and others who had seen them.

It is noteworthy that he mentions that the God whom **you serve continually will deliver you.** This reference to his consistent devotional life is important in light of the context, because this is the very reason he is being put in the lion's den, his unwillingness to stop serving his God continually.

Dan 6:17 Then a stone was brought and laid on the mouth of the den, and the king sealed it with his own signet ring and with the signets of his lords, that the purpose concerning Daniel might not be changed.

> "A stone was placed over the opening of the den and sealed with the signet rings of the king and his nobles so that no one would dare attempt to rescue Daniel ("so that Daniel's situation might not be changed"). Soft clay was attached to the chains draped over the stone, and the king and his nobles made their personal marks (seals) by pressing their rings into the clay.[63] After the clay hardened, the chains could not be removed without breaking the seals. Surely no one would attempt to remove the chain containing the names of the king and some of his highest officials. Daniel was now in the den, and all possibility of escape was cut off."[9]

God Rescues Daniel from the Lions

Dan 6:18 Now the king went to his palace and spent the night fasting; and no musicians were brought before him. Also his sleep went from him.
Dan 6:19 Then the king arose very early in the morning and went in haste to the den of lions.

The king really liked Daniel. He wanted to put him over all of Babylon, and he also thought he was an honest man and maybe even a friend. There might have also been a bit of guilt and perhaps fear of Daniel's God for being a party to the killing of an innocent men. Any one of these might be a reason for the king's distress this night.

It says he arose very early and made haste to the lion's den. I love this, as it shows the reckless abandon and even faith that it was at least possible that Daniel could have survived the night.

> "Lacocque comments: "Perhaps we should see the king's hasty return early the next morning… in the perspective of the ancient Babylonian custom that the victim would be pardoned if he were tortured and had not died"[10]

Dan 6:20 And when he came to the den, he cried out with a lamenting voice to Daniel. The king spoke, saying to Daniel, "Daniel, servant of the living God, has your God, whom you serve continually, been able to deliver you from the lions?"
Dan 6:21 Then Daniel said to the king, "O king, live forever!
Dan 6:22 My God sent His angel and shut the lions' mouths, so that they have not hurt me, because I was found innocent before Him; and also, O king, I have done no wrong before you."
Dan 6:23 Now the king was exceedingly glad for him, and commanded that they should take Daniel up out of the den. So Daniel was taken up out of the den, and no injury

whatever was found on him, because he believed in his God.

So he calls in and he hears a reply back! What a relief it must have been for him.

Daniel says that God had sent an angel to accomplish this deliverance.

God also sent an angel to free Peter from prison, as well as a huge number of other jobs in the Old and New Testament. We are to understand angels as on a mission from God to accomplish a task. They are not doing something out of their own will but are servants of God's will on earth.

One thing that I think should be highlighted here is Daniel's commitment to using these opportunities for glorifying God, one might even say evangelism. I sense a kind of premeditation in these speeches Daniel gives when he knows he has an opportunity to glorify God.

Consider when he was on his way to Nebuchadnezzar's throne room in Daniel Chapter 2. He had the answer in hand, he had been given the interpretation in the prayer meeting. I don't think Daniel was practicing how he was going to present the dream. Instead, I think he was practicing how he would glorify God before and after he gave the dream.

I can imagine that Daniel was thinking of what he would say to the king all night, as opportunities for evangelism like this did not come every day and Daniel intended to make the most of it.

Dan 6:24 And the king gave the command, and they brought those men who had accused Daniel, and they cast *them* into the den of lions—them, their children, and their wives; and the lions overpowered them, and broke all their bones in pieces before they ever came to the bottom of the den.

This should not have come as a surprise to these men after seeing that the king saw through their plot.

Being fed to the lions was a known part of the Persian Empire. The picture here demonstrates the miraculous nature of Daniel's deliverance; this was not a matter of the lions being full. They were in fact very hungry, which is reasonable, that is to keep them hungry, if you were using them for a form of execution.

Dan 6:25 Then King Darius wrote: To all peoples, nations, and languages that dwell in all the earth: Peace be multiplied to you.
Dan 6:26 I make a decree that in every dominion of my kingdom *men must* tremble and fear before the God of Daniel. For He *is* the living God, And steadfast forever; His kingdom *is the one* which shall not be destroyed, And His dominion *shall endure* to the end.
Dan 6:27 He delivers and rescues, And He works signs and wonders In heaven and on earth, Who has delivered Daniel from the power of the lions.
Dan 6:28 So this Daniel prospered in the reign of Darius and in the reign of Cyrus the Persian.

So much like the case of Nebuchadnezzar, a written proclamation of Yahweh is put out by Darius, expressing many of the revelations of God that Nebuchadnezzar only realized late in his life, namely that God is the one who rules men and his kingdom is an everlasting one.

This again is the realization that we all must come to. Darius realized it quicker than Nebuchadnezzar.

Chapter 7

Daniel has a Vision of Four Animals

Daniel 7 is considered by some to be the most important chapter in the Book of Daniel. Others even consider it the most important chapter in the entire Old Testament for reasons which we will get into later, but certainly one of those reasons is because of its prophetic significance.

In Daniel Chapter 7, Daniel has a vision of four beasts: a lion, a bear, a leopard and a "diverse beast." These beasts are identified as kings and/or kingdoms by the angel who interprets Daniel's dream starting in verse 17.

The question is which kingdoms are being referred to with these beasts.

Most conservatives believe that Daniel 7 is simply a retelling of Daniel 2. In other words, the dream that Nebuchadnezzar had in Daniel 2 of a multi-metal statue which represented the four kingdoms of Babylon, Medo-Persia, Greece, and Rome are again described here in Daniel 7.

I don't agree with that view, but I do agree with them that the fourth beast in Daniel 7 is the kingdom of Antichrist. However, because of their insistence that this chapter is simply a mirror image of Daniel 2, they are forced to defend the position that the Antichrist must somehow come from something they call the Revived Roman Empire (RRE), because in Daniel Chapter 2 the last section of the statue is clearly talking about Rome. So if this chapter is the same as that one, then the fourth beast in this chapter, the Antichrist beast, is Rome.

But as I will demonstrate, not only is that not necessary; it could cause many people to miss the signs of the Antichrist's kingdom. For more information on why the belief of the RRE is based on a bad exegesis of Daniel Chapter 2, please see chapter 2 of this book.

I would also recommend a four-part paper by Charles Cooper, who is a former professor of Hermeneutics at Moody Bible Institute, called "Daniel 2 and Daniel 7: Equal or not Equal."

In the traditional view, the beasts of Chapter 7 are succeeded in time by the next beast. For example, the lion, the first beast (who they say represents Babylon) would be followed after much time by the bear (who they say represents Medo-Persia) since Babylon was conquered by Medo-Persia, and then the leopard (Greece) would conquer the bear after that, and so on. I believe there are significant reasons to challenge this view of the kingdoms being in temporal succession of one another. In other words, to challenge the idea that these beasts existed one after the other instead of all at the same time.

In this study I will propose that this vision of the four beasts in Daniel 7 is not simply a picture of four kingdoms that have come and gone in the past, but rather this is a picture of the four kingdoms that will be on the earth **at the same time** when the Antichrist begins his reign. If this is the case, then this chapter, along with the latter half of Daniel 11 and Revelation 13, gives the church its best chance to recognize the geo-political precursors to the rise of Antichrist.

A large number of reasons for viewing these beasts as contemporaneous as opposed to successive will be presented in this study, but I will mention a few notable ones so that you can get an idea of the types of problems the traditional view has.

Daniel 7:11-12 describes the Antichrist who is thrown into the lake of fire after his reign is completed. Few conservatives would debate this point. However, after he is thrown into the lake of fire, the mentioning of the previous three beasts show that they are still around at that time. In fact, it says specifically that they are allowed to live on after that.

110

I watched then because of the sound of the pompous words which the horn was speaking; I watched till the beast was slain, and its body destroyed and given to the burning flame. As for the rest of the beasts, they had their dominion taken away, <u>yet their lives were prolonged for a season and a time.</u> - Dan 7:11-12

In what sense can Neo-Babylonia or Medo-Persia be spoken of as living on after the Antichrist is destroyed? Traditional scholars give no compelling explanations for their presence and prolonging of their life at this point. I will show you why the contemporaneous view explains this verse with many confirmations from the text.

Additionally there are several grammatical and contextual indications that make it plain that these kingdoms exist at the same time in history.

The following then is an overview of the key points that we will find in this vision as understood by what I will call the contemporaneous beast view:

There is a dividing of the world into four parts in the time just before the Antichrist begins his rule (figure 1.) The Antichrist eventually takes control of one of those four kingdoms which has 10 rulers (figure 2.) He eventually conquers all four kingdoms through war and effectively rules the entire world in a new amalgamated beast as seen in Revelation 13:1-2 (figure 3.)

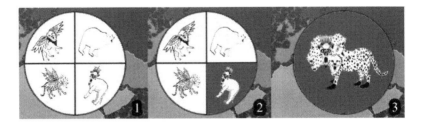

His initial ruling of only a fourth part of the earth is perhaps why in Revelation 6:8 power is given to "Death and Hades" over only a fourth part of the earth. This point is especially important if one understands that Revelation 6 may be the most complete description of the Antichrist's torment of people before the wrath of God begins. In other words Revelation 6 would be the perfect place to describe the Antichrist's dominion as only covering a fourth of the earth, even though he will eventually subdue all of the other three kings and control the entire world system, which brings me to my next point.

This view suggests that Daniel Chapter 11:36 and following essentially links Daniel Chapter 7 with Revelation 13. Let me explain what I mean by all that, and it may take me a minute to do so, so bear with me.

Daniel 11:36-45 describes how the Antichrist will be conquering all kinds of lands and kingdoms, then at some point he will declare himself to be higher than God Himself in the "Holy Place" in Jerusalem, at that point the last 3.5 years of his reign will begin. But before this, he is busy making war, conquering other kingdoms and establishing his domain. Here is a sampling of his military career during that time as told in Daniel 11.

> Thus he shall act against the strongest fortresses with a foreign god, which he shall acknowledge, *and* advance *its* glory; and he shall cause them to rule over many, and divide the land for gain. "At the time of the end the king of the South shall attack him; and the king of the North shall come against him like a whirlwind, with chariots, horsemen, and with many ships; and he shall enter the countries, overwhelm *them,* and pass through. He shall also enter the Glorious Land, and many *countries* shall be overthrown; but these shall escape from his hand: Edom, Moab, and the prominent people of Ammon. He shall stretch out his hand against the countries, and the land of Egypt shall not escape. He shall have power over the treasures of gold and silver, and over all the precious things of Egypt; also the Libyans and Ethiopians *shall follow* at his heels. But news from the east and the north shall trouble him; therefore he shall go out with great fury to destroy and annihilate many. - Dan 11:39-44

This is perhaps why the book of Revelation says that one of the reasons the world marvels at the Antichrist is because of his war-making capability. They say of him in the Book of Revelation:

> So they worshiped the dragon who gave authority to the beast; and they worshiped the beast, saying, "Who *is* like the beast? Who is able to make war with him?" - Rev 13:4

How it is that we have come to see the Antichrist as a man of peace, I do not know. He will be a man of war without question.

Arguably the chapter that gives the most detail of the Antichrist is Revelation 13. The first two verses of that chapter say:

> Then I stood on the sand of the sea. And I saw a beast rising up out of the sea, having seven heads and ten horns, and on his horns ten crowns, and on his heads a blasphemous name. Now the beast which I saw was like a leopard, his feet were like *the feet of* a bear, and his mouth like the mouth of a lion. The dragon gave him his power, his throne, and great authority. - Rev 13:1-2

This is an unambiguous reference to our chapter in Daniel Chapter 7. The fact that we have a lion, a bear, and a leopard in the same place all in context of the Antichrist is enough to pay attention, but when you see that it has seven heads and ten horns, a direct correlation to Daniel 7, the possibility of this being a coincidental similarity is not a reasonable option.

Let me show you why this is significant.

If you take the beasts in Daniel 7, that is a lion with wings, a bear, a four headed leopard, and a ten-horned beast, and you combined them all into one beast, you would have a seven-headed ten-horned beast with characteristics of a bear, a leopard and a lion, exactly what we see in Revelation 13.

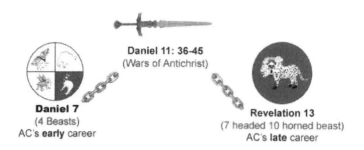

Daniel 11: 36-45
(Wars of Antichrist)

Daniel 7
(4 Beasts)
AC's **early** career

Revelation 13
(7 headed 10 horned beast)
AC's **late** career

In other words I am proposing to you that what you are looking at in the first few verses of Revelation 13, when a seven-headed, ten-horned lion/leopard/bear beast comes out of the sea, is the Antichrist, now done with his conquest of the other three world powers, and is the uncontested ruler of the world. Revelation 13 is understood by most conservatives to be the Antichrist's final 3.5, years not his first 3.5 years.

So back to what I said earlier: the view that I will be promoting, the contemporaneous beast view, suggests that Daniel Chapter 11:36-45 (which describes the wars of Antichrist) essentially links Daniel Chapter 7 (the Antichrist pre-wars, where he is only one of four powers) with Revelation 13 where he is the uncontested ruler of all world powers.

So these three chapters spread out all over the Bible, more or less provide a before, during and after conquests snapshot of the Antichrist.

And here in Daniel 7 it gives us details on what to look for in the world just prior to and during the beginning of Antichrist's assent to power. Daniel 11:36-45 gives us what his conquests of the other powers will look like. And Revelation 13 tells us what it will look like once he has gained complete control.

Dan 7:1 In the first year of Belshazzar king of Babylon, Daniel had a dream and visions of his head *while* on his bed. Then he wrote down the dream, telling the main facts.

In the first year of Belshazzar king of Babylon

Daniel gives us a time stamp of this vision. He says it is in the first year of Belshazzar. We might remember Belshazzar from Chapter 5 and the writing on the wall episode. This may be significant as this would mean that this vision takes place well after Nebuchadnezzar's death and only 10 or so years before Babylon would ultimately fall. We will discuss this as it relates to the first beast in a moment.

Then he wrote down the dream, telling the main facts.

Some translations say that Daniel tells us the "sum of the matter." In other words there are details of this vision that were not given in this account. He instead gives us the most important or "main" facts.

Dan 7:2 Daniel spoke, saying, "I saw in my vision by night, and behold, the four winds of heaven were stirring up the Great Sea.
Dan 7:3 And four great beasts came up from the sea, each different from the other.

The four winds of heaven were stirring up the Great Sea.

The picture of the **Great Sea** where these beasts come from is not debated much, as scripture in many places describes sinful humanity as the sea (cf. Isa 17:12–13; cp. Rev 13:1 with 13:11 and Rev 17:1 with 17:15).

The sea in which the beast (the Antichrist) sits and came out of in Rev 13 is interpreted by the angel in Revelation 17:15 as being representative of the people of the earth:

> Then he said to me, "The waters which you saw, where the harlot sits, are peoples, multitudes, nations, and tongues. - Rev 17:15

Therefore these beast kingdoms arise from the water which represents humanity. In other words these four kingdoms are four kingdoms produced by humanity.

The four winds is often used to figuratively denote the entire known world in Scripture: Jer. 49:36; Dan 8:8; 11:4, Matt 24:31; and Mark 13:27; Targ[um] Isa 11:12.

The phrase **the four winds** is often associated in that context with the four cardinal points of the compass, i.e. North, South, East, and West. The cardinal points are even directly being referred to in several instances of the phrase the four winds in the Book of Daniel: Daniel 8:8 and 11:4. Cooper in his paper spends a lot of time tying each of the four kingdoms here to a compass direction.

Here we also find one of the many grammatical clues that suggest that these four kingdoms will appear at the same time. The phrase "were stirring up" referring to the four winds stirring up the sea actually means bursting forth suddenly as opposed to over time. I will quote from Stephen Miller of the New American Commentary, who gives this fact even more weight because he holds to the traditional view and not the one I am proposing. He says:

> "Four winds of heaven" were "churning up" the sea, as in a time of sudden storm. The participle "churning up" can also mean "bursting forth,"[14] and the idea seems to be that these winds suddenly burst forth upon the sea."[11]

So I would suggest that this verse is saying that there will be four kingdoms produced in four different parts of the earth quite suddenly.

Dan 7:4 The first *was* like a lion, and had eagle's wings. I watched till its wings were plucked off; and it was lifted up from the earth and made to stand on two feet like a man, and a man's heart was given to it.

The traditional view has this beast being Babylon, and specifically, Nebuchadnezzar. For example they say that wings being plucked off and its being made to stand on two feet and given a heart of a man is referring to the humbling experience that God gave to Nebuchadnezzar in Chapter 4 where

Nebuchadnezzar was forced to act like an ox for several years until he recognized the sovereignty of God and then was restored to his right mind.

This part of the interpretation has many problems, the first being that Nebuchadnezzar was dead at the time of this vision based on verse 1, and it seems strange therefore, that Daniel would see Nebuchadnezzar coming out of the sea, and providing more details about his life or kingdom.

The picture the traditional view paints is that the lion represents Nebuchadnezzar when he was forced to act like a beast and then the plucking of the lion's wings, making it stand on two feet and giving it a man's heart is symbolic of God restoring Nebuchadnezzar to his right mind at the end of Daniel 4. This would suggest that the reason for these four beings being described as "beasts" is because of similar situations like that of Nebuchadnezzar's. Are we to understand then that the king of Medo-Persia or Greece or Rome are also described as beasts because they too were forced to act like beasts by God? If so, they were apparently not restored to sanity as Nebuchadnezzar was, since no man's heart was given to them.

The description of the first beast here in Daniel 7 doesn't really even fit what happened to Nebuchadnezzar in Chapter 4. The clear intent in Daniel 7 is that the lion was always a lion, but was given a "man's heart" and thus changed. The lion was not restored to its natural state by the plucking of its wings and making it stand on two feet. It was permanently transformed and the intent of the text, as we will see, is that it was a downgrade for the lion, not an upgrade. Nebuchadnezzar's situation was exactly reversed if you analyze this closely.

And again we have the problem of continuity. If the reason the first beast is a beast is because of Nebuchadnezzar thinking he was an ox once then where does that leave us hermeneutically if we are trying to be consistent with the other beasts.

Surely the term "beast" is to be understood the same way it is understood in other prophetic scriptures; that is, a way to denote an unusually evil nation or king.

The traditional view also will say things like "the winged lion is the traditional symbol for Babylon, evidence of this can be seen on the Ishtar Gate from Babylon."

To start out with, there is no evidence to suggest that winged lions were considered to be a symbol of Babylon. Lions in general, regardless of wings, were associated not with Babylon but with the goddess Ishtar. This is partly because of the reference to her loving lions in the Epic of Gilgamesh which states of Ishtar:

> "'Thou has loved the lion, mighty in strength'"

For this reason Ishtar was often depicted with lions in sculptures and reliefs; only occasionally are the lions winged and for reasons we will get to later. This is why lions appear on the famous Ishtar gate of Babylon, because of their association with Ishtar, but Ishtar was not even the main goddess of Babylon. She was in some traditions however considered to be married to Marduk, who was the main god of Babylon, thereby making her the queen of Babylon by marriage in those traditions.

There are other winged animals on the gate, like the bull, though most of the bulls do not have wings. In fact the other two animals depicted on the gate (bulls and dragons) vastly outnumber the lions. There were 120 lions compared to 575 dragons and bulls. Incidentally, Nebuchadnezzar was really proud of the bulls and dragons on the front of the gate (where you won't find any lions). He even mentions them specifically in his inscription about why he built the gate, but he does not mention the lions at all.

All that to say that many commentators who try to make this point that winged lions are symbols of Babylon do so despite the historical evidence that winged lions are quite simply not symbols of Babylon at all, and when they do show up in Babylon they exceedingly rare. Most of the lions depicted are without wings. Wings or not, lions are almost exclusively associated with Ishtar who is only tangentially related to the Babylonian kingdom, and by most accounts was only a minor goddess in the Babylonian culture. And to make matters worse, she was a goddess whose worship and association with lions goes back 1000 of years before this to a different kingdom altogether.

People trying to make this winged lion in Verse 4 be Babylon are often thinking of the so-called Lamassu. A Lamassu is a representation of a protective deity, not from Babylon but rather thousands of years before this in the Akkadian and then Assyrian kingdoms. And although there are occasions where Lamassu have been depicted with lions' bodies, the vast majority of them are with bulls' bodies. There is some evidence that the Assyrian tradition of putting Lamassu, their protective deities, on city gates was why certain animals on other gates in later periods were given wings, as a kind of tip of the hat to the older Akkadian traditions regarding these protective deities.

So the problems with the idea that winged lions are symbols of Babylon are as follows:

They are not symbols of Babylon according to the Babylonians, and are never referred to as such that I know of in their writings; the Ishtar gate has lions on it because lions are a symbol of Ishtar, and even then they are not depicted on the gate nearly as much as the other animals. The concept of Lamassu was mostly represented with a bull's body and had virtually nothing to do with Babylon since they were Assyrian.

I also think this interpretation causes a hermeneutical problem as well. If one is going to say that we should look for a culture's symbol for itself to decipher the following beast kingdoms, then how are we to deal with the rest of the beasts? There is not a shred of evidence that, for example, the Medo-Persians symbolized themselves with a bear. I don't even think any traditional commentators try to suggest this, probably because of the obvious lack of evidence, nor did Greece make statues or reliefs symbolizing itself as a leopard, let alone Rome as the odd beast that Daniel describes in this chapter.

In other words if you're going to say that the deciphering of the beasts/kingdoms in Daniel 7 can be done by looking at the artwork of the kingdom in question and seeing what symbols they described themselves with, then it needs to be consistent.

119

There is a similar problem with the next point which is brought up by proponents of the traditional view, which is that Nebuchadnezzar is called both a lion and an eagle in Scripture. This is the best of the point that the traditional view has to offer in favor of their view for any of the four beasts. But even so it should be considered that Scripture also calls Shalmaneser, the king of Assyria, a lion and an eagle too in Hosea 8:1 and Jeremiah 50:17.

A simple study of the usage of lions or eagles or any other beast in scripture will reveal that they are used to designate characteristics and are often widely interchangeable among individuals or nations as long as those individuals or nations display the characteristics of that animal described in scripture. For example, when used in a negative sense in, lions are, among other things, strong (Prov 30:30), fearless (Prov 28:1; 30:30), stealthy (Psalm 17:12), frightening (Ezra 19:7; Hosea 11:10; Amos 3:8), destructive (1 Sam 17:34; Micah 5:8), and territorially protective (Isa 31:4).

Satan is described as walking around like a lion seeking whom he may devour.

The same can be done with eagles. According to one Bible Encyclopedia, it is:

> " ..Referred to for its swiftness of flight (Deut. 28:49; 2 Sam. 1:23), its mounting high in the air (Job 39:27), its strength (Ps. 103:5), its setting its nest in high places (Jer. 49:16), and its power of vision (Job 39:27-30)."

> This "ravenous bird" is a symbol of those nations whom God employs and sends forth to do a work of destruction, sweeping away whatever is decaying and putrescent (Matt. 24:28; Isa. 46:11; Ezek. 39:4; Deut. 28:49; Jer. 4:13; 48:40).[12]

So consider that when lions or eagles are used of kings, it is used of different kings and often different kingdoms, but the unifying factor is that they were instruments of God in the judgment of

Israel and displayed the characteristics of the animals laid out in scripture.

Again, the traditional view would fail at the point of trying to apply this hermeneutic to the other three beasts. For example, there is no reference to Alexander the Great or Greece as a leopard in Scripture, or to Cyrus or Medo-Persia as a bear.

I would suggest that we should attempt to interpret the first beast the same as we would with the others, and the most scriptural way to do that is by understanding the symbolism of the beasts by the different characteristics of that particular animal provided by scripture.

The first *was* like a lion, and had eagle's wings.

A kingdom that is like a lion and has wings like an eagle would seem to suggest a strong and swift nation. 2 Samuel 1:23 says:

> Saul and Jonathan were beloved and pleasant in their lives, And in their death they were not divided; They were swifter than eagles, They were stronger than lions. - 2Sa 1:23

We could go on to apply the other characteristics of these two animals to these beasts for more clarity, but I think the important part in terms of interpretation comes with the following lines:

I watched till its wings were plucked off; and it was lifted up from the earth and made to stand on two feet like a man, and a man's heart was given to it.

I think that both the wings being plucked off as well as the lion being forced to act like a man are to be understood as a bad thing, for this kingdom, not an upgrade.

The wings being plucked is pretty obvious: If the kingdom was swift like an eagle but its wings were plucked, it would not be to the nation's advantage.

The being given a man's heart should in my opinion be understood as having its lion's heart changed into a weaker heart. Scripture is clear that a lion's heart is better than a man's in regard to boldness or fearlessness.

> And even he who is valiant, whose heart is like the heart of a lion, will melt completely. For all Israel knows that your father is a mighty man, and those who are with him are valiant men. - 2Sa 17:10

> The wicked flee when no one pursues, But the righteous are bold as a lion. - Pro 28:1

So if I was looking for this kingdom, I would be looking for a kingdom who was strong and fast, but their swiftness was taken away from them, and they were not as bold as they once were.

Charles Cooper in his paper on this subject ties the lion king here to the King of the south in Daniel Chapter 11 which will attack the Antichrist in Verse 40 but whom the Antichrist who will easily subdue him.

It is not my goal in this study to provide the interpretation of which modern day nations or coalition of nations are represented here. I am not sure that we have seen the referent on the world scene yet, and more political maneuverings might be necessary before these verses can be applied to their geopolitical counterparts.

I am doing this study so that others will be able to make the connections when the time comes. I am not saying that it is not worth looking for right now, but it is not obvious to me if the national referents can be known, though that could be because of my lack of information about geopolitics, or because the referents are not yet in the form being described here. But one thing I am sure of is that when it comes it will be obvious if you are looking for it, and we don't have to look for cryptic fulfillments of these prophecies. If you have the right interpretation it will click, and if you don't, it won't.

Dan 7:5 "And suddenly another beast, a second, like a bear. It was raised up on one side, and *had* three ribs in its mouth between its teeth. And they said thus to it: 'Arise, devour much flesh!'

The next beast Daniel describes is like a bear. In the traditional view this must be Medo-Persia because again they believe that this is a retelling of Daniel 2 in which the second part of the statue is indeed Medo-Persia.

As we have already noted none of the ideas they apply to the lion work for the bear. There is nothing to indicate any Medo-Persian king had a humbling experience which made them think like a beast, nor is there any indication whatsoever that the Medo-Persian empire identified itself symbolically or any other way with a bear, and there is never a reference to any Medo-Persian king as a bear in Scripture.

It was raised up on one side

Proponents of the traditional view will say that the bear being raised up on one side is symbolic of the uneven relationship between the Medes and Persians in their coalition. The Medes were initially the dominant party but later the Persians were the more dominant of the two parts of this empire.

It should be noted that the word "raised up" here is passive; that is, that it was raised up on one side by another force not of its own doing. Much like the lion having its wings plucked and being stood up, etc., this bear is being raised up on one side by another party, probably also the group that is ordering it to "devour much flesh." It says: **And they said thus to it: 'Arise, devour much flesh!'** The **they** here could be a reference to the winds of the earth which stir up the sea in Verse 1.

And *had* three ribs in its mouth between its teeth.

The three ribs in its mouth according to the traditional view represent three notable conquests of the Medo-Persian Empire. But because there are more than three notable conquests of the Medo-Persian Empire, there is much argument among those

123

holding to this view as to which three should be considered the most important. I of course don't think this has anything to do with the Medo-Persian Empire and so we should not concern ourselves with why this is not a perfect description of their military conquests -- that is because it isn't.

One interesting verse is found in Hosea 13:7-8 in which God describes Himself as all of the beasts in this chapter, the only other time these beasts are found together other than in Revelation 13, and I think it will give us an idea of what these ribs are:

> So I will be to them like a lion; Like a leopard by the road I will lurk; I will meet them like a bear deprived *of her cubs;* I will tear open their rib cage, And there I will devour them like a lion. The wild beast shall tear them. - Hos 13:7-8

The bear here is described as tearing open a rib cage, and so I think the basic hermeneutic applied to the bear by the traditional view is correct; that is, the ribs represent initial conquests by this kingdom that are three in number.

I would also note that almost every time a bear is figured in scripture the idea of it being, as it says here, "deprived of her cubs," is mentioned. That is the biblical bear is the most ferocious when its offspring is threatened. This is such a consistent thing that I would be surprised if the nation or nations that the bear represents is not acting out of a real or perceived sense of defense.

And they said thus to it: 'Arise, devour much flesh!'

I think that this phrase is very important as it helps to weaken the case that this beast represents Medo-Persia, because after the conquests of Cyrus the Great and his son Cambyses II, which occurred relatively quickly and very early in the Medo-Persian history, there would be 200 years of no conquering at all until the empire was defeated by Alexander the Great. The empire would spend most of its existence simply struggling to maintain the lands that were initially conquered for it by Cyrus and his son in the first few years.

So if this bear already with the main conquests in its mouth is supposed to be Medo-Persia, then it either chose not to go and devour any more flesh, as it was ordered to, or it is simply not talking about the Medo-Persian Empire.

Charles Cooper connects the bear king to the king of the North in Daniel 11 who is said to try to make war with the Antichrist. It says:

> … and the king of the North shall come against him like a whirlwind, with chariots, horsemen, and with many ships; and he [the Antichrist] shall enter the countries, overwhelm *them,* and pass through. - Dan 11:40b

In the past people have tried to make the "King of the north" in Daniel 11 be Russia. This was due more to Russian being the current geopolitical "boogey man" at the time that Hal Lindsey wrote his books more than any reason from the text.

Dr. J Paul Tanner, Professor of Hebrew and Old Testament Studies at the Jordan Evangelical Theological Seminary, wrote an article called *"Daniel's 'King of the North': Do We Owe Russia An Apology?"* He concludes:

> "To be hermeneutically consistent, the "king of the North" ought to be interpreted in light of the meaning the phrase has had throughout the chapter."

Tanner has a very logical argument, and I would highly recommend his paper to you. He ultimately concludes this way:

> "I would like to submit that the "King of the North" is a confederation of northern Arab nations that will attack the Antichrist and his forces in this military conflict centered in the Middle East."

125

So like the lion, I am not prepared to suggest to you the specific nations that are represented by the bear, but I think it's highly likely that to go looking for it in the current climate would be a fruitless endeavor, as I believe these coalitions will arise quickly and possibly as a result of factors that have not yet occurred or are only beginning to occur. That being said I would not let that keep any of you from being watchmen in this regard.

Dan 7:6 "After this I looked, and there was another, like a leopard, which had on its back four wings of a bird. The beast also had four heads, and dominion was given to it.

The leopard with four bird wings and four heads is the Greek Empire in the traditional view. Again it has the same problems as the bear, as Alexander the Great was not humbled by having his mind turned into a beast's mind, nor is the symbol of the leopard associated with the Greek Empire nor is Alexander the Great or Greece referred to as a leopard in the Bible.

I would agree with them, however, that the four wings on the leopard probably represent a very fast-moving empire.

One of the biggest problems with this view is the four heads of this beast. The traditional proponents say that these heads represent the four generals who Alexander the Great gave his Empire to after he died.

Even a casual student of history knows that the Greek Empire did nothing but diminish, and diminish greatly after Alexander the Great died. The traditional view then has scripture attributing the fast and ferocious conquests of the Grecian Empire to the four generals; no mention of Alexander is present. This is problematic to say the least. Even if you were to assume that Alexander was somehow involved, perhaps he was the torso, to give such prominence to the generals is completely inconsistent with history and with the way that scripture uses the head/kingdoms motif.

Cooper makes the case that the leopard is speaking of the king of the east, or the source of the "news" from the east that will trouble the Antichrist in Daniel 11:44 but who it appears Antichrist will also subdue.

> But news from the east and the north shall trouble him; therefore he shall go out with great fury to destroy and annihilate many. - Dan 11:44

How does Scripture speak of leopards?

They tear into pieces (Jer 5:6), swift (Hab 1:8), lie in wait for its prey (Jer 5:6, Hos 13:7).

I think we are looking for an exceedingly fast coalition of four kings or kingdoms or even four leaders of the same kingdom. It may make an agreement with the king of the north, and because of the consistent use in scripture, I think this kingdom will have some quality that can be described as lying in wait or being patient before striking.

The leopard is found only about six times in Scripture and the only time it seems to apply to any nation or king is in Revelation 13, where we see that all four of the beasts have been combined as they rise out of the sea for the final 3.5 years of Antichrist's rule, suggesting again that we are to understand these kingdoms in Daniel 7 as somehow being represented again all the way in Revelation 13.

Dan 7:7 "After this I saw in the night visions, and behold, a fourth beast, dreadful and terrible, exceedingly strong. It had huge iron teeth; it was devouring, breaking in pieces, and trampling the residue with its feet. It *was* different from all the beasts that *were* before it, and it had ten horns.
Dan 7:8 I was considering the horns, and there was another horn, a little one, coming up among them, before whom three of the first horns were plucked out by the roots. And there, in this horn, *were* eyes like the eyes of a man, and a mouth speaking pompous words.

Here the traditional view has Rome in view. All of their reasons for this are very general and can apply to any of the previous

127

kingdoms; that is strength and being fearful because of its might. I think any and every world empire would be able to claim these characteristics. The idea that it was **different** from the previous ones also can be applied to any kingdom on the list depending on how you define different.

There are major differences in the fourth empire described here and the last empire described in the statue vision back in Daniel 2, For instance in this verse the strength of the empire is clearly the main focus; not a hint of weakness is detected. Contrast that with the last empire of Daniel 2 in which the Bible spends verse after verse describing the divided nature and inherent <u>weakness</u> of that kingdom. I would call that a very big difference: the one in Daniel 2 is divided and weak and the one in Daniel 7 is described as invincible.

The main thing that people see as the clincher here is the reference to the ten horns which they say corresponds to the ten toes in Daniel 2. But I beg the reader to realize that there is no mention of ten toes in Daniel 2. That idea has been read back into the text by people who assume these two chapters are the same.

In Chapter 2, the feet and toes are one unit, a fact easily demonstrated not just by the descriptions of them being one unit in the text, but also by the rock striking the feet, not the toes, in order to destroy it.

If the Bible wanted to make a big deal out of the ten toes, it would have said, "By the way, there are ten toes," but it does not. There is no mention of the number of toes in the text. For example I believe we are supposed to pay attention to the three ribs in the bear's mouth. And in the next chapter, the two horns on the ram's head, or even the ten horns on this beast's head. But when a number is not mentioned, we should not read it into the text. For example, no one tried to draw attention to the ten fingers on the hands of the statue which represent Medo-Persia, because there is no correlation there. It is taking the analogy too far. We wouldn't note that there are two eyes and ears on the head either. When the Bible is silent we should be too.

That being said, I do have some agreement with the traditional view at this point, in that I think that the kingdom that the Antichrist comes from will have ten kings because of this passage in Daniel 7 and because of its interpretation by the angel, which we will get to later.

Perhaps it might even be like representatives of the European Union or a similar organization in a different region, and he will subdue three of them before ultimately talking over the whole organization. I think that this organization will be associated with the west in some way, as does Charles Cooper, but it is not required to be the "Revived Roman Empire." And I hope you will see chapter 2 to find out why I say that.

There are two grammatical clues in this verse that support the overall premise that the four beasts are contemporaneous and not successive.

The first is the use of the word "before" in Verse 7:

> "It *was* different from all the beasts that *were* before it"

The word "before" here is the Aramaic word *qodam which is only used in a* spatial *sense and never in a temporal sense.*

*In other words it is never used in the time sense, like "he tied his shoes before he ran." It is only used in the sense of being in f*ront of something, *like "I put some food before the king."*

One example of how this word is used is in Daniel 2:25:

> Then Arioch quickly brought Daniel before the king, and said thus to him, "I have found a man of the captives of Judah, who will make known to the king the interpretation." - Dan 2:25

There is a totally different word if you wanted to speak of something happening before something else as in time.

So when it says "It *was* different from all the beasts that *were* **before** it," it must mean grammatically that the other beasts are spatially in front of it, which means that these beasts must be on the earth at the same time.

This brings me to the second grammatical clue in this verse:

This phrase: **trampling the residue with its feet.** We will see that this also supports the idea that these beasts are contemporaneous.

Charles Cooper says the following on this point:

> "The importance of the translation of this verse is evident by examining several Bible translations:
>
> > A fourth beast, dreadful and terrifying and extremely strong; and it had large iron teeth. It devoured and crushed and trampled down the remainder with its feet. (NASB)
> >
> > A fourth beast, terrifying and dreadful and exceedingly strong. It had great iron teeth; it devoured and broke in pieces and stamped what was left with its feet. (ESV)
> >
> > a fourth beast, dreadful and terrible, and strong exceedingly; and it had great iron teeth: it devoured and broke in pieces, and stamped the residue with the feet of it. (1895-KJV)
> >
> > a fourth beast – terrifying and frightening and very powerful. It had large iron teeth; it crushed and devoured its victims and trampled underfoot whatever was left. (NIV)
>
> The reader should discern that the translations, with the exception of the NIV, place the final clause as the object of all three verbs. Does "what was left" go with the final verb to stamp or with all three verbs: to

devour, to break in pieces, and to stamp? The answer to this question along with the question regarding the meaning of the clause "what was left" support our contention that the four kings/kingdoms of Daniel 7 reign upon the earth at the same time. If the clause "what was left" applies only to the verb to stamp, we would have to conclude that the clause refers to the things the beast did not devour or break in pieces. In other words, "what was left" is everything else the beast is not able to devour or break in pieces. If the beast could not "eat" it or "break" it, he stamped on it.

The other option is to take "what was left" as the object of all three verbs: to devour, to break in pieces, and to stamp, which is reflected in most translations. Taken in this sense, "what was left" represents everything the first three beasts do not control. In other words, the four kings/kingdoms divided the world up between them. The lion-king, the bear-king, the leopard king, and the diverse-king each get a fourth. In context, "what was left" is best taken to refer to that part of the earth that did not fall under the control of the first three beasts/kings/kingdoms."

Dan 7:8 I was considering the horns, and there was another horn, a little one, coming up among them, before whom three of the first horns were plucked out by the roots. And there, in this horn, *were* eyes like the eyes of a man, and a mouth speaking pompous words.

I would have an identical interpretation of this verse as most conservative scholars. There are many points that are made of this little horn that are clearly talking about the Antichrist. He appears to start his ascent to power by doing something to three of the ten kings. This too would be something that should be quite evident to the watchman when it happens.

Dan 7:9 "I watched till thrones were put in place, And the Ancient of Days was seated; His garment *was* white as snow, And the hair of His head *was* like pure wool. His throne *was* a fiery flame, Its wheels a burning fire; Dan 7:10 A fiery stream issued And came forth from before Him. A thousand thousands ministered to Him; Ten thousand times ten thousand stood before Him. The court was seated, And the books were opened. Dan 7:11 "I watched then because of the sound of the pompous words which the horn was speaking; I watched till the beast was slain, and its body destroyed and given to the burning flame.

Daniel now shifts his attention to a new character in the vision: the Ancient of Days. This is a reference to YHWH, though the same description is applied to Jesus in Revelation. Later we will see the Son of Man whom Jesus identified with interacting with the Ancient of Days. This is one of the go-to passages for the "two powers in heaven" idea which is described well by Dr. Michael Hesier.

There is much to discuss about this idea but it is out of the scope of this study which is focused on the prophetic implications of this chapter so I will leave you to study this section further, which I highly recommend.

Daniel is now going to watch the Ancient of Days destroy the beast with the little horn by giving it to the burning flame.

These verses are very important for our discussion, because they correspond directly to events in the Book of Revelation.

If we compare the two books, we will see that Daniel is giving us very specific information about the timing of the events being described in this chapter.

Let's start with the first phrase: **I watched till thrones were put in place.**

I will read from the last part of Revelation 19 to the first part of Revelation 20. Remember there are no chapter breaks in the original languages, and I want you to notice a few different things that correspond directly to our verse.

First you will see the Antichrist is cast into the lake of fire, just as it happens in our passage:

> Then the beast was captured, and with him the false prophet who worked signs in his presence, by which he deceived those who received the mark of the beast and those who worshiped his image. These two were cast alive into the lake of fire burning with brimstone. - Rev 19:20

Then we read that thrones are set up after that, which corresponds with Daniel as well:

> And I saw thrones, and they sat on them, and judgment was committed to them. - Rev 20:4a

These thrones are for some or all believers in Christ who will judge angels and men at this time. Paul says the following in 1 Corinthians:

> Do you not know that the saints will judge the world? And if the world will be judged by you, are you unworthy to judge the smallest matters? Do you not know that we shall judge angels? How much more, things that pertain to this life? - 1Co 6:2-3

The comparisons to the time just before the millennial reign of Christ are very important and Daniel will continue to make unambiguous references to it as we will see. One reason I want to show you this is because I think it helps to explain the next verse.

Dan 7:12 As for the rest of the beasts, they had their dominion taken away, yet their lives were prolonged for a season and a time.

As for the rest of the beasts

There is no doubt that the other beasts of Daniel 7 are in view here; that is, the lion, the bear and the leopard. It says that their dominion is taken away but their lives are prolonged for a time.

This verse is very difficult to get around if you still hold the traditional view because the other beasts are long gone by this point. Stephen Miller of the New American Commentary who holds to the traditional view offers the following to try to explain this most serious problem:

> "How could these beasts lose their authority and still exist? The explanation is that their dominance ceased, but they continued to live because they were absorbed into the next empire. For example, Greece was conquered by Rome; and although Greek dominance came to an end, the nation continued to live by being absorbed into another one of the earthly kingdoms, the Roman Empire."[13]

So according to Miller, when Daniel says **As for the rest of the beasts, they had their dominion taken away, yet their lives were prolonged for a season and a time.** He means that there would still be Neo-Babylonian or Medo-Persian <u>blood</u> on the earth in the last days, which is almost impossible to believe, for purely genetic reasons. This also presumes that the Bible sees kingdoms in a purely ethnic sense, which is very difficult when dealing with kingdoms like the Romans who were very ethnically diverse.

I have another explanation for this problem.

After the Antichrist is destroyed at Armageddon there will still be people and indeed nations on earth who will populate the 1000-year period after the sheep and goat judgment. This has explicit Biblical support.

We know that there will be specifically identifiable nations in the millennium. For example in Zechariah 14:16-19 Egypt is mentioned. In fact in that same passage it specifically says that some of the same nations that were a part of the final battles would be serving the Lord during this time:

"And it shall come to pass, that <u>every one that is left of all the nations</u> which came against Jerusalem shall even <u>go up from year to year to worship the King</u>.

One more interesting fact about this is the mention of some of the 3 (non-antichrist) animals which represent nations in Daniel Chapter 7 being mentioned in the verses about the 1000-year period in Isaiah 11:

The wolf also shall dwell with the lamb, <u>The leopard</u> shall lie down with the young goat, The calf and the young lion and the fatling together; And a little child shall lead them. The cow and <u>the bear</u> shall graze; Their young ones shall lie down together; And <u>the lion</u> shall eat straw like the ox. - Isa 11:6-7

We shouldn't build doctrine on things like that, but given the other scriptures; I think it is very interesting.

Dan 7:13 "I was watching in the night visions, And behold, *One* like the Son of Man, Coming with the clouds of heaven! He came to the Ancient of Days, And they brought Him near before Him.
Dan 7:14 Then to Him was given dominion and glory and a kingdom, That all peoples, nations, and languages should serve Him. His dominion *is* an everlasting dominion, Which shall not pass away, And His kingdom *the one* Which shall not be destroyed.

***One* like the Son of Man, Coming with the clouds of heaven!**

This again is pointing to the specific period of time in which these events happen. This vision of the Son of Man is not out of chronological context with the destruction of the final beast. This phrase "one like the Son of Man coming on the clouds" is a technical term used very often by the Lord and it is referring not to the rapture but rather to Revelation 14:14-20, in which the cloud rider and the angels destroy the wicked earth dwellers.

Then I looked, and behold, a white cloud, and on the cloud sat *One* like the Son of Man, having on His

135

head a golden crown, and in His hand a sharp sickle. And another angel came out of the temple, crying with a loud voice to Him who sat on the cloud, "Thrust in Your sickle and reap, for the time has come for You to reap, for the harvest of the earth is ripe." So He who sat on the cloud thrust in His sickle on the earth, and the earth was reaped. Then another angel came out of the temple which is in heaven, he also having a sharp sickle. And another angel came out from the altar, who had power over fire, and he cried with a loud cry to him who had the sharp sickle, saying, "Thrust in your sharp sickle and gather the clusters of the vine of the earth, for her grapes are fully ripe." So the angel thrust his sickle into the earth and gathered the vine of the earth, and threw *it* into the great winepress of the wrath of God. And the winepress was trampled outside the city, and blood came out of the winepress, up to the horses' bridles, for one thousand six hundred furlongs. - Rev 14:14-20

Other references to this occasion of "one like the Son of Man" coming on the clouds for the purpose of judgment can be found in Matthew 13:41, Matthew 26:64, Mark 13:26, Mark 14:61-62 and Luke 21:27.

I am making a distinction between this coming on the clouds event in Daniel 7 and Revelation 14 from the rapture which happens a significant amount of time before this event. The rapture is described in similar terms but there are distinct differences. I think it is proper to look at this as two reaping events, one for the righteous called the rapture and a later one for the destruction of the wicked, typified by verses like this:

The Son of Man will send out His angels, and they will gather out of His kingdom all things that offend, and those who practice lawlessness, and will cast them into the furnace of fire. There will be wailing and gnashing of teeth. - Mat 13:41-42

All of this to say that this chronology would constitute further proof that the allowing of the other three kingdoms to live on after this time must be a reference to the millennium based on the context, and that the other three kingdoms must therefore all be on the earth at the same time, and therefore the traditional interpretation of these beasts must be wrong.

Dan 7:15 "I, Daniel, was grieved in my spirit within *my* body, and the visions of my head troubled me.
Dan 7:16 I came near to one of those who stood by, and asked him the truth of all this. So he told me and made known to me the interpretation of these things:

Daniel is shaken up by the vision. He asks a heavenly being to help him understand it. He is then given the heavenly interpretation of the vision so we can now check our interpretation with that of the angel and make sure our interpretations lines up with Scripture.

Dan 7:17 'Those great beasts, which are four, *are* four kings *which* arise out of the earth.
Dan 7:18 But the saints of the Most High shall receive the kingdom, and possess the kingdom forever, even forever and ever.'

The angel starts by giving a very broad overview of the vision. It is summed up in only two verses.

Those great beasts, which are four, *are* four kings *which* arise out of the earth.

The first thing that the angel does is confirm that these beasts represent kings or kingdoms. Later on in Verses 23 and 24, the angel refers to these beasts as kingdoms, not just kings. It is therefore almost universally accepted that "kings" and "kingdoms" are interchangeable in much of Daniel's prophetic writing.

The angel then jumps all the way to the end to declare that these four kingdoms will be displaced ultimately by the kingdom given to the saints of the Most High.

137

But the saints of the Most High shall receive the kingdom, and possess the kingdom forever, even forever and ever.

This mention of the saints receiving a kingdom is extremely important: this event is specifically noted three more times in this chapter. It is a probably a reference to the saints who rule with Christ during the millennial reign as in Revelation 20:4:

> And I saw thrones, and they sat on them, and judgment was committed to them. Then *I saw* the souls of those who had been beheaded for their witness to Jesus and for the word of God, who had not worshiped the beast or his image, and had not received *his* mark on their foreheads or on their hands. And they lived and reigned with Christ for a thousand years. - Rev 20:4

It is a fulfillment of the promise of the Lord in the letters to the seven churches in Revelation:

> And he who overcomes, and keeps My works until the end, to him I will give power over the nations— 'HE SHALL RULE THEM WITH A ROD OF IRON; THEY SHALL BE DASHED TO PIECES LIKE THE POTTER'S VESSELS'— as I also have received from My Father; - Rev 2:26-27

So once again we have specific language regarding the millennial kingdom giving us a time stamp for these events in Daniel 7.

Dan 7:19 "Then I wished to know the truth about the fourth beast, which was different from all the others, exceedingly dreadful, *with* its teeth of iron and its nails of bronze, *which* devoured, broke in pieces, and trampled the residue with its feet;
Dan 7:20 and the ten horns that *were* on its head, and the other *horn* which came up, before which three fell, namely, that horn which had eyes and a mouth which spoke pompous words, whose appearance *was* greater than his fellows.

Daniel inquires of the angel to know more about the fourth beast and little horn.

A few extra details are mentioned in this recapping of the events of the vision that were not mentioned initially. For example the beast had:

Nails of bronze

So in addition to iron teeth, nails of bronze are mentioned. Based on the other uses of bronze or brass in scripture I would suggest this simply means the feet will be strong. A very similar use of bronze feet or in this case hooves smashing things can be seen in Micah 4:13:

> Arise and thresh, O daughter of Zion; For I will make your horn iron, And I will make your hooves bronze; You shall beat in pieces many peoples; I will consecrate their gain to the LORD, And their substance to the Lord of the whole earth. - Mic 4:13

This extra detail of bronze feet may help someone find out which nations or coalition of nations are in view in the fourth beast, or it may simply be just a symbolic way to show the ability and skill the nation has at destroying.

**Dan 7:21 "I was watching; and the same horn was making war against the saints, and prevailing against them,
Dan 7:22 until the Ancient of Days came, and a judgment was made *in favor* of the saints of the Most High, and the time came for the saints to possess the kingdom.**

And the same horn was making war against the saints, and prevailing against them

Another detail is mentioned here by Daniel that was not mentioned before; that is, that this horn made war against the saints and prevailed against them. This is a clear reference to the Antichrist in Revelation 13:7:

It was granted to him <u>to make war with the saints</u> and to overcome them. And authority was given him over every tribe, tongue, and nation. - Rev 13:7

And the time came for the saints to possess the kingdom

This is another reference to the saints receiving the millennial kingdom., There will be at least one more such reference in Verse 27 showing the theological importance of the idea that the saints will be given the dominion that is taken from the Antichrist.

Dan 7:23 "Thus he said: 'The fourth beast shall be A fourth kingdom on earth, Which shall be different from all *other* kingdoms, And shall devour the whole earth, Trample it and break it in pieces.

The angel is now interpreting the fourth beast for Daniel. It too is a kingdom. It is again noted that it is different in some way from the other kingdoms, though we are not told how. The new information that the angel gives us is that this beast will ultimately devour the whole earth which is also noted of the Antichrist in Revelation 13:7-8.

Dan 7:24 The ten horns *are* ten kings *Who* shall arise from this kingdom. And another shall rise after them; He shall be different from the first *ones,* And shall subdue three kings.

We learn many things here: First, that the ten horns on the fourth kingdom's head were ruling the kingdom first.

This could be a system in which many representatives rule over one kingdom equally, it could develop quite quickly.

The angel then tells us that three of the ten will be subdued; some translations say humiliated. The root word means to make lower, or humble. If it weren't for the initial vision showing them uprooted, suggesting a complete disregarding of them, I would suggest based on the word itself that these kings are simply put in a much lower place by the Antichrist, though I am not dogmatic on any of these points at this time.

Dan 7:25 He shall speak *pompous* words against the Most High, Shall persecute the saints of the Most High, And shall intend to change times and law. Then *the saints* shall be given into his hand For a time and times and half a time.

He shall speak *pompous* words against the Most High

Speaking blasphemies against God is a very consistent description of the Antichrist in Scripture:

(Dan 7:8, Dan 7:20, Dan 8:24-25, Dan 11:28, Dan 11:30-31, Dan 11:36-37; Isa 37:23; 2Th 2:4; Rev 13:5-6, Rev 13:11.)

Shall persecute the saints of the Most High

The persecution of saints by the Antichrist is mentioned almost as many times as the blasphemies, as defining characteristics of the Antichrist:

(Rev 6:9-10, Rev 11:7-10, Rev 13:7-10, Rev 14:12, Rev 16:6, Rev 17:6, Rev 18:24)

And shall intend to change times and law

The words "times" and "law" here are pretty general and they are used a number of different ways in scripture. **Times** is sometimes rendered "seasons", and **law** can mean a decree from God or from man, and it is used both ways. In my research I tried to find some pattern of their usage in scripture but came to the conclusion that the interpretation of this phrase is more simple than complex.

Some people say that this changing of the times and seasons is related to Antichrist changing or taking away the holidays like Christmas or Passover for the Jews.

I think that there are several possibilities for this and I will list a few of my best guesses.

That the changing of the times and seasons is a reference to the many instances of reforms that we are told the Antichrist makes in the end times, some examples being his forbidding to marry and the commanding to abstain from foods (1 Tim 4:3), (though this is only said to happen in the "last days" it is not necessarily attributed to the Antichrist), his ending of the daily sacrifices (Dan 12:11; 2Th 2:4), his causing all people to receive a mark in order to buy or sell (Rev 13:16).

It could also be a reference to his trying to increase the time he is given by God to persecute the saints, that is 3.5 years. Almost every time this period of persecution is spoken of it mentions that the time is given to him and allotted to him by God. We know that Satan does not want his time to be limited to 3.5 years, and in fact in Revelation 12:12 we are told that one of the reasons his wrath will be so great is because he knows his time is short.

One of the reasons I suggest that this might be a reference to his attempt to lengthen his time is because of the context. This idea is sandwiched contextually with 3.5-year persecution references. In addition one point might be made that it says that he only "intends" or attempts to change the time and decree. It could be that he is never successful at this attempt.

I think either of these is a valid argument, or it could be a reference to something altogether different.

Then *the saints* shall be given into his hand For a time and times and half a time.

This is a reference to the 3.5-year time period given to the Antichrist to persecute the saints. In the original language it is clear that the time, times and half a time essentially means 3.5 years. But thankfully this time period in confirmed in many way throughout scripture. One almost identical verse to this one is found in Revelation 13:5. It says:

> And he was given a mouth speaking great things and blasphemies, and he was given authority to continue for forty-two months. - Rev 13:5

This 3.5 years begins when the Antichrist declares himself to be higher than God in the temple in Jerusalem. Jesus describes how the greatest persecution that the world has ever seen will begin immediately after this event in Matthew 24.

Some say that the saints here is only a reference to those left after the rapture, that is people saved after the rapture. But people that believe this believe it without a scriptural basis. And I would suggest that it is in direct conflict with many verses, such as 2 Thessalonians 2:1-11 and Matthew 24: 29-31.

The church will see the persecution of Antichrist, which will begin at the midpoint of the seven-year period. But at some unknown point after that time, the church will be raptured out of that persecution and the wrath of God or the Day of the Lord will begin on the wicked on that same day. This is the standard "prewrath" view which I and many others hold to. It is also the earliest view of the church, that is that the church would encounter the Antichrist before the rapture.

Dan 7:26 'But the court shall be seated, And they shall take away his dominion, To consume and destroy *it* forever.

A reference to the judgment of Antichrist.

Dan 7:27 Then the kingdom and dominion, And the greatness of the kingdoms under the whole heaven, Shall be given to the people, the saints of the Most High. His kingdom *is* an everlasting kingdom, And all dominions shall serve and obey Him.'

It is interesting that this chapter has been so emphatic that the kingdom is given to the saints of the Most High. In many ways the Bible is the story of God making a new nation, a new kingdom made up of His people, people who chose to love Him.

I never have considered how much He was planning on giving his people at the end of time until this study.

Dan 7:28 "This *is* the end of the account. As for me, Daniel, my thoughts greatly troubled me, and my countenance changed; but I kept the matter in my heart."

Daniel is worn out by the experience. He says he kept the matter in his heart, probably meaning that he didn't immediately broadcast what he had seen in the vision but thought much about it.

Chapter 8

Daniel Has a Vision of a Goat and a Ram

Chapter 8 continues in Hebrew after about five chapters of the underlying text having been written in Aramaic. Some commentators say this is because it is now done talking about gentile history and that the rest of the book is about Jewish history. This idea I think loses a measure of credibility due to the accepted fact that this chapter as well as Chapter 11 will extensively deal with the history and future of nations like Persia, Greece, Egypt and other nations which are obviously gentile nations. So although there may be significance for the change in languages at this point, I am not convinced that is the reason for it.

The events that will be prophesized here and in the next few chapters would not occur for hundreds of years after the time that Daniel wrote them; though many of these events are history to us, they were future to Daniel and his readers.

Many commentators have an issue with the prophecies here and in the following chapters simply because they are extremely accurate. There are many worldviews in the academic world that can't allow for the accurate foretelling of the future, and so, based solely on this prophecy's accuracy, many have argued that these next few chapters were written after the facts that they detail - a theory that strains credulity because the book of Daniel appears in the Septuagint which can be shown to be in wide use, a demonstration that it was an accepted part of the Hebrew canon, around the same time as these events.

These prophecies also were probably of great encouragement to the Jews who at this time were still in captivity. They would have been hearing about all kinds of rumors of wars, such as the impending war with Persia, and it would be comforting for them to know that although many nations would rise and fall, Israel would remain, even in the distant future. They would not have to wait much longer for this prophecy to begin to be validated either. In just a little over a decade they will be allowed to return home to Israel, and there would indeed be a Persian king on the throne just as this chapter says.

However, as we will see, there is a large portion of this prophecy that is relevant and important to us today, especially in relation to the so-called Antichrist.

Dan 8:1 In the third year of the reign of King Belshazzar a vision appeared *to* me—to me, Daniel—after the one that appeared to me the first time.

In the third year of the reign of King Belshazzar

This vision occurs way before **Belshazzar's** drunken feast on the night of the fall of Babylon recorded in Chapter 5. So we are going backwards chronologically here in Chapter 8. In fact this vision would have taken place more than 11 years before the feast detailed in Chapter 5.

When Daniel says "**after the one that appeared to me the first time**." He is referring to the vision of the four beasts in Daniel 7.

Dan 8:2 I saw in the vision, and it so happened while I was looking, that I *was* in Shushan, the citadel, which *is* in the province of Elam; and I saw in the vision that I was by the River Ulai.

Daniel is seeing this vision as if he was in Shushan. It could be that he was physically or spiritually transported there such as in the case of Ezekiel (Ez 8: 2-4) or it could be that he really was actually there when the vision took place, or that he simply saw the vision as if he was there. The text is not clear, though I favor the former explanation, that he was spiritually or physically transported such as Ezekiel based on the grammar and context.

146

Shushan or Susa was a city to the east of Babylon, where some believe that Daniel lived during the exile and in fact they believe his tomb is there today. The King Nabonidus stayed there often too. The city was later taken by the Persian King Cyrus and became one of the four capitals of the Persian Empire, specifically the winter capital.

Dan 8:3 Then I lifted my eyes and saw, and there, standing beside the river, was a ram which had two horns, and the two horns *were* high; but one *was* higher than the other, and the higher *one* came up last.

Later on in verse 20 the angel will give us the interpretation of this **ram** which is the kingdom of Medo-Persia.

The two horns represent the two divisions of that empire. The longer horn (which probably represents greater strength or notability) came up later. This no doubt corresponds to how Persia, which had very little territory or power at the beginning, came to be the much more dominant part of the Medo-Persian alliance.

Miller, in the New American Commentary, says that the ram is a fitting symbol for the Medo-Persians because:

> "According to Ammianus Marcellinus (10.1; fourth century A.D.), the Persian ruler carried the gold head of a ram when he marched before his army.[14]"

I would not be so quick to suggest these types of reasons for the animal symbols used here, as it is an interpretive methodology that we have seen break down in our study of Daniel 7, where according to Miller and most others, the Medo-Persians are there represented by a bear - not a goat.
In that case Miller says a bear is an apt symbol for the Medo-Persian Empire, not because of any bear idols carried into battle, but rather because of "its great size and fierceness in battle."[15]

This would also mean that in a few verses we should look for a similar connection between Greece and goats in order to be hermeneutically consistent, which very few commentators attempt to do as there is no clear connection between Greece and a goat.

I am not necessarily opposed to this method of interpretation, and it may well prove to be the correct one in the end, but I think that an interpretation based on the biblical data regarding any animal must first be exhausted before going to historical factors. In addition, I am not at all convinced that we need to find a deeper meaning to the animals represented here as kingdoms anyway. It could simply be that these animals, a ram and a goat, who often fight in nature, are used for that reason alone. As we will see, it is the fact that they clash with one another that is of the most importance here contextually.

Dan 8:4 I saw the ram pushing westward, northward, and southward, so that no animal could withstand him; nor *was there any* that could deliver from his hand, but he did according to his will and became great.

Pushing westward, northward, and southward
These are the directions of the conquests of Medo-Persia:

> **Westward** - Persia conquered westward Babylon, Mesopotamia, Syria, Asia Minor.
> **Northward** - Colchis, Armenia, Iberia, and the dwellers on the Caspian Sea.
> **Southward** - Judea, Egypt, Ethiopia, Libya; also India, under Darius. He does not say *eastward,* for the Persians themselves came from the east (Is 46:11).[16"]

Cyrus the Great created the largest empire the world had ever known at that time, and may be to this day the largest empire ever. The directions that it expanded are perfectly in line with this prophecy as you can see on any map of the Achaemenid (Medo-Persian) Empire.

So that no animal could withstand him; nor *was there any* that could deliver from his hand, but he did according to his will and became great.

Cyrus was obviously skilled in battle, and judging by the size of his empire alone, few who **could withstand him**, but he was even more skilled in diplomacy. He was often seen as a liberator to the countries he conquered. To this day he is called the "father" in many of the countries he conquered because he was seen as a father figure by his empire.

And became great

Not only did he become **great,** he is one of the few people remembered by that name, "Cyrus the Great," and many historians such as Stanford University's Professor Patrick Hunt[17] believe he is more deserving of the title than the next person we are about to look at, who also has been remembered with the same epitaph, "Great."

Dan 8:5 And as I was considering, suddenly a male goat came from the west, across the surface of the whole earth, without touching the ground; and the goat *had* a notable horn between his eyes.

This **male goat** charging from the west is again interpreted for us in verse 21 by the angel. It is the empire of Greece and the **notable horn between his eyes** is revealed by the angel to be its first king whom we know was Alexander the Great.

Without touching the ground

This is probably a reference to speed. Speed is an appropriate designation for Alexander the Great and the Grecian Empire for several reasons:

1.) The speed in which he conquered the known world. (He died a young man at age 33, after only 13 years of military campaigns, an unprecedented and unequaled feat.)

2.) His army was known for its ability to traverse great distances very quickly.

3.) Once at the battle, the intentionally small army was able to quickly outmaneuver their opponents using the Greek Phalanx, a fighting style developed by Alexander's father.

Dan 8:6 Then he came to the ram that had two horns, which I had seen standing beside the river, and ran at him with furious power.
Dan 8:7 And I saw him confronting the ram; he was moved with rage against him, attacked the ram, and broke his two horns. There was no power in the ram to withstand him, but he cast him down to the ground and trampled him; and there was no one that could deliver the ram from his hand.

So the Goat (Alexander and Greece) attacks the Ram (Medo-Persia) and defeats it. This event took place a mere three or so years after Alexander became king.

Terms like **"with furious power"** and **"he was moved with rage against him"** probably speak of the extreme hostility Alexander, and for that matter, all of Greece had against the Persians at this point.

Alexander's father was planning an invasion of Persia when he was murdered. This grudge against the Persians that Alexander and all of Greece were nursing was in part because of the Persians' conquests of the mainland of Greece after the famous battle of Thermopylae. To make a long story short, the proud Grecians absolutely hated being conquered by the Persians, and when Alexander took the throne he made a bee line for Persia for revenge.

Dan 8:8 Therefore the male goat grew very great; but when he became strong, the large horn was broken, and in place of it four notable ones came up toward the four winds of heaven.

The uncanny accuracy of this prophecy continues. Here is says that the Grecian Empire will grow very great but when it

becomes strong the horn (Alexander) will be broken, and four other horns (or rulers) of the goat will succeed him.

Alexander died at the height of his power due to a fever. His famous last words concerning who to give his empire to were: "give it to the strong," which after a few murders of Alexander's children and brother, was interpreted as "give it to my four generals."

These four generals split up the empire four ways. The phrase **"four winds of heaven"** is appropriate. The phrase "four winds of heaven" is often a way for scripture to speak of the cardinal directions, though it is also often used to allegorically describe the entire world.

Dan 8:9 And out of one of them came a little horn which grew exceedingly great toward the south, toward the east, and toward the Glorious *Land.*

In my opinion this verse is the beginning of a transition from things that have already happened in history to things that are yet to come.

This idea of a transition here is not an arbitrary decision. We are given a hint that this shift happens at this point in the text by the angel, when, in his interpretation of this vision in verse 23, after telling us about how the ram is in fact Medo-Persia and that the goat is Greece and about the four empires that will succeed it, he stops and says the following before going on to explain the verse we are about to study:

> "And in the latter time of their kingdom [speaking of the four empires that follow Greece], When the transgressors have reached their fullness, A king shall arise, having fierce features, who understands sinister schemes." Dan 8:23

I will explain when we get to verse 23 why I think the phrase "When the transgressors have reached their fullness," is a reference to an eschatological fulfillment of the following verses.

In addition there are other phrases said by the angel referring to this portion of the prophecy that have long led scholars to argue that an eschatological fulfillment is at least partially required here. Phrases such as "The vision *refers* to the time of the end" in verse 17 and "in the latter time of the indignation; for at the appointed time the end *shall be*" in verse 19 give us solid ground for our interpretation that these next verses are intended to begin to speak of the end times.

And out of one of them came a little horn

This little horn can be shown to have been fulfilled in some ways by Antiochus IV or Antiochus Epiphanes of the Seleucid Empire (one of the four broken up empires of Greece), but many conservative scholars also see the following verses as a "type" of the Antichrist as well.

The challenge for the prophecy interpreter when dealing with prophecies that have dual or more fulfillments or types is to judge what aspects of the type should be delegated to which near or far referent. I tend to take a very conservative approach to this. That is, I wait for clear biblical support before I will allow an aspect of a type to be applied to its yet future referent.

We will see in Chapter 11 for instance that the text is clearly speaking of Antiochus until about verse 36 when it no longer applies to Antiochus, but does apply to what we know about the Antichrist. This is a very common thing in prophetic scriptures. Take for example Ezekiel 28 where it starts out talking about the King of Tyre, but ends up speaking of Satan in obvious terms, saying that he was in the Garden of Eden, something that obviously did not apply to the King of Tyre.

Often though there is a transitional period between the near and far aspects, a time in which the text could apply to both. David Guzik explains it as being like a fade effect in film, one frame overlaps another frame and both can be seen for a moment until only one remains. In biblical prophecy there also can be a fade-in that never quite fades out; in other words, once it fades in it continues to have an overlapping meaning, usually a near and far application. Such is the case here.

I feel for reasons we will see in a moment that although the following verses are fulfilled by Antiochus, the most literal fulfillment of these verses will be fulfilled by the Antichrist.

I differ from some commentators slightly here because I put the emphasis more on the Antichrist in this chapter where others may put the emphasis on Antiochus, though I think they are both legitimate. I simply think I can demonstrate that the text is more precise when speaking of the Antichrist than it is of Antiochus in these verses, especially toward the end.

Out of one of them

Them grammatically must refer back to one of the four empires broken up from Alexander's Empire. Those four empires, the Ptolemaic Kingdom of Egypt, the Seleucid Empire in the east, the Kingdom of Pergamon in Asia Minor, and Macedon.

Antiochus IV or Antiochus Epiphanes, who will be in view in the next few verses, was king of the Seleucid Empire which encompassed Afghanistan, Syria, Lebanon, Iran and Iraq, plus parts of Armenia, Turkey, Turkmenistan, Uzbekistan and Tajikistan, though its capital, Antioch, was in Syria.

This has led many to speculate that the Antichrist will be from one of these countries that made up the former Seleucid Empire. I would not say that it is scripturally certain. One reason is because this is right at the moment of that fade-in / fade-out process that I was talking about earlier, and to build doctrine on this would be unwise.

For instance in Ezekiel 28 I would not say that Satan was literally the king of Tyre in Ezekiel's day because at that point in the prophecy it was not yet speaking of Satan, yet I would have no hesitation stating for doctrine that Satan was perfect when he was created, something that we learn almost exclusively from that passage in Ezekiel. The difference was the distance from the fade. At this point I am not sure we are safely out of the historical or near application territory, partially because of the phrase **"which grew exceedingly great toward the south, toward the east, and toward the Glorious _Land_,"** which I think may even be pre-Antiochus, that is speaking of his great-great-great-grandfather Seleucus (see next section), though I am not ruling out the possibility that this also could refer to Antichrist.

We should be careful especially as we proceed in the next few chapters of Daniel not to say for certain about the Antichrist that which is not certain in the text. That being said, if all the other information that we discover about the Antichrist in this study fits, I would have no problem with the idea that, for example, the Antichrist comes from the former Seleucid Empire, a theory that is very popular these days, but if it is contradicted in the more clear passages regarding the Antichrist, then this type of proof text must be disregarded as it does not rest solid enough ground to build a foundation.

Came a little horn which grew exceedingly great toward the south, toward the east, and toward the Glorious _Land_.

This idea of a little horn which grew can refer to the Seleucid Empire itself. One of the four generals of Alexander, Seleucus I, started out with pretty much just Babylon after Alexander died, but he expanded his portion of Alexander's kingdom to include much of Alexander's near eastern territories. In fact the Seleucid Empire came to be the largest of the four empires because of his post-Alexander conquests. If you look at it on a map you can see that it expanded just as it is said here, toward the south, east and toward Israel.

Indeed it could, as most commentators have it, also be referring to the great-great-great-grandson of Seleucus, Antiochus Epiphanes who ruled the Seleucid Empire that his ancestor conquered many years earlier and who **is** clearly in view in later verses.

These commentators explain that Antiochus started small [little horn] in that he killed his brother in order to inherit the throne.

It could be said of Antiochus that he expanded toward the south and east and toward Israel as well, but he inherited a huge empire from his fathers. His conquests of Egypt (to the south) and Miller says "Persia, Parthia, Armenia" to the east, were very limited at best -he really didn't even actually conquer Egypt in the end. At any rate his conquests were certainly not **exceedingly great.**

It is my view that though it begins to zero in on Antiochus in the next verse I don't think it has quite gotten to him just yet, and that these verses are for the purpose of directing us to one of the four successive kingdoms of the Alexander Empire. i.e., the Seleucid Empire. This is given support when one considers that throughout the course of Chapter 11 the "king of the north" and "king of the south" titles are applied to many different generations of rulers of these same empires (Seleucid's and Ptolemy's).

I think that these, as well as the following verses, are best seen as being fulfilled in the Antichrist, though the historical fulfillments are also intended.

For example, the Antichrist is also said to start out small (little horn):

We saw in Daniel 7 that the Antichrist will start out as only one of ten rulers of only one beast (Dan 7: 7-8), yet we saw that by the time he is ready to declare himself to be higher than God in the temple he will have conquered not just those ten kings, but the other three beasts as well (Rev. 13:1-2). (See the discussion on Daniel 7 if you are not used to the idea that the four beasts of Daniel 7 are contemporaneous.)

So I think the idea of him starting off small, or as a **little horn,** is one doctrinal certainty we can say of the Antichrist.

We can also see that the Antichrist's conquests will similarly be southward (Daniel 11: 40, 43) and eastward (Daniel 11:44) and also toward the **Glorious Land** which is the exact phrase used when speaking of the Antichrist in Daniel 11:41.

> He shall also enter the Glorious Land - Dan 11:41

So what I am saying is that we can find explicit teaching in scripture regarding the Antichrist that exactly fits this as well as many other things in this chapter. The next verse is a good example.

Dan 8:10 And it grew up to the host of heaven; and it cast down *some* of the host and *some* of the stars to the ground, and trampled them.

Of Antiochus this is said to be referring to his terrible persecution of the Jews. The idea is that the terms like "hosts" and "stars" which usually refer to angels are here referring to Jews, and that idea can be accepted in more allegorical sense as there is some scriptural support for it and I do think that Antiochus terrible persecution of the Jews is in view here.

The literal side of this dual prophecy however, that is its reference to the Antichrist has much more scriptural support and it can be easily taken at face value.

For example notice the phrases used here and there counterparts regarding the Antichrist:

And it grew up to the host of heaven:

> And there was war in heaven: <u>Michael and his angels</u> fought against the dragon; and the dragon fought and <u>his angels</u>, And prevailed not; neither was <u>their</u> place found any more in heaven. - Rev 12:7-8
> For thou hast said in thine heart, I will ascend into heaven, I will exalt my throne <u>above the stars of God:</u> I

will sit also upon the mount of the congregation, in the sides of the north - Isa 14:13

And it cast down *some* of the host and *some* of the stars to the ground

> And the great dragon was cast out, that old serpent, called the Devil, and Satan, which deceiveth the whole world: he was cast out into the earth, and his angels were cast out with him. - Rev 12:9

It seems that just before Satan is thrown to earth he starts a literal war in heaven. We know that this war is future because of Rev 12:12 and following which puts this particular "fall" at the 3.5 year mark of the seven- year period coinciding with the so-called "abomination of desolation" that would spark the persecution known as the Great Tribulation.

It is also clear from the context of Revelation 12 that the Antichrist, not just Satan, is in view toward the end of that prophecy. Some think that it is at the middle of the 70th week after Satan's fall "to earth" and he "knows his time is short" that the Antichrist is possessed by Satan himself though I'm not sure if that is necessary.

Dan 8:11 He even exalted *himself* as high as the Prince of the host; and by him the daily *sacrifices* were taken away, and the place of His sanctuary was cast down.

In reference to Antiochus, this occurred when he (most likely) had the godly high priest Onias III killed in favor of Hellenistic men who simply paid Antiochus for the job, men like Jason and later Menelaus.

The idea of the high priest being called a **prince** can be seen in the following verse:

> Therefore I will profane the **princes of the sanctuary**; I will give Jacob to the curse, And Israel to reproaches. - Isa 43:28

The Keil and Delitzsch Commentary on the Old Testament says that the idea of "princes" here is referring to the highest levels of priests [which included the high priest] that were divided by lot in 1 Ch 24:5.

It is notable also because it calls them in this verse the "princes of the sanctuary" because from what I can gather from the Hebrew this is the intended meaning of the phrase "**and the place of His sanctuary was cast down.**" In other words, the high priest, who was the prince of the sanctuary, had the sanctuary he was prince over (**his sanctuary**) cast down, in this case by Antiochus, who although didn't destroy the temple, defiled it so mightily that it closed down for just over three years.

It should be noted here that the capital "H" as in "His sanctuary" has been added by the translators to reflect their position that "His" is referring to God, not because of any grammatical clue. And I think they are right, especially in the far fulfillment of this prophecy because, as has been the case with the others, I feel the best and most literal fulfillment of this prophecy will be found in the Antichrist.

For example:

Exalted *himself* as high as the Prince of the host:

> Who opposes and <u>exalts himself above all that is called God</u> or that is worshiped, so that <u>he sits as God in the temple of God, showing himself that he is God</u>. - 2Th 2:4

See also: Dan 11:36, Rev 13:6

Dan 8:12 Because of transgression, an army was given over *to the horn* to oppose the daily *sacrifices;* and he cast truth down to the ground. He did *all this* and prospered.

158

So it is saying that an **army** or "host" is given to Antiochus (and or the Antichrist) to oppose the daily sacrifices. A parallel to this verse can be found two chapters later when these events are spoken of in greater detail. It says:

> And forces shall be mustered by him, and they shall defile the sanctuary fortress; then they shall take away the daily *sacrifices,* and place *there* the abomination of desolation. - Dan 11:31

The forces or armies of Antiochus indeed did defile the sanctuary. This they did by sacrificing a pig on the altar and setting up an altar to a pagan deity in the Holy of Holies. The reasons he did this will be discussed in more detail in Chapter 11. But it should be noted that Antiochus' armies, not Antiochus himself did all that.

As far as the Antichrist is concerned, when he sits in the temple declaring himself to be higher than God, he will be backed by his military in some capacity or another. One scripture that comes to mind about this is:

> "But when you see Jerusalem surrounded by **armies**, then know that its **desolation** is near." - Luk 21:20

I am not sure that in the case of the Antichrist the abomination of desolation will seem all that "abominable" to the people in Jerusalem, as the near fulfillment was during Antiochus's time. The future Jerusalem may in fact view it as a good thing, as if the Messiah had come, though it will certainly be an abomination from God's perspective and something far worse than an idol in the temple and some swine's blood.

Dan 8:13 Then I heard a holy one speaking; and *another* holy one said to that certain *one* who was speaking, "How long *will* the vision *be, concerning* the daily *sacrifices* and the transgression of desolation, the giving of both the sanctuary and the host to be trampled underfoot?"

In Daniel's vision there are angels talking to one another. Some think that one of these "Holy Ones" is a Christophany, though it does not appear certain from the text.

"How long *will* the vision *be, concerning* the daily *sacrifices* and the transgression of desolation, the giving of both the sanctuary and the host to be trampled underfoot?"

This question is asked for the benefit of Daniel and us because, as we will see, the angel gives the answer to Daniel - not to the one who asks the question.

The question is about the desolation of the temple which ended the daily sacrifices. The angel asks essentially "how long will there be no daily sacrifices?" The fact that the **daily sacrifices** are of particular concern is important for reasons we are about to see.

Dan 8:14 And he said to me, "For two thousand three hundred days; then the sanctuary shall be cleansed."

It should first be noted that the word "**days**" does not appear in the original language. The words that do appear are "evenings," which in Hebrew is "ereb," and "mornings," which in Hebrew is "boger".

The fact that some Bible translators decided to translate these two words as "days" despite the absence of the Hebrew word for "day", "Yom," has caused some trouble.

Why? Well, a few reasons: The first is the so called "day-year theory." That is the idea that when you see a day in prophecy, it is okay to assume that a year is meant. This has been the basis for several date-setting movements in the past century.

There are a lot of problems with this, besides the fact that the word "day" does not even show up here and therefore is not even a candidate for a day-year prophecy.

I would suggest that in every single case that a prophecy gets interpreted within the Bible itself by another person in the Bible, it is interpreted literally by them. In other words in a non-day-year fashion.

In other words days are days, and years are years in prophecy according to biblical figures. For example, Daniel in the next chapter realizes that based on the prophecy written by Jeremiah that the Jews will get out of captivity after 70 years of exile. Daniel would not have calculated this properly if he used any other method of interpretation other than a literal one. If we took all the prophecies in the bible that have come true and applied a day-year-theory to them, like the prophecies of the Messiah, they would cease to be accurate. So day-year theorists are arbitrarily selective as to when to apply this hermeneutic and, as far as I know, this is the only place that they deem it necessary.

There is a much better way to understand this prophecy, but we must go back to the idea of "ereb" and "boqer," the Hebrew words for "evenings" and "mornings". Why such a strange way of saying "days" if indeed "days" was meant?

Every day there were two sacrifices at the temple, a morning and an evening sacrifice. This is described in Exodus 29:38-43

The angel was simply answering the question "how long will the daily sacrifices be forgone?"
The answer is given as the number of sacrifices that would be actually missed, i.e., "2300 evening and morning sacrifices will be missed before the sanctuary will be cleansed and they can start up again."

If the angel was saying there would be a total of 2300 morning and evening sacrifices missed before they would resume again, then it would be a total of 1150 days (2300 total sacrifices divided by 2 sacrifices per day = 1150 days).

There is a good debate on this issue, and I believe that in part the reason there is confusion is because whether 2300 days are meant or 1150 days, there are some problems with perfectly matching either of those dates up to Antiochus or the Antichrist, for that matter.

Let's review some history first so we know what we are looking for.

Antiochus comes back from an unsuccessful campaign in Egypt in a rage, and on his way home to Syria he had to pass through Jerusalem. This is when the defilement of the temple occurred, which included a religious idol being put in the Holy of Holies, etc.

This ultimately caused a rebellion of the Jewish people, led by a prominent family called the Maccabees.
They ultimately defeated the Greek forces, cleansed the temple, and reinstated the daily sacrifices.

We know the exact dates in which the sacrifices were ended by Antiochus's armies, and when they were restored again by the Maccabees. This is a matter of historical certainty;

I Maccabees, though not a canonical book, is widely agreed by scholars to be historically accurate and its dates match other data we can gather about this event and in Chapter 1, verse 54, it says:

> "On the 15th day of the 9th month of the 145th year [of the kingdom of the Greeks] king Antiochus set up the abominable idol of desolation upon the altar of God."

The termination is established in the same book I Mac. 4:52, 53

> "And they arose before the morning of the 25th day of the 9th month of the 148th year, and they offered sacrifices according to the law upon the new altar..."

But now here is the problem: if you do the math on the number of days, which *should* come up to 1150 if our theory is correct, it actually only comes to 1105, which is 45 days short.

This has led many to say things like: well, perhaps the sacrifices were stopped sometime before the idol was set up. This I suppose is possible, but we have no record of it, and it would seem to run contrary to certain occasions in scripture when the abomination of desolation is mentioned as being **the reason** that the sacrifices are stopped - not because of some preceding event. This at least seems certain of the end-times version of the abomination of desolation such as in Matthew 24:15.

This almost-but-not-quite interpretation has left others to pursue the possibility that perhaps 2300 evenings and mornings really was just speaking of 2300 days. In other words it would be like saying 2300 **groupings** of evenings and mornings.

This camp then needs to try to find a fulfillment that lasts about 6.3 years. They will say that from the assassination of the high priest until the cleansing of the temple by the Maccabees is right around 6 years (though they will usually admit not exactly 6.3 years) and that this general period should be viewed as the entire Maccabean "tribulation."

This view has a major problem in that it has to take the assassination of the high priest or some other event as the starting point even though the ending of the sacrifices is explicitly said to be the starting point by the angel.

Both views are lacking as they do not come to a literal and perfect resolution, which is especially troubling since the dates of the events in question have been so well preserved for us.

The answer to this conundrum, I believe is simple - we are using the wrong calendar. Most of these calculations are using a 365 day calendar when, as we will see, that is not always the way the Bible renders time.

We will discuss calendars more when we look at Daniel 9, and we will see that the Bible can be shown conclusively to use at least three calendars at different times for different reasons. But for right now, what we need to know is that the Bible often uses a 360-day calendar to render prophecy.

You may be familiar with the idea that the Book of Revelation gives us the last 3.5 years of the famous seven- year period in various formats in several places. For instance in Revelation 13:5 it speaks of it as 42 months, in Revelation 12:6 it is 1260 days, and in 12:14 as a "time times and half a time" [or 3.5 years]. All of this gives us certainty that we are dealing with 360-day years in that prophecy, which deals with the end times abomination of desolation.

We will show more examples of the Bible's use of 360-day years, and some thoughts as to why it does this in Chapter 9. But for right now I want to focus in on the Greek world at that time, and show that it too used the 360-day year, as I think that the Greek way of keeping time here will help us solve this problem.

Herodotus the so called father of history has a number of quotes about the Greek calendar that lets us know that there are 360 days in a Greek year, but he also has a few quotes that tell us about the so-called intercalary months, this is the extra month thrown in at different times in order to keep calendars on pace with the seasons. He said the following:

> "Take seventy years as the span of a man's life. Those seventy years contain 25,200 days without counting intercalary months. Add a month every other year to make the seasons come round with proper regularity, and you will have 35 additional months which will make 1050 days. Thus the total days of your seventy years is 26,250 and not a single one of them is like the next in what it brings."

I will quote Fred P. Miller for the calculations based on these numbers.

> "Using the Greek calendar according to Herodotus and assuming that the years 146 and 148 were intercalary years, we come up with the following calculation: 9-15-145 to 9-25-148, the dates given in Maccabees from the desecration to the cleansing, is three years and ten days.

Thus, the math sentence following the Greek calendar which was in use at the time the prophecy was fulfilled would be: (3 X 360) + (2 X 30) + 10. Let's diagram it.

3 x 360 equals *******************1080 days
2 x 30 (2 intercalary months)***********60 days
From 15th to 25th equals **************10 days

Total ****************************1150 days"

So in other words if each year is 360 days and if there is an extra 30 days every other year (which Herodotus said there was) then all of this fits. It would seem to me that the problem is solved.

How this relates to the Antichrist is an open question for me at this point. The problem is that in Daniel 12, when it is certainly talking about the Antichrist's desolation in the end times, it says it will be "1290 days," which is a difference of 140 days from this calendar.

> "And from the time *that* the daily *sacrifice* is taken away, and the abomination of desolation is set up, *there shall be* one thousand two hundred and ninety days. - Dan 12:11

We will see when we get to this that there is a very interesting reason for the additional 30-day and 45-day period tacked onto the last seven- year period. But if you want to get started on this, I suggest Dr. Elbert Charpie's presentation on Daniel's 30- and 45-day period.

So I will at this point say that I can see the significance of the 2300-day prophecy for Antiochus, but have not yet determined its relationship to the Antichrist.

My hunch is that the overwhelming evidence in scripture that points to there being a 3.5 year period from abomination to the restoration is also in view in the 2300 evenings and mornings prophecy, but that it is being rendered in this way for one reason or another.

But until that is confirmed I will assume this is a separate prophecy from the 3.5-year period, perhaps never intended to apply to the Antichrist but only to Antiochus, which seems unlikely given the context, or that it will make sense as a distinct prophecy of the Antichrist when the events come to pass.

An Angel Interprets Daniel's Vision

Dan 8:15 Then it happened, when I, Daniel, had seen the vision and was seeking the meaning, that suddenly there stood before me one having the appearance of a man.
Dan 8:16 And I heard a man's voice between *the banks of* the Ulai, who called, and said, "Gabriel, make this *man* understand the vision."
Dan 8:17 So he came near where I stood, and when he came I was afraid and fell on my face; but he said to me, "Understand, son of man, that the vision *refers* to the time of the end."
Dan 8:18 Now, as he was speaking with me, I was in a deep sleep with my face to the ground; but he touched me, and stood me upright.
Dan 8:19 And he said, "Look, I am making known to you what shall happen in the latter time of the indignation; for at the appointed time the end *shall be.*

Miller believes this one with the "appearance of a man" to be God himself, perhaps a Christophany:
I explain why I don't believe it is in the discussion on Daniel 10:4-6

Latter time of the indignation

This is a prophetic theme spoken of often, with the phrases like "appointed time." The concept appears often in Daniel (Dan 8:17, Dan 8:23, Dan 9:26-27, Dan 11:27, Dan 11:35-36, Dan 12:7-8). The time of God's wrath against the wicked is appointed; it will come about with certainty.

166

Latter time

Not just a late time, as in a few hundred years from now (i.e., Antiochus) but latter as in eschatological or final time, though both are probably in view but again the more literal referent is Antichrist.

Dan 8:20 The ram which you saw, having the two horns— *they are* **the kings of Media and Persia.**
Dan 8:21 And the male goat *is* **the kingdom of Greece. The large horn that** *is* **between its eyes** *is* **the first king.**
Dan 8:22 As for the broken *horn* **and the four that stood up in its place, four kingdoms shall arise out of that nation, but not with its power.**

Here we find that our interpretation of the animals that represent kingdoms were correct. We also take note here of the fantastic accuracy of God's word. God, who is the Alpha and Omega, can easily tell us history in advance.

Dan 8:23 "And in the latter time of their kingdom, When the transgressors have reached their fullness, A king shall arise, Having fierce features, Who understands sinister schemes.

When the transgressors have reached their fullness

In an eschatological sense the transgressors should here be understood as all those that will be recipients of God's wrath during the Day of the Lord.

This idea that transgression can reach a "**fullness**" is also a consistent theme in scripture. It would seem that God has an allotment of sinfulness that can occur before judgment is sent.

> Then He said to Abram: "Know certainly that your descendants will be strangers in a land that is not theirs, and will serve them, and they will afflict them four hundred years. And also the nation whom they serve I

> will judge; afterward they shall come out with great possessions. Now as for you, you shall go to your fathers in peace; you shall be buried at a good old age. But in the fourth generation they shall return here, <u>for the iniquity of the Amorites is not yet complete."</u> - Gen 15:13-16

Abraham would not see the fulfillment of his promised land in his day because the people who were already in the land, the Amorites, had not yet reached their allotment of sinfulness. In fact it would be another 400 years before they did. Our God is indeed a longsuffering God.

It is unlikely, as some commentators have it, that this **fullness of transgressions** occurred in Antiochus's day as contextually the transgressors would be the Israelites, and we know from the words of Jesus that their sin had not reached its fullness even in his day, for he said after their rejection of Him:

> Fill up, then, the measure of your fathers' guilt. - Mat 23:32

So they are still awaiting their allotment to come due. I personally think this allotment is detailed in Revelation 17 and 18, and if you are inclined you can see my book *Mystery Babylon When Jerusalem Embraces the Antichrist.*

Dan 8:24 His power shall be mighty, but not by his own power; He shall destroy fearfully, And shall prosper and thrive; He shall destroy the mighty, and *also* the holy people.

Though we can make a case for Antiochus with each of these points, as I have been saying this is far more about the Antichrist than Antiochus at this point.

His power shall be mighty, but not by his own power

This is paralleled in:

Now the beast which I saw was like a leopard, his feet were like the feet of a bear, and his mouth like the mouth of a lion. [He is mighty…but] The dragon gave him his power, his throne, and great authority. [not by his own power] - Rev 13:2

He shall destroy fearfully, And shall prosper and thrive; He shall destroy the mighty, and *also* the holy people.

"It was granted to him to make war with the saints and to overcome them. And authority was given him over every tribe, tongue, and nation." - Rev 13:7

"I was watching; and the same horn was making war against the saints, and prevailing against them" - Dan 7:21

"For then there will be great tribulation, such as has not been since the beginning of the world until this time, no, nor ever shall be. And unless those days were shortened, no flesh would be saved; but for the elect's sake those days will be shortened." - Mat 24:21-22

Dan 8:25 "Through his cunning He shall cause deceit to prosper under his rule; And he shall exalt *himself* in his heart. He shall destroy many in *their* prosperity. He shall even rise against the Prince of princes; But he shall be broken without *human* means.

Through his cunning He shall cause deceit to prosper under his rule

This was described in the vision as one who "understands sinister schemes" also in Daniel 11:21, and here we must again be careful not to put too much emphasis on "types" but it says of Antiochus: "but he shall come in peaceably, and seize the kingdom by intrigue."

This perhaps could relate to the "covenant with many" spoken of in Daniel 9 but it is not clear to me.

It does seem however that we can be certain that the Antichrist's initial coming to power was not through warfare; though once he has a measure of power, warfare will certainly be the way he gains more of it.

In this verse, however, the emphasis seems to be that deception itself will be prominent during his rule. This is echoed in many places in the New Testament, one of particular note is:

> Now the Spirit expressly says that in latter times some will depart from the faith, giving heed to deceiving spirits and doctrines of demons, speaking lies in hypocrisy, having their own conscience seared with a hot iron - 1Ti 4:1-2

But he shall be broken without *human* means.

The Antichrist does not meet his end by human means but only by the "breath of the mouth" of the returning Christ. (Rev 19:19-21, 2 Thes 2:8)

Dan 8:26 "And the vision of the evenings and mornings Which was told is true; Therefore seal up the vision, For *it refers* to many days *in the future.*"

A reiteration is given regarding the truthfulness of the 2300 evenings-and-mornings vision. Miller postulates a reason for this:

> " the detail concerning the "evenings and mornings" evidently was singled out because it told the exact length of the persecution period, information that would be of great interest to those suffering this ordeal."[18]

Therefore seal up the vision, For *it refers* to many days *in the future.*"

See the discussion on Daniel 12:4 for more about the meaning of the "sealing" here.

Dan 8:27 And I, Daniel, fainted and was sick for days; afterward I arose and went about the king's business. I was astonished by the vision, but no one understood it.

This sickness is interesting, it could be said that the reason for the sickness was the grief of having seen the future of his people, and the destruction that would come upon them. It is evident from Daniel's prayer in Daniel 9 that he was a man of passion for his people. This vision then would indeed make such a man "sick."

It could also be that the mere presence of the beings made him sick, or the sheer exhaustion that would occur in such an encounter would leave him that way. It is evident in some cases in scripture that angels had to "strengthen" the people that they talked to. Or of course it could be a combination of both, or neither, the text is not explicit on *why* exactly Daniel was sick here.

Chapter 9

Daniel Prays for His People

Dan 9:1 In the first year of Darius the son of Ahasuerus, of the lineage of the Medes, who was made king over the realm of the Chaldeans

Daniel says he received this vision "**In the first year of Darius the son of Ahasuerus**". There are a lot of different views about who this is, and it actually will play a significant role in the chronology of the prophecy that Daniel is about to receive, so we should look at it in detail.

At the moment there is no historical record of such a king. There are two main options that conservative scholars take here. They say that because this King Darius is apparently the same one who began ruling directly after the fall of Babylon according to Daniel 5: 30-31

> In that night was Belshazzar the king of the Chaldeans slain. And **Darius the Median** took the kingdom, *being* about threescore and two years old.

This conjoined with the historical fact that it was Cyrus II "the Great" was the Persian king who ruled after the fall of Babylon, many scholars simply say that Darius was just a title, another way for Daniel to reference Cyrus. This seems plausible until you realize that it would mean that Daniel got his facts wrong when calling Cyrus **of the lineage of the Medes** which he does in this passage as well as in Daniel 5:31.

The other view conservatives take is that there really was a king named Darius who was a Mede that ruled Babylon as a kind of co-regent with Cyrus, others who hold to this basic view cast Darius less of a co-king than they do a governor of the province of Babylon.

In other words after Cyrus took over, he appointed governors over the new parts of his empire - Darius the Mede being the new governor of Babylon.

Charles Cooper in his book *God's Elect and the Great Tribulation* points out that Daniel says explicitly in several places that the kingdom being referred to here would be a combined Median and Persian empire, and that according to Daniel 8: 3-4, 20 although the Medes would be less influential than, and basically controlled by, the Persian half of this empire, they still would be co-ruling together, and that each of them would have a king.

So in this telling, Darius would be a king along with Cyrus. In other words Darius was more than a governor; he was co king, albeit a king who was subordinate to Cyrus. This would explain a number of things, including the phrase "[Darius the Mede..] who <u>was made king</u> over the realm of the Chaldeans" Darius was "made" king. This is a strange wording unless he was given his kingdom. And while it is true that this could speak of the sovereignty of God who makes and deposes all kings, a few other points make me think it is simply talking about Cyrus' appointing Darius as **King over the realm of the Chaldeans.**

One such reason is found in the last verse of Daniel 6:

> So this Daniel prospered in the reign of Darius, <u>and</u> in the reign of Cyrus the Persian. - Dan 6:28

This seems to be a very clear indication that Daniel believed that the rule of Darius and Cyrus the Persian occurred simultaneously. Though those that try to say Darius and Cyrus are the same person suggest that this should be translated:

> So this Daniel prospered in the reign of Darius, <u>even</u> the reign of Cyrus the Persian.

They claim this is a valid translation even though no Bible version that I checked - and I checked seven of them - translates this verse in that way. All of the ones I checked use the word "and," not "even," suggesting Daniel was talking about two individuals ruling at the same time.

Believing that these two kings were the same person, as so many conservatives do, and forcing this "even" instead of "and" on the text has the problem of Daniel being wrong at least twice in this book when he clearly calls Darius a Mede, and not just from there but "of" as in descended from Medians, something that was definitely not true of Cyrus, who Daniel clearly calls "The Persian" in 6:28.

Holding to the contemporaneous-kings view also helps to solve the various discrepancies in the ancient world about the list of kings for this empire.

Daniel's prophecy in 11:1-2 reads as follows:

> "Also in the first year of Darius the Mede, I, even I, stood up to confirm and strengthen him. And now I will tell you the truth: Behold, three more kings will arise in Persia, and the fourth shall be far richer than them all; by his strength, through his riches, he shall stir up all against the realm of Greece." - Dan 11:1-2

Daniel seems to suggest here that there would be just five kings of Medo-Persia from Darius until Alexander the Great conquers the empire. Yet this would conflict with most historians who believe there were 10-13 kings during this time.

Most commentators who accept the 10-13 kings chronology of modern scholarship say things like Stephen Miller does in his New American Commentary.

> "Kings after Xerxes are not mentioned [by Daniel], apparently because the later Persian rulers were not germane to [his] purpose."[19]

Charles Cooper points out that this list of kings of the Medo-Persian Empire that modern scholarship accepts is based on one single writer, and that many other historians from the period have differing accounts regarding the number of these kings. These sometimes wildly divergent lists of Persian kings are due in part to the destruction of Persian historical texts by Alexander the Great after his conquest of Persia.

Cooper suggests that the problem is resolved by there being two lines of kings in the Medo-Persian Empire, one of Media and one of Persia, and he demonstrates that this view is also backed up in several places in scripture.

This also accounts for major discrepancies by scholars in the length of the Persian Empire, some accounts differing as much as 156 years.

This and many other issues are discussed in Charles Cooper's Commentary of Daniel 9 from his book *God's Elect and the Great Tribulation*, a book which I will heavily rely on for this chapter.

Dan 9:2 in the first year of his reign I, Daniel, understood by the books the number of the years *specified* by the word of the LORD through Jeremiah the prophet, that He would accomplish seventy years in the desolations of Jerusalem.

Understood by the books

Daniel was reading either Jer 25:12 or Jer 29:1. The former seems to be the original prophecy that told Israel that their exile would last for 70 years. It reads:

> 'Then it will come to pass, when seventy years are completed, *that* I will punish the king of Babylon and that nation, the land of the Chaldeans, for their iniquity,' says the LORD; 'and I will make it a perpetual desolation'. - Jer 25:12

Though it is also quite likely that Daniel was reading what was then a letter sent by the prophet Jeremiah to the exiles in Babylon recorded in Jer 29:10 which reiterates the earlier prophecy but also contains elements that make me think that it was of particular interest to Daniel. That letter starts off this way:

> Now these *are* the words of the letter that Jeremiah the prophet sent from Jerusalem to the remainder of the elders who were carried away captive—to the priests, the prophets, and all the people whom Nebuchadnezzar had carried away captive from Jerusalem to Babylon. - Jer 29:1

Jeremiah, in this letter, tells the captives a few things that are worthy of noting. He tells them that while they are in Babylon they are to build houses, plant gardens, take wives, have children, and to seek peace in Babylon. He basically tells them to be good citizens and they will be rewarded. He tells them that God has good plans for them, and for them not to worry about all the false prophets who are prophesying doom to them in Babylon.

It is this context that Jeremiah reiterates the earlier prophecy from Jer 25 that they were only to be there for 70 years.

This section is also a proclamation of judgment on the kings of Israel for their idolatry as well as the false prophets. It also details the many sins of Israel and some of the reasons for their exile.

Of particular note about this letter of Jeremiah is that it seems as if these good plans God had in store for them and even the 70 years exile coming to an end reads as if it is almost conditional on earnest prayer from the Israelites.

> Then you will call upon Me and go and pray to Me, and I will listen to you. And you will seek Me and find *Me,* when you search for Me with all your heart. I will be found by you, says the LORD, <u>and I will bring you back from your captivity;</u> I will gather you from all the

nations and from all the places where I have driven you, says the LORD, and I will bring you to the place from which I cause you to be carried away captive. - Jer 29:12-14

We will confirm later through Leviticus 26 that the idea of the return to the covenant and the land of Israel was in fact conditional on a particular type of prayer. And that is the reason that Daniel begins here to very earnestly pray, in sackcloth and ashes, for the prophecy of Jeremiah to come to pass, because he realized that their return was conditional on a particular prayer.

The word of the LORD through Jeremiah the prophet

The word Lord here is YHWH. This is one of the many uses of the covenant name YHWH in Daniel 9, which is the only place that it appears in Daniel. This is probably because Daniel is essentially referring to Jeremiah 29 here which uses the covenant name YHWH extensively. In fact the idea of calling it the **word of the LORD through Jeremiah the prophet** probably comes from Jeremiah 29:4 which makes the same claim about the ultimate authorship of that prophecy:

> Thus says the LORD of hosts, the God of Israel, to all who were carried away captive, whom I have caused to be carried away from Jerusalem to Babylon: - Jer 29:4

He would accomplish seventy years in the desolations of Jerusalem.

The word "accomplish" here in Hebrew is Strong's number H4390 and it basically means to fulfill or finish. So it's saying that seventy years of desolations needed to be finished out. Jeremiah 25:11 implies that this **desolation** that needed to be finished out was referring to the land when it says:

> And this whole land shall be a desolation and an astonishment, and these nations shall serve the king of Babylon seventy years. - Jer 25:11

In 2 Chronicles 36 we are told that this land desolation that needed to be fulfilled 70 years was the required amount of rest the land was supposed to have received according to the law of Moses and the so-called land Sabbaths.

> And those who escaped from the sword he carried away to Babylon, where they became servants to him and his sons until the rule of the kingdom of Persia, to fulfill the word of the LORD by the mouth of Jeremiah, until the land had enjoyed her Sabbaths. As long as she lay desolate she kept Sabbath, to fulfill seventy years. - 2Ch 36:20-21

Every seventh year the land was not to be worked by farmers; according to the Mosaic Law, it was supposed to be given rest. This apparently had never been done by the Israelites for 490 years. If you divide 490 by 7, to determine how many seven-year cycles that would be, you get 70. It seems clear that the number of years that Israel was exiled was the number of years that the land was supposed to have laid rest over that 490-year period.

This sabbatical cycle may have some application in the 70 weeks prophecy which also is 490 years long, as we will see later on.

Dan 9:3 Then I set my face toward the Lord God to make request by prayer and supplications, with fasting, sackcloth, and ashes.

Then I set my face toward the Lord God

This may mean that he was facing Jerusalem, toward the place where the temple, the so called "house of God" stood. This we have seen was Daniel's habit while praying (Dan 6:10). It also probably should be taken in a spiritual sense, that is that Daniel began to **face** God; that is approach him in the sense of fervent prayer - in other words to turn his attention to God.

Prayer and supplications

There is a slight difference between these two words. "**Supplication**" usually means a request is being made. "**Prayer**" can also include requests but it is not necessarily so. In other words prayer can also include worship, thanksgiving, and confession of sins. I think based on the outline of Daniel's prayer which starts out with all of these things before going into his requests, that this is the reason Daniel uses these two words, "prayer" and "supplications." In other words praise and confession and then requests.

With fasting, sackcloth, and ashes.

These are all things that would be done in fervent prayer. I think that Daniel was responding to the Word of the Lord in Jeremiah which called for fervent prayer:

> Then you will <u>call upon Me</u> and go and <u>pray to Me</u>, and I will listen to you. And you will <u>seek Me</u> and find *Me, <u>when you search for Me with all your heart.</u>* - Jer 29:12-13

Daniel here is praying to God with all of his heart. He does this with **fasting, sackcloth, and ashes.**
God's word suggests many times that fervent prayer gets his attention. One of my favorite examples of this is in Psalm 34.

Again as we will see when we look at Leviticus 26, there is a specific reason for this fervent prayer that Daniel is about to make.

Dan 9:4 And I prayed to the LORD my God, and made confession, and said, "O Lord, great and awesome God, who keeps His covenant and mercy with those who love Him, and with those who keep His commandments,
Dan 9:5 we have sinned and committed iniquity, we have done wickedly and rebelled, even by departing from Your precepts and Your judgments.
Dan 9:6 Neither have we heeded Your servants the prophets, who spoke in Your name to our kings and our princes, to our fathers and all the people of the land.

Dan 9:7 O Lord, righteousness *belongs* to You, but to us shame of face, as *it is* this day—to the men of Judah, to the inhabitants of Jerusalem and all Israel, those near and those far off in all the countries to which You have driven them, because of the unfaithfulness which they have committed against You.
Dan 9:8 "O Lord, to us *belongs* shame of face, to our kings, our princes, and our fathers, because we have sinned against You.
Dan 9:9 To the Lord our God *belong* mercy and forgiveness, though we have rebelled against Him.
Dan 9:10 We have not obeyed the voice of the LORD our God, to walk in His laws, which He set before us by His servants the prophets.

O Lord, great and awesome God

Daniel begins this prayer with praise. This too is how the Lord told us to begin our prayers.

"Our Father who art in Heaven, hallowed be Thy name."

We have sinned

Daniel then begins to confess his sins and the sins of the people of Israel.
There is a very good reason that we will discuss later that Daniel spends so many verses confessing Israel's sins.

Daniel includes himself in the nation's sins, as we see by his use of the word "we," even though, as we saw in Daniel Chapter 6, even Daniel's enemies found no fault in Daniel, so they had to make prayer to God illegal in order to accuse him of something.

> "As Daniel confesses Israel's sin he prays as if he is as bad as the rest of Israel. This is a confession of **we**, not *they*. In this sense, *they* prayers never really reach God; genuine **we** prayers see self correctly and see our fellow saints with compassion."- Guzik

Dan 9:11 Yes, all Israel has transgressed Your law, and has departed so as not to obey Your voice; therefore the curse and the oath written in the Law of Moses the servant of God have been poured out on us, because we have sinned against Him.

Dan 9:12 And He has confirmed His words, which He spoke against us and against our judges who judged us, by bringing upon us a great disaster; for under the whole heaven such has never been done as what has been done to Jerusalem.

Therefore the curse and the oath written in the Law of Moses the servant of God have been poured out on us

This curse is referring to Leviticus 26:14-38 which details what exactly will happen to the Israelites if they break the covenant.

It begins this way:

> 'But if you <u>do not</u> obey Me, and <u>do not</u> observe all these commandments…' - Lev 26:14

The Law of Moses had a list of blessings if they kept the covenant as well as a list of curses if they broke it. The curses detailed in Leviticus 26 were poured out on Israel during the Babylonian captivity as a result of their breaking the contract of the Law of Moses. In other words the exact punishment for breaking the covenant was detailed 490 years earlier. It is my view that part of Daniel's epiphany while reading Jeremiah's prophecy was that Israel's current situation in Babylon was the fulfillment of Leviticus 26:14-38. Part of the reason I think this is because of the next verse.

Dan 9:13 "As *it is* written in the Law of Moses, all this disaster has come upon us; yet we have not made our prayer before the LORD our God, that we might turn from our iniquities and understand Your truth.

Yet we have not made our prayer before the LORD our God

Daniel is saying "look, the Leviticus 26 curse has come upon us, **yet we have not made our prayer!**" He is referring to a specific prayer; a prayer given in Leviticus 26 after the curse part of the chapter. The prayer is given as the remedy for the curse. This remedy starts in verse 39 and goes through verse 45

> And those of you who are left shall waste away in their iniquity in your enemies' lands; also in their fathers' iniquities, which are with them, they shall waste away. 'But if they confess their iniquity and the iniquity of their fathers, with their unfaithfulness in which they were unfaithful to Me, and that they also have walked contrary to Me, and that I also have walked contrary to them and have brought them into the land of their enemies; if their uncircumcised hearts are humbled, and they accept their guilt—then I will remember My covenant with Jacob, and My covenant with Isaac and My covenant with Abraham I will remember; I will remember the land. The land also shall be left empty by them, and will enjoy its sabbaths while it lies desolate without them; they will accept their guilt, because they despised My judgments and because their soul abhorred My statutes. - Lev 26:39-43

Remember that was written at least 490 years before the Babylonian captivity, So again I believe that Daniel's prayer is not inspired so much by the realization that the 70 years was almost up, as so many say, but rather by the realization that Israel had not yet made the prayer required of them by Leviticus 26 to restore the covenant in the event that they break it. This would also explain the conditional language in the prophet Jeremiah's letter to the exiles in Babylon that was discussed earlier, that seemed to suggest that fervent prayer was required before the captivity could end.

The next two verses close out the confession portion of this prayer:

Dan 9:14 Therefore the LORD has kept the disaster in mind, and brought it upon us; for the LORD our God *is* righteous

in all the works which He does, though we have not obeyed His voice.
Dan 9:15 And now, O Lord our God, who brought Your people out of the land of Egypt with a mighty hand, and made Yourself a name, as *it is* this day—we have sinned, we have done wickedly!

After this point Daniel moves from praise and confession to supplications or requests. It should also be noted that the so-called Lord's Prayer in the New Testament also has a section just for our requests when it says:

> "Give us this day our daily bread"

I take that to be an invitation from God to spend time asking Him for the many things we need in this life.

Daniel's supplication is focused on the restoration of the temple, city and holy people. This fact is worthy of noting because the answer to this prayer that the angel gives, which we will discuss in another episode, concerns these exact things that Daniel prayed for, and there are some errors that come about regarding the upcoming 70 weeks prophecy by not realizing the point that what Daniel prays for here is also the main point in God's answer to that prayer.

Dan 9:16 "O Lord, according to all Your righteousness, I pray, let Your anger and Your fury be turned away from Your city Jerusalem, Your holy mountain; because for our sins, and for the iniquities of our fathers, Jerusalem and Your people *are* a reproach to all *those* around us. "

The first part of his supplication is regarding the city of Jerusalem and its restoration as well as the peoples'.

Dan 9:17 Now therefore, our God, hear the prayer of Your servant, and his supplications, and for the Lord's sake cause Your face to shine on Your sanctuary, which is desolate.

The second part of his request is concerning the temple and its restoration

Dan 9:18 O my God, incline Your ear and hear; open Your eyes and see our desolations, and the city which is called by Your name; for we do not present our supplications before You because of our righteous deeds, but because of Your great mercies.

For we do not present our supplications before You because of our righteous deeds.

I think that because of the terms "we" and "our" used here by Daniel that he was conscious to the fact that he was - right there, right then – making the necessary prayer required in Leviticus 26 on behalf of the people of Israel in order to restore the covenant.

Dan 9:19 O Lord, hear! O Lord, forgive! O Lord, listen and act! Do not delay for Your own sake, my God, for Your city and Your people are called by Your name.

Here we see that Daniel only mentions the city and the people, yet we know that in verse 17 the temple was also included. This seems like a minor point but it will come up as we study the next section.

A Prophecy of Seventy Weeks

Dan 9:20 Now while I *was* speaking, praying, and confessing my sin and the sin of my people Israel, and presenting my supplication before the LORD my God for the holy mountain of my God,
Dan 9:21 yes, while I *was* speaking in prayer, the man Gabriel, whom I had seen in the vision at the beginning, being caused to fly swiftly, reached me about the time of the evening offering.

Now while I *was*

Daniel's great prayer is interrupted by Gabriel. This is interesting because as we will see, the answer to Daniel's prayer that Gabriel gives concerns something Daniel asked for only at the end of his prayer. In other words, God knew what Daniel was going to pray before he prayed it and had dispatched His divine answer before Daniel actually made that specific request. This reminds us of Matthew 6:8 which states:

> "For your Father knows the things you have need of before you ask Him."

However it also tells us that God was waiting for Daniel to start the prayer as we see in verse 23:

> "At the beginning of your supplications the command went out, and I have come"

I think one lesson from this is that though God does know what you need, He still wants you to ask for it in prayer. Sometimes we can make the error of thinking that since God knows we need such and such a thing so He will do it for us, but we forget that our petitions and prayers are what scripture tells us moves the hand of God, and in particular prayers of the whole heart like we see with Daniel's.

For the holy mountain of my God

This is how Daniel sums up what his entire prayer was about. He refers to Jerusalem and the area around the temple by using this phrase "**holy mountain of my God.**" This is interesting because this is yet another occasion where we see what Daniel considered his prayer to be about, that is to say Jerusalem and the temple. Not even the people are mentioned here, just the temple area, though the people are in verse 24, but the holy mountain is singled out here by Daniel as the main thing he was praying about. A quick look at the request portion of his prayer reveals the fact that the city and the temple were at the center of Daniel's prayer.

> Now therefore, our God, hear the prayer of Your servant, and his supplications, and for the Lord's sake

cause Your face to shine <u>on Your sanctuary, which is desolate.</u> - Dan 9:17

This is important to keep in mind as we progress; there are many errors that can come by not realizing that Daniel's prayer and the answer to his prayer were very temple centric.

The man Gabriel

Daniel calls Gabriel a **man** because he appears in human form. We see back in chapter 8 where Gabriel first appeared to Daniel, which is what is meant by the phrase: **"whom I had seen in the vision at the beginning,"** that Gabriel had only "the appearance of a man."

Also when we see Gabriel in the New Testament, we are there told explicitly that he was an "angel":

> And the angel answered and said to him, "I am Gabriel, who stands in the presence of God, and was sent to speak to you and bring you these glad tidings. - Luk 1:19

Being caused to fly swiftly

This would be one of the few places in the Bible where we are told that angels fly. Stephen Miller thinks that it is possible that this is supposed to be written "in my extreme weariness" such as the NASB has it, and further that it refers to Daniel - not the angel.

> While I was still speaking in prayer, then the man Gabriel, whom I had seen in the vision previously, came to me <u>in my extreme weariness</u> about the time of the evening offering. – NASB

Miller defends the view this way:

> "The Hebrew supports the reading "in extreme weariness." A conjectural Hebrew verb is necessary to produce "in swift flight."19 (2) Some angels (i.e.,

cherubs and seraphs), it is true, are portrayed in
Scripture as having wings and flying (cf. Exod 25:20;
Isa 6:2; Ezek 1:6, 11, 19, 24), but Goldingay observes
that Scripture does not indicate that ordinary angels
have wings but appear rather in human form.20 The
text states specifically that Gabriel appeared in the
form of a "man," and men do not have wings.21 (3)
Although the idea of Gabriel flying swiftly to bring
an urgent message to Daniel would suit the context,
Daniel's utter exhaustion after a prolonged period of
fasting and prayer (cf. 9:3) fits the situation even
better (cf. 10:2, 8)."[20]

Though I am not sure of the grammatical points that Miller
makes here, I can say that this is the only time in scripture that
this Hebrew word is translated as "**fly**" or anything like it. Every
other time it has to do with faintness or weariness which in my
opinion gives more weight to the NASB translation here.

**Dan 9:22 And he informed *me,* and talked with me, and
said, "O Daniel, I have now come forth to give you skill to
understand.**
**Dan 9:23 At the beginning of your supplications the
command went out, and I have come to tell *you,* for you
are greatly beloved; therefore consider the matter, and
understand the vision:**

I have now come forth to give you skill to understand.

It's interesting that Daniel didn't really ask to understand
anything about the desolation of Jerusalem and the temple. He
wanted something done about it, and indeed, as we will see, his
request for something to be done about the temple will also be
granted. But God also gives Daniel understanding about it. This
is perhaps because the situation was not as simple as Daniel
probably wanted it to be, and God wanted Daniel and us to
understand the details of this complex matter.

Daniel learns in the following revelation that indeed the temple
and city will be built again, but he also learns it will be destroyed

188

again, and for similar reasons as the first time. Then he learns it
will be rebuilt once more, and yes, destroyed once more, all
before a final more permanent one will be consecrated.

This was probably bittersweet news for Daniel who finds out
here that although the wheels are going to be put in motion for
the temple's reconstruction, something he would have loved to
hear, this new temple's eventual demise was also foretold.
Sometimes God wants to give us understanding of why
something bad happens in our lives rather than stopping that bad
thing from happening altogether.

For you *are* greatly beloved;

Commentators have long noted the interesting connection
between Daniel and the Apostle John in this regard. This idea of
being greatly loved or in John's case the "disciple who Jesus
loved" could be the reason that both Daniel and John are given
the great apocalyptic revelations in the Bible. Is there a
connection to this love and the giving of great Revelations to
them? I'm not sure we can be certain from the text, but it is
interesting enough to note.

Therefore consider the matter, and understand the vision:

We are about to consider one of the most difficult and disputed
sections in all of scripture. And I will be taking a position that is
probably like nothing you have heard before. I will be drawing
heavily from Charles Cooper's book *God's Elect and the Great
Tribulation*, although I will be expanding on many points he
makes and slightly modifying others. I want to encourage
everyone to test the things I will say and understand that I am not
dogmatic about the interpretation that I am about to present,
though I do firmly believe it to be the correct one.

It should also be said that although I am about to put forward a
different view than one commonly believed, I am **not** doing it for
theological reasons. If you examine the many different
interpretations of this passage from Bible commentators you will
see that the reason people come up with different explanations

for it is mainly because of their underlying theologies that they bring to the text.

For example, if you are an amillennialist or some version of a preterist, believing that all or mostly all prophecy was fulfilled in 70 AD, you must see this text very differently than a futurist who believes that many of the prophesies in the Bible have not yet come to pass. These particular presuppositions are the main reason people differ on this text. They often bring these presuppositions, fully formed to this text and make it say what they have already determined it should say. There is almost no other text where you can determine a person's underlying denominational theology by their interpretation of it as with this one.

On this point I think my interpretation gains some validity. I have no problem theologically with this text being a prophecy of Jesus' entering into the gates of Jerusalem, or his baptism or death, or many similar views that are proposed by futurists. My overall theology would not change one single bit if that were really what this text were about. So I am not taking a different position on this so that my theology will fit, I am taking a different position because I think the text and context demand it, and I hope to demonstrate to you that at the very least, there is another very logical interpretation of this text that is not often articulated.

Believe me, I would have much rather blown through this chapter quickly with a few quotes from Sir Robert Anderson's *A Coming Prince* and moved on to the next chapters which I find absolutely fascinating rather than spending about two months in study and writing almost 19,000 words on a passage that really doesn't affect my theological bottom line, but the mere fact that I believe that the interpretation I'm going to present is correct demands it.

Dan 9:24 "Seventy weeks are determined For your people and for your holy city, To finish the transgression, To make an end of sins, To make reconciliation for iniquity,

To bring in everlasting righteousness, To seal up vision and prophecy, And to anoint the Most Holy."

Seventy weeks

This word "**weeks**" loosely translates to "sevens." A good analogy would be to our English word for dozens except instead of 12, it is 7.

Seventy sets of sevens have been determined. Scholars understand this to be speaking of seventy sets of seven years; in other words, 490 years. This is so universally agreed upon to be speaking of 490 years by scholars of all denominations and positions that I will not go into too much detail as to why, but it should be noted that there are some scholars who choose to see this 70 sets of seven years as "indefinite periods of time."

However, if we just consider this chapter, we see for example that Daniel was reading Jeremiah who prophesied of a specific 70-year period, which was taken literally by Daniel and fulfilled literally in history. In addition the 70 years of exile was also based on a literal 490-year neglect by Israel of the land Sabbath law, and this is just one of the many reasons that the literal view of this time period enjoys the vast majority of support from scholars.

For your people and for your holy city

These 70 weeks are determined for the **holy people** and the **holy city**. This is yet another reiteration of the focus of this prophecy. It will concern Jerusalem.

If we review some of the phrases in the next three verses which constitute this prophecy I think it will be clear that indeed the holy city is in view throughout.

> Verse 25 says "The street shall be built again, and the wall, Even in troublesome times." Clearly this is referring to Jerusalem.

Verse 26 says "prince who is to come Shall destroy the city and the sanctuary" again information about the city and the temple is in view.

Verse 27 the final verse contains the phrase "He shall bring an end to sacrifice and offering." Referring to the temple sacrifices; no matter what your interpretation of this verse is, the fact is that it is referring to something at the temple ending, i.e. sacrifices, is evident.

I have quoted these lines from the three verses that make up this prophecy to show that although other things may be discussed in this prophecy, the fact that it has Jerusalem and the temple unambiguously in view throughout all three verses is obvious to anyone regardless of what else they may say about this difficult section of scripture.

To finish the transgression, To make an end of sins, To make reconciliation for iniquity, To bring in everlasting righteousness, To seal up vision and prophecy, And to anoint the Most Holy.

70 weeks are determined for the people and the holy city in order to accomplish these six things.

There are some, like preterists, for example, that say that these six things were fulfilled with Christ and His atoning death at Calvary, and there can be no doubt that a few of these six things could easily be said to have occurred at that point. But I don't believe the majority of these prophecies can be shown to have occurred already, though they can be shown to refer to prophecies of the kingdom age, sometimes called the millennium.

Let's take each of these six things and see first if they can be said to have occurred already in history, and second discuss if there is scriptural support to see them in view of an ultimate future fulfillment of the Jewish People, Jerusalem, and the Temple.

To finish the transgression

The word for **transgression** is *pesha* and it basically means
rebellion. The word for finish *kala'* means to restrain. This is one
of the more difficult of the six to try to say has already occurred
in history. The preterist will play up the idea that the word for
finish does not seem to say that it is ended for good, but rather
that transgression is restrained; they would say that after Christ's
death, rebellion is restrained. They would do this despite clear
warnings that rebellion will continue to increase in the last days:

> But know this, that in the last days perilous times will
> come: For men will be lovers of themselves, lovers of
> money, boasters, proud, blasphemers, disobedient to
> parents, unthankful, unholy, unloving, unforgiving,
> slanderers, without self-control, brutal, despisers of
> good, traitors, headstrong, haughty, lovers of pleasure
> rather than lovers of God, having a form of godliness
> but denying its power. And from such people turn
> away! - 2Ti 3:1-5

And this passage in 2 Timothy is probably speaking of the state
of those claiming to be Christians contextually. If I were to quote
some passages about the state of the unsaved in the last days we
would also see that transgression will not be restrained there
either. It seems that in the "last days" rather than sin being
restrained, it is let off its leash!

No matter which way you choose to interpret whose
transgression will be restrained, it doesn't work. The context of
this passage seems to demand that ethnic Jews will have their
transgressions restrained; and we know based on the current state
of rebellion of the Jews and their rejection of Christ, that we
cannot say this has occurred.

If we were to say that this applies to the saved individual, I
would give it some credence despite the complete departure from
context. There is a sense in which the Holy Spirit partially
restrains us from sinning in the form of conviction of sins, but it
does not altogether restrain us from sinning; which is the idea
here.

To make an end of sins

Here we have more support for what is meant in the previous prophecy; that is a finishing or ending of sins. Here the word for *end* is much stronger. In all 64 uses of the word it means to finish, to put a final complete end to; in other words, it is never used as simply a restraint of anything. Therefore the preterist has a much more difficult time with this one than the previous.

Both of these first two are not speaking of an end to the consequences of transgression or sin, or an end of the power of sin or some other thing that would be easy to explain in light of Calvary and the new covenant. No, here we are told without reservation that transgression and sin themselves will be finished. There is no theology that can account for this other than a futurist view. The futurist position not only has the ability to explain this, but it has explicit scriptural support for these two ideas.

A direct reference to this is found in Ezekiel 37 in a prophecy of the millennium. We will see that Daniel seems to be drawing heavily from this prophecy of Ezekiel, who was a contemporary of Daniel.

> Then say to them, 'Thus says the Lord GOD: "Surely I will take the children of Israel from among the nations, wherever they have gone, and will gather them from every side and bring them into their own land; and I will make them one nation in the land, on the mountains of Israel; and one king shall be king over them all; they shall no longer be two nations, nor shall they ever be divided into two kingdoms again. They shall not defile themselves anymore with their idols, nor with their detestable things, nor with any of their transgressions; but I will deliver them from all their dwelling places in which they have sinned, and will cleanse them. Then they shall be My people, and I will be their God. - Eze 37:21-23

Here we have a direct prophecy of God ending Israel's transgression. This is a complete end. He says that they will not
194

defile themselves anymore with their idols, or any of their transgressions. This is the exact language used back in Daniel. We don't have to pretend that sin or transgression has stopped if we simply take God's word at face value. It has not happened yet, but it will. Again we will have confirmation later that essentially the six prophecies in view in Daniel 9 are taken directly from Ezekiel 37, a passage clearly speaking of the millennium, where Christ rules on earth.

John in the book of Revelation gives us another picture of what this "restraining of transgression" and "end of sins" looks like. And it is not a coincidence that it appears in the quintessential millennium passage of Revelation 20.

> Then I saw an angel coming down from heaven, having the key to the bottomless pit and a great chain in his hand. He laid hold of the dragon, that serpent of old, who is *the* Devil and Satan, and bound him for a thousand years; and he cast him into the bottomless pit, and shut him up, and set a seal on him, so that he should deceive the nations no more till the thousand years were finished. But after these things he must be released for a little while. - Rev 20:1-3

The amillennialist, who believes we are living in this time right now, where Satan is bound, has a difficult time explaining that Satan is no longer able to tempt a person currently, especially in light of verses like 1 Peter 5:8 which explains that Satan, like a lion, is looking for people to devour. This difficulty as well as a great many others would disappear if one simply takes the Bible at face value - that these great events have not occurred yet, but we can be sure they will, as they are foretold in holy scripture.

To make reconciliation for iniquity

Of all six prophecies of Daniel 9:24 this one, and to a lesser extent the next one are the only ones I would say without reservation have indeed already occurred. Christ on the cross has reconciled us to God (2 Cor 5:18.19) by taking upon himself the wrath of God which we deserved for our iniquity, thereby giving us peace with God and reconciliation.

So in that sense I would give one point out of six to the preterist. But I would submit that if we look at this in context, this is a prophecy about the Jews and Jerusalem. And we know that indeed they will one day be saved, as Paul the apostle prophesied, as we will see, and when they are saved they will be saved in the same way we have been, by grace through faith in the atoning work of the person of Jesus Christ. So the language of making "reconciliation for iniquity" is just as appropriate for them in a future context as it is for us if we are saved.

For the preterist who does not believe this future reconciliation for the Jews is going to happen, I will refer you to the Apostle Paul. Please notice that in this passage in Romans 11 that Paul reiterates the millennial prophecies by quoting Isaiah and particularly one of the many prophecies of the future ending of sins in the kingdom age just as we saw in Daniel.

> For I do not desire, brethren, that you should be ignorant of this mystery, lest you should be wise in your own opinion, that blindness in part has happened to Israel until the fullness of the Gentiles has come in. And so all Israel will be saved, as it is written: "THE DELIVERER WILL COME OUT OF ZION, AND HE WILL TURN AWAY UNGODLINESS FROM JACOB; FOR THIS IS MY COVENANT WITH THEM, WHEN I TAKE AWAY THEIR SINS." - Rom 11:25-27

This is a very important point. Paul, who was obviously writing after Christ's death and resurrection, is saying that there is a yet future "turning away of ungodliness" and a "taking away of sins" from national Israel.

Anyone that says that all of Daniel 9:24 occurred on the cross has a different theology than Paul the Apostle. Paul is going out of his way here to tell you that the promise given to Daniel, that Israel will be saved and their rebellion will end, was not a promise taken away from them. It will happen after the "fullness
196

of the gentiles" comes in. This is a mystery that Paul does not want you to be "ignorant" of or "conceited" about.

To bring in everlasting righteousness

This is the only other one of the six prophecies that I would agree with the preterist by saying that it could indeed be said that everlasting or perpetual righteousness came in with Christ's atoning death. Our righteousness is in Christ and is not dependent upon ourselves anymore if we are saved and therefore is everlasting. However this again has the weakness of requiring you to divorce this from the context of having to do with the Jews and Jerusalem.

The best explanation, like the others, is to see this in light of the promises given to the prophets about the future of Jerusalem and the Jewish people.

This idea of bringing in everlasting righteousness, like the idea of a future ending of sins, is a common theme found in promises to Jerusalem about the future kingdom age. As we read a few of these promises God makes about the everlasting righteousness of Jerusalem in the millennium, keep in mind how difficult it would be to imagine God not keeping this particular promise because of the way He says it.

> For Zion's sake I will not hold My peace, And for Jerusalem's sake I will not rest, Until her righteousness goes forth as brightness, And her salvation as a lamp *that* burns. The Gentiles shall see your righteousness, And all kings your glory. You shall be called by a new name, Which the mouth of the LORD will name. - Isa 62:1-2

This new naming of Jerusalem mentioned in Isa 62:2 is foretold in the last verse of Ezekiel.

After Ezekiel spends nine chapters detailing the millennium, he ends his description of an obviously different city in terms of structure by saying:

> All the way around *shall be* eighteen thousand *cubits;*
> and the name of the city from *that* day *shall be:* THE
> LORD *IS* THERE. - Eze 48:35

The words THE LORD *IS* THERE are sometimes transliterated
as Yahweh Shamah. So Jerusalem will indeed have a new name
in the millennium.

How preterists and others can read a verse like this "And for
Jerusalem's sake I will not rest, Until her righteousness goes
forth as brightness, And her salvation as a lamp *that* burns.", and
simply say that God has not done nor will ever do what He said
He would do I will never understand.

The point being made by the Lord through Isaiah here is much
the same as Paul when he quoted Isaiah in Romans 11; that God
will take away the sins and make Israel righteous, and they will
never again go astray after other gods.

It is difficult to underestimate the importance of this
eschatological idea of the future righteousness of Israel. It is
repeated in many places and in many ways, always in an
eschatological sense.

It is so important that it is the one idea that Paul picks out of all
prophecies of the future of the Jews to passionately reinforce will
take place. The idea again is that the ending of sins and future
righteousness of Israel is yet future and that it will indeed take
place just as Isaiah, who he quotes, said it would.

It is with this in mind that the next prophecy **To seal up vision
and prophecy** should be understood.

The prophecies of Jerusalem and its future judgment and
subsequent restoration and reconciliation are the completion of
Bible prophecy. If you don't believe me, read the last three
chapters of the Bible, Jerusalem is referred to almost 20 times in
those chapters! The very last words of the Bible, which even a
partial preterist would admit is still future, refer to a prophecy in
Isaiah 11 being fulfilled. Isaiah 11 is another quintessential

millennium passage. In that passage it refers to Jesus as the root of Jesse.

While running the risk of being redundant I think the best way to demonstrate that the sealing up, or finishing vision and prophecy, is to again quote Paul in Romans 11:

> For I do not desire, brethren, that you should be ignorant of this mystery, lest you should be wise in your own opinion, that blindness in part has happened to Israel until the fullness of the Gentiles has come in. And so all Israel will be saved, as it is written: "THE DELIVERER WILL COME OUT OF ZION, AND HE WILL TURN AWAY UNGODLINESS FROM JACOB; FOR THIS IS MY COVENANT WITH THEM, WHEN I TAKE AWAY THEIR SINS." - Rom 11:25-27

Paul is saying "look guys, we still have all that stuff in Isaiah about Israel and its future that has not come to pass yet, and it is still going to come to pass, just as it was written, but not until the fullness of the gentiles happens first."

In other words the eschatological promises to Israel are the final things that need to occur to complete vision and prophecy, things which Paul clearly did not believe had happened yet.

And to anoint the Most Holy.

The final thing that will occur for the people and the holy city after 70 weeks is that the **Most Holy** will be anointed.

The preterist would like to have this refer to Jesus and His anointing, possibly at His baptism. While this is a technical possibility, there is no use in scripture of this phrase speaking of a person but only a thing.

The idea that this is speaking of an anointing of the most holy place (not a person) is therefore almost universally agreed upon by scholars of many different backgrounds, and most Bible translations translate this as "most holy place" accordingly.

199

The preterist takes this to refer to Jesus despite the grammatical difficulty.

They might even try to point to Hebrews where Jesus is said to minister in the holy place as a kind of compromise recognizing that this must refer to the temple; that is, they might say that in a sense Jesus is kind of like the Holy of Holies. But if you think about that theologically there is no sense that Christ is like the Holy of Holies or the temple. He is the spirit that goes in the temple or the Holy of Holies but he is not the temple itself - that is the church which He indwells, theologically speaking.

Again there is a much better explanation if one is willing to look at prophecies of the kingdom age or millennium as yet future.

The temple that Ezekiel spends almost nine complete chapters describing at the end of his book has obviously never been built. The size of it would be equal to the entire current city of Jerusalem. A temple the size of a city is a big temple! The preterist is left with saying that it will never be built, basically saying it could have been built if the Jews had accepted the Messiah, but since they didn't, it won't. Alternately they might say that it is only symbolic of the new covenant. But if you take Ezekiel at face value, and there is no reason why we shouldn't, the "anointing" of the temple that Daniel is talking about is referring to the dedication of that temple in Ezekiel, this immense structure that is said to be built in the millennium. This will be incredibly important as we proceed, but for now just know that there is law in Exodus which told Moses how to **anoint** a temple in order to inaugurate its use.

In other words this prophecy of **anointing the most holy place** is saying that there will be 70 weeks before the inauguration of the kingdom age temple of Ezekiel 40-48, a temple that must be built in order to fulfill prophecy - a temple that all Jews who believe the old scriptures are currently awaiting.

Dan 9:25 "Know therefore and understand, *That* from the going forth of the command To restore and build Jerusalem Until Messiah the Prince, *There shall be* seven

weeks and sixty-two weeks; The street shall be built again, and the wall, Even in troublesome times."

At this point I will deal less with the preterist viewpoint as they more or less believe what most conservatives do about the following verses (that is, that they refer to Christ), that is until the last verse, which we will discuss when we get to it. The preterist however is typically unconcerned with getting any of the following dates right as they view all the talk of "7 weeks" and "62 weeks" etc. as basically irrelevant and should only be seen as symbolic numbers referring, as RC Sproul says, to the "fullness of time."[21]

I would also like to say that when I first heard of the theory I'm about to express put forth by Charles Cooper in his book, I rejected it solely on the grounds that I had been told time and time again that this passage was the best prophecy of the Messiah in the Old Testament, fulfilled to the very day, and so I didn't want to lose what I thought was a great apologetic argument.

I even told Mr. Cooper at a conference that I agreed with most of his conclusions about many things but not on this. My reasoning at that point was not based on any evidence to the contrary that I had, but rather that I just didn't like the idea of losing what I thought was a great apologetic argument.

After studying this passage in depth, I found that he made a very compelling case that I had a hard time arguing with. I also found that the idea that this prophecy was perfectly fulfilled to the day that Jesus entered into Jerusalem on a donkey was not at all accurate. And because of the complex mathematics involved in such a study, almost no one was checking to see if it was accurate; and therefore, almost everyone that has a position about this holds it out of more or less blind faith in the person who told them that it was accurate.

I also believe this prophecy is accurate to the day, but that is has to do with what the angel said it would have to do with, i.e. Daniel's people and the Holy City (Jerusalem).

That from the going forth of the command To restore and build Jerusalem

Here we come to a very important point in the text if we are going to attempt to find an accurate fulfillment of this 70 weeks. This is trying to tell us when to start the 70 weeks clock. It says that we start it from **the going forth of the command To restore and build Jerusalem.** The word for *command* is sometimes translated *decree.*

There are about four events in scripture that have been proposed as candidates for this decree (and you thought this was going to be easy).

Most commentators and scholars say that this decree occurred when Artaxerxes gave Nehemiah permission, safe passage and supplies to return to Jerusalem to rebuild the city walls in 445 B.C. (Neh 2:1-8)

There a number of problems with this that we will look at later, but one notable one is that by saying this event is the decree, they are ignoring that this was not a decree or command given by Artaxerxes but rather simply his giving them permission and supplies. This would seem to be a minor point until you realize that there is an alternative that is being overlooked which is obviously a decree in the truest sense.

Daniel at the time of writing this "70 weeks" prophecy in Babylon was about 80 years old. The Babylonian Empire he had been taken captive by when he was a teenager had just been overthrown by the Persians, and what's more, the name of the Persian king who now ruled the world was named Cyrus!

There were two reasons that that fact must have been absolutely astounding to Daniel. The first is that 200 years before his time, the prophet Isaiah prophesied about a future king which would be named Cyrus.

> "Thus says the LORD to His anointed, <u>To Cyrus,</u>
> whose right hand I have held— To subdue nations
> before him And loose the armor of kings, To open

before him the double doors, So that the gates will not be shut: 'I will go before you And make the crooked places straight; I will break in pieces the gates of bronze And cut the bars of iron. I will give you the treasures of darkness And hidden riches of secret places, That you may know that I, the LORD, Who call *you* by your name, *Am* the God of Israel. For Jacob My servant's sake, And Israel My elect, I have even called you by your name; I have named you, though you have not known Me. - Isa 45:1-4

This prophecy written 200 years before Cyrus, essentially tells the Persian King that his recent conquest of Babylon was a gift to him from God, not of his own doing.

But this prophecy in Isaiah 44 and 45 goes even further. It then says the following:

I have raised him up in righteousness, And I will direct all his ways; He shall build My city And let My exiles go free, Not for price nor reward," Says the LORD of hosts. - Isa 45:13

And just before that in chapter 44 is says:

Who says of Cyrus, '*He is* My shepherd, And he shall perform all My pleasure, Saying to Jerusalem, "You shall be built," And to the temple, "Your foundation shall be laid."- Isa 44:28

So now God's message to Cyrus, written 200 years in advance, tells Cyrus that he was going to make a decree that the city of Jerusalem and the temple (which in Daniels day was totally destroyed) would be rebuilt.

Okay, so you can imagine that someone showed the book of Isaiah to Cyrus at some point, right? Well, we don't have to wonder if Cyrus got the message or not because there is literally a copy of the decree that he made, which would have been posted all around the known world, recorded in the Bible.

> In the first year of King Cyrus, King Cyrus issued a
> decree *concerning* the house of God at Jerusalem:
> "Let the house be rebuilt, the place where they
> offered sacrifices; and let the foundations of it be
> firmly laid, its height sixty cubits *and* its width sixty
> cubits, - Ezr 6:3

This is also mentioned in 2 Chronicles which says:

> Now in the first year of Cyrus king of Persia, that the
> word of the LORD by the mouth of Jeremiah might
> be fulfilled, the LORD stirred up the spirit of Cyrus
> king of Persia, so that he made a proclamation
> throughout all his kingdom, and also *put it* in writing,
> saying, Thus says Cyrus king of Persia: All the
> kingdoms of the earth the LORD God of heaven has
> given me. And He has commanded me to build Him a
> house at Jerusalem which is in Judah. Who *is* among
> you of all His people? May the LORD his God *be*
> with him, and let him go up! - 2Ch 36:22-23

Now back to Daniel, who has been praying for the city and the
temple to be rebuilt, who realizes that the time is close. After all,
the 70 years Jeremiah predicted is almost up, and there is a man
named Cyrus on the throne, just like Isaiah said there would be.
Daniel, because of his familiarity with scripture, would have
known that Cyrus was about to make a decree, even before
Cyrus did!

The argument against the 70 weeks starting with the decree of
Cyrus is based on one idea and one idea alone. They say that in
the text of the decree in Ezra 6 and 2 Chronicles, which we just
read, there is no mention of the <u>city</u> being decreed to be rebuilt,
only the temple, and that is true - in the written decree recorded
in Ezra and 2 Chronicles, there is no mention of Cyrus decreeing
that the city be rebuilt. After all, the angel told Daniel "from the
going forth of the command to rebuild the <u>city</u>," not the temple.
Cyrus in Ezra 6 never mentioned the city. Case closed, right?

There is a major flaw with that argument. If you look at what God said Cyrus would do in Isaiah 44 and 45, He says explicitly that the decree would also concern rebuilding the city.

> Who says of Cyrus, '*He is* My shepherd, And he shall perform all My pleasure, Saying to Jerusalem, "You shall be built," And to the temple, "Your foundation shall be laid."- Isa 44:28

In that verse the city and the temple are mentioned as a part of what Cyrus will decree. To make matters worse in the next chapter, which is a reiteration of the same decree, only the city is mentioned:

> I have raised him up in righteousness, And I will direct all his ways; He shall build My city And let My exiles go free, Not for price nor reward," Says the LORD of hosts. - Isa 45:13

So if God says that Cyrus' decree was to rebuild the city, then Cyrus' decree was to rebuild the city. Case closed.

Cooper says of this:

> "This passage alone is sufficient to prove that Cyrus did decree concerning Jerusalem "She will be rebuilt." Otherwise God's word has failed which is a conclusion we are not prepared to accept."

I have never heard anyone who holds to the other views deal with this adequately. They point out that the text of the decree recorded in Ezra and 2 Chronicles doesn't specifically mention the city but they keep Isaiah 44 and 45 out of the discussion as they prove that the Cyrus' decree was indeed to rebuild the city as well as the temple.

The real reason people pretend Isaiah 44 and 45 aren't there and push the beginning of the 70 weeks up about 83 years or so is because they have already decided what the outcome of this prophecy "should" be, that is having something or other to do with Jesus. Though exactly what depends on the mathematical gymnastics that each individual commentator does, whether it's His baptism or death or triumphal entry, will depend on who has the calculator, since these dates are by no means fixed in history and so each commentator has some wiggle room if they need it.

But the problem is that there are no acrobatics, no matter how skilled they are with a calculator which would allow them to make this prophecy have to do with Jesus if they started the 70 weeks with Cyrus' decree, so they must look for something else that would allow them to get closer to the time of Christ. It's a clear case of confirmation bias.

A few other problems with starting the 70 weeks with Artaxerxes and Nehemiah in 445 (the most commonly held view among conservatives) are as follows:

The exact date for this is not recorded in scripture.
One would think that if we were to get this right to the very day we should be given the very day that it started. This as we will see can be ascertained in the case of the Cyrus' decree, but with Artaxerxes in 445 we are simply given the month and year it occurs. In Sir Robert Anderson's *The Coming Prince*, which is the book cited by nearly all proponents of the 445 view, Anderson simply chooses the first day in the month more or less arbitrarily.

Another problem with the Artaxerxes 445 view is that Nehemiah was sent to build a wall, not a city. That wall was built in 52 days we are told; a city was not built in 52 days, nor was it claimed to have been by the text.

Speaking specifically of Sir Robert Anderson's view that this ended with the triumphal entry, there are problems with his theory as more data comes out regarding the date of Passover for that year derived from the so-called Elephantine Papyrus, which makes even the recent improvements on Anderson's view impossible according to some.[22]

Stranger still is the fact that this would mean that this prophecy totally ends a good 30-plus years before one would think it would end contextually speaking, that is at the fall of Jerusalem
206

and the destruction of the temple. I mean the prophecy is unambiguously supposed to be about the city and the temple, and to just leave a 30-plus year gap seems unlikely.

Granted the destruction of the temple is required to occur <u>after</u>, not during, the 69th week according to verse 26 but you would think that it would be a little more precise, especially given how precise the rest of the prophecy is, as we will see.

Know therefore and understand, *That* **from the going forth of the command To restore and build Jerusalem Until Messiah the Prince,** *There shall be* **seven weeks and sixty-two weeks;**

Here we run into probably the single biggest problem as to why everyone thinks this has something to do with Jesus. That is that the translators of certain Bible versions also believed that. And they inserted things that are not in the Hebrew text to make their personal views prominent.

I'm sure that the translators thought they were doing us a favor by doing this and I am not accusing them of doing anything dishonest, but this will be the first of many places in the next three verses that the translators do things that the underlying text never required them to do.

This phrase **Messiah the Prince** here in the NKJV and many other versions capitalizes the M and the P, which is a translator choice, as there is no such idea of capitalization in Hebrew, It is simply the translators expressing their opinion about the identity of this anointed prince. At least the NKJV is toned down from the ASV which says it should be translated "THE anointed one" adding the definite article "The" as if it was saying "The Messiah." If it were the case that the Hebrew definite article was present here, "ha," then we would have no choice but to say this is referring to Jesus, as he is only person that could fit such a designation.

But the Hebrew does not have the definite article, and modern translations reflect this and translate the verse like this:

> (ESV) Know therefore and understand that from the
> going out of the word to restore and build Jerusalem
> to the coming of an anointed one, a prince, there shall
> be seven weeks. Then for sixty-two weeks it shall be
> built again with squares and moat, but in a troubled
> time.

> (NET) So know and understand: From the issuing of
> the command 64 to restore and rebuild Jerusalem 65
> until an anointed one, a prince arrives, 66 there will
> be a period of seven weeks 67 and sixty-two weeks.
> It will again be built, 68 with plaza and moat, but in
> distressful times.

The difference here is clear; there is no reason that the anointed
ruler must be Jesus.

The term *anointed* in Hebrew, where we get the term *Messiah*, is
something that a modern Christian only associates with Jesus,
but a simple word search in a concordance shows that the word
in the Old Testament is almost never referring to the messiah but
to kings or priests and even once to Cyrus who we have already
mentioned:

> "Thus says the LORD to His anointed, To Cyrus,
> whose right hand I have held— To subdue nations
> before him And loose the armor of kings, To open
> before him the double doors, So that the gates will
> not be shut: - Isa 45:1

Here Cyrus, a pagan Persian king, is referred to as a "messiah;"
that is, an anointed one. In this case the anointing he had was to
do certain things to advance God's plan, including letting the
people go, commanding the temple and the city to be rebuilt.

The word is found in several contexts in the Old Testament,
mostly referring to rulers and priests who do God's bidding in
one way or another, either in the military, political or religious
sense.

Also in verse 24 the word *messiah* is spoken of again, but in this case it is referring to the Holy of Holies:

"And to <u>anoint</u> the Most Holy."

So just in this one chapter, we have in view a Gentile, probably unsaved king, who God called a messiah in Isa 45, as well as a part of the temple called messiah. I hope this is enough to suggest to you that Daniel can say the word *messiach* without it necessarily referring to Christ.

Again I don't mind this being about Jesus. I love Jesus. I think he is The Messiah, "Ha Messiach", but I think if we understand that *messiah* is just a word that means anointed in the Hebrew language, we can discover the real meaning of this text.

I believe that we do not have to guess about this and that scripture gives us the confirmation we need to be sure we are on the right track with this thinking. But to be able to understand who this anointed prince is, we need to clear up another problem created by some overzealous translators. This problem arises as a result of the following translation:

***There shall be* seven weeks and sixty-two weeks;**

Almost without exception commentators will tell you that this is a way of saying 69 weeks. In other words 7 plus 62 equals 69 or 483 years. When asked why scripture wouldn't simply say 69 weeks instead of making you add 7 weeks and 62 weeks to get 69, there is usually no answer. It is just some extra homework Gabriel wanted to give to us, I suppose.

I submit that there is a very good reason that scripture mentions two distinct sets of weeks here: first a set of 7 and then a set of 62. We should not simply add them up and pretend that they are to be taken as one large block of time.

The problem is one of punctuation. The meaning of this verse changes drastically depending on where you end the sentence. The Masoretic text, which the Old Testament is based on, calls for a period after the 7 weeks, which would make this verse read as follows:

> Know therefore and understand that from the going out of the word to restore and build Jerusalem to the coming of an anointed one, a prince, there shall be seven <u>weeks. Then</u> for sixty-two weeks it shall be built again with squares and moat, but in a troubled time. - Dan 9:25

But the problem with following those rules for a translator is that if you did so it would mean that from the going forth of the decree until an anointed prince arrived there would only be 7 weeks or 49 years, this would make it impossible to speak of Christ because he obviously didn't appear 49 years after Cyrus' decree or Artaxerxes' decree, or any other option available.

The NET Bible has a fascinating footnote on this point

> "The accents in the MT indicate disjunction at this point [Meaning a period after the 7 weeks], which would make it difficult, if not impossible, to identify the "anointed one/prince" of this verse as messianic. The reference in v. 26 to the sixty-two weeks as a unit favors the MT accentuation, not the traditional translation. If one follows the MT accentuation, one may translate "From the going forth of the message to restore and rebuild Jerusalem until an anointed one, a prince arrives, there will be a period of seven weeks. During a period of sixty-two weeks it will again be built, with plaza and moat, but in distressful times." The present translation follows a traditional reading of the passage that deviates from the MT accentuation."

So it's basically saying, "If we translated this the way we should, we couldn't have this be Jesus, so we're not going to translate it that way."

The ESV however, picking up on this, is the first version that I know of to apply the correct punctuation even though it makes it impossible to see the fulfillment of this as being messianic.

> Know therefore and understand that from the going out
> of the word to restore and build Jerusalem to the coming
> of an anointed one, a prince, there shall be seven weeks.
> Then for sixty-two weeks it shall be built again with
> squares and moat, but in a troubled time. - Dan 9:25
> (ESV)

So again the difference is that we now must look for an anointed
ruler exactly 49 years from the decree, and that anointed ruler
obviously can't be Jesus because it is far too early. And the 62
weeks

is speaking of the entire time that the city and the temple will
exist before its destruction, which we will get to later. But for
now we must discover who this ruler is.

Before we can know who shows up 49 years after Cyrus' decree,
we need to know when that decree happened. We can ascertain
this date in part because we know that there would be exactly 70
years from the fall of Jerusalem by Nebuchadnezzar until the
decree of Cyrus

Since we know the date for the fall of Jerusalem by
Nebuchadnezzar, we can count 70 years from that date in order
to arrive at the very date of Cyrus' decree, the beginning of the
70 weeks prophecy. From there we can calculate exactly 49
years (7 weeks) and we arrive at the 28th day of the 4th month of
the ancient Jewish civil year of Tammuz. This is <u>the exact date</u>
that Nehemiah arrived in Jerusalem to build the walls,[23] a feat
which he accomplished in 52 days.

It interesting that Nehemiah's arrival in Jerusalem is the
fulfillment of this and that the very day of that arrival is
mentioned in scripture, because that is exactly what we were
supposed to look for according to Daniel 9:25; that is, the *arrival*
of an anointed ruler. This is perhaps why Anderson and others
opt for the triumphal entry even though it certainly wasn't the
Lord's first arrival in Jerusalem. In other words they knew that in
order to be legit, it had to have something to do with someone
arriving in Jerusalem.

This is impressive and a bit of a relief for me because scripture gives us a way to check our facts and make sure we are on the right path before moving on to much more difficult areas in which we will have to rely on extra-biblical sources for dates. So this is kind of a check point where you can find the exact dates without leaving the pages of scripture. We know the date of Cyrus' decree and we know the exact date of Nehemiah's arrival and they are exactly 49 years (7 weeks) apart. Yep, we are on the right track.

So we can see that Nehemiah was at the right place at the right time. But how exactly was he an anointed prince?

The prince part is easy. The word for prince is *Nagid*. It is a general term used of leaders whether military, political or religious. It is translated as governor, leader, captain, noble, prince and ruler in different places in the Bible.

Nehemiah was the governor of Israel:

> And Nehemiah, who was the governor, and Ezra the priest and scribe… - Neh 8:9

This word for governor is a title used on only a few occasions in the Bible. It comes from a Persian word meaning something like "To be feared." And it's clear that he was what we would consider the governor or main political leader. So yeah, Nehemiah definitely fits the bill for a *Nagid*. But was he an anointed Nagid.

Well if we look at it in general terms, Nehemiah was certainly anointed by God to do what he did.

But as I was looking more closely into the ministry of Nehemiah I found that he too also prayed the specific Leviticus 26 prayer that Daniel prayed which I made such a big deal about at the beginning of this chapter. In the first chapter of Nehemiah, before he makes his request to the king, he prays the very same prayer that Daniel prayed, asking for the forgiveness of their forefathers. It seems then that Nehemiah is also linked to this 70-weeks timeline through his prayer.

212

The Idea that Nehemiah was anointed is clearly evident in the
book of Nehemiah. Before entering into the presence of the king
to ask for money and material and leave to go build the walls,
Nehemiah prays:

> "O Lord, let your ear be attentive to the prayer of
> your servant, and to the prayer of your servants who
> delight to fear your name, and give success to your
> servant today, and grant him mercy in the sight of
> this man." Now I was cupbearer to the king. - Neh
> 1:11

God granted this request from Nehemiah as well as paved the
way for complete success in his accomplishing the Lord's will in
Jerusalem, even amidst great trials.

To understand Nehemiah's importance and why he should be
pointed to as an integral part of the 70-weeks prophecy it should
be recognized that there are even a few books of the Bible was
written about the stalled building progress after Cyrus' decree.
The Book of Haggai and Zechariah for example were written to
Israel after Cyrus' decree, but before Nehemiah to encourage the
Jews who had zealously begun to rebuild the temple and city
after Cyrus' decree, but because of setbacks and fears, and too
much focus on their personal lives, the work had stalled.

The ministry of Haggai and Zechariah did encourage the people
to continue their work which resulted in the finishing of the
temple only a few years later, but after that the people of Israel
fell into the same trap with rebuilding the city around the temple.
The lack of walls made the city a dangerous place to live and
therefore not too much migration back to the city was happening.

I think this is why scripture points to the leadership of Nehemiah
and his wall-building project as such an important part of this
process. That is, that although Cyrus, years before, had let the
Israelites go home and had permission to rebuild the city and
temple, and had even made some progress, there was no real
leadership to get God's project moving, and for all intents and
purposes it was totally stalled and the people were back in sin
having forgotten the law of God.

Nehemiah was the guy you can point to and say after him and his walls which made the city safe for families to inhabit again, and therefore effectively beginning the migration back to Israel, as well as his spiritual leadership which literally taught the people the law of God again and restarted the priesthood and the temple services, God's project of bringing Israel back from the ashes really got underway, and the city grew and grew until it was eventually destroyed…well…434 years later.

Then for sixty-two weeks it shall be built again with squares and moat, but in a troubled time. (ESV)

After Nehemiah there would be 62 weeks or 434 years. The text does not seem to suggest anything too specific will happen during this time other than it **will be built again with squares and moat but in troubled time**. Though we find out from the next verse that the 434 years seems to be designating a time after which the city and temple would be destroyed, it says:

> And after the sixty-two weeks, an anointed one shall be cut off and shall have nothing. And the people of the prince who is to come shall destroy the city and the sanctuary. Its end shall come with a flood, and to the end there shall be war. Desolations are decreed. - Dan 9:26

In other words it seems as if it is saying during the 434 years, the city and the temple will exist until it is once again destroyed. The NET Bible seems to agree with the idea that the 434 years is not saying that it will take 434 years for the temple and city to be rebuilt but rather that it is a period of time in which the city will return before its destruction. The footnote where they address this says:

> "it will return and be built." The expression is a verbal hendiadys.[24]

Squares and moat

The term for **squares** is sometimes translated plaza or square. It is interesting that in the early times before the city was
214

completely rebuilt the main place that is mentioned in Nehemiah and Ezra that was built in which people met was a big plaza by the Water gate.

> And all the people gathered as one man into the square before the Water Gate. And they told Ezra the scribe to bring the Book of the Law of Moses that the LORD had commanded Israel. - Neh 8:1

Moat is translated "wall" in some versions but there doesn't seem to be any reason for thinking that it should be "wall." Most translations have this as "moat" or something similar.

The word means sharp or cut and can mean something like a moat or a ditch which is pretty much the opposite of wall, and if it was "wall" that would be the only time the word would have been used that way.

It's an interesting word and it is only used a few times in scripture. Oddly it is translated as "gold" more times than anything else when used as a noun.

But in a troubled time

Whether this is referring to the building of the walls that Nehemiah undertook, which according to the narrative had tremendous opposition, or it is simply referring to the troublesome next 434 years of the 2nd temple age, with oppression from the Greeks and then later the Romans, they would both fit as they are both equally true, though I tend to favor the latter explanation.

Dan 9:26 And after the sixty-two weeks, an anointed one shall be cut off and shall have nothing. And the people of the prince who is to come shall destroy the city and the sanctuary. Its end shall come with a flood, and to the end there shall be war. Desolations are decreed.

And after the sixty-two weeks

Two things are supposed to happen after -- not during but after -- these 434 years:

> 1) An anointed one shall be cut off
> 2) The city and the temple will be destroyed.

To make this point more clear, we do not have an exact date for when both of these things are supposed to happen, only that they will be <u>after</u> the 434 years, though one would expect them to be very close to the end of that time. One thing is for sure from the text - they cannot happen before the 434 years is up.

An anointed one shall be cut off and shall have nothing

This verse is usually taken to mean that after 434 years Christ will be crucified. Again the translators' personal beliefs, despite the absence of textual reasons, have perpetuated this idea.

An anointed one

This particular variation of the word *mashiyach*, here translated as "anointed" appears 39 times in the Old Testament and in every case except for this one what is being referred to is clearly identified, whether it was a king or priest or whatever. This is the <u>only</u> case in the Bible where that information is not provided. The NKJV inserts the word "one" here as if a person is in view, but that is a decision on the part of the translator and not in the actual text.

In addition Charles Cooper points out that in the Greek versions of the Old Testament the instance of this word was understood by the ancient translators not to be referring to a person at all:

> "In both versions [the Septuagint and the Theodotion] the term chrisma (oil for anointing or action of anointing) occurs for the Hebrew term mashiyach (see Exodus 29:7, 30:25). The word refers to that which the anointing is preformed, the unguent or ointment.

There are two oddities about the Greek translation here. First chrisma is a neuter singular noun instead of a masculine noun as in the Hebrew Bible. This indicated that the Greek translators did not interpret the Hebrew mashiyach to refer to a person. If the Greek translators had understood Daniel to be referring to a person christos would have been more appropriate, since it refers to a person. Second neither version has the article therefore an appropriate translation is "an anointing" [as opposed to "an anointed one" and certainly not Messiah with a capital M which is clearly wrong].

As a side note this could just as easily be translated "an anointed place" as we will see later.

Shall be cut off

So an anointing or anointed place is cut off, what could that possibly mean? Well, for starters we need to look at what the idea of "cut off" means in scripture.

It can be used literally, that is to cut off a piece of fabric or something. It is also sometimes used to refer to someone being separated or removed or destroyed; in other words, killed.

I am going to suggest to you that this idea of an anointing being cut off is referring to a prophecy that God gave to Solomon after the temple he just built was dedicated and anointed. That prophecy contained a warning that if they rebelled against God then He would cut off the people and the temple which he anointed.

As I read from 1 Kings 9:6-7 remember the context. Solomon has just built the first temple ever. He has just had a huge party dedicating that temple. Now the celebrations were all over and God gives him this message which concerns the temple he just dedicated.

> *But* if you or your sons at all turn from following Me, and do not keep My commandments *and* My statutes

217

> which I have set before you, but go and serve other
> gods and worship them, <u>then I will cut off Israel</u> from
> the land which I have given them; <u>and this house</u>
> [The Temple] which I have <u>consecrated</u> for My name
> <u>I will cast out of My sight.</u> Israel will be a proverb
> and a byword among all peoples. - 1Ki 9:6-7

In order to fully appreciate what is being said here and how it
applies to our verse in Daniel 9 we will need to go back to the
beginning of the 70-weeks prophecy, where Gabriel tells Daniel
that one of the things that was to be accomplished at the end of
the 70 weeks was a <u>most holy place</u> was to be <u>anointed.</u>

> Seventy weeks are decreed about your people and
> your holy city ......<u>to anoint a most holy place.</u>
> (ESV)

Every temple had to be anointed with very special oil when it
was dedicated. This is described in Exodus 30:

> And you shall make from these a holy anointing oil, an
> ointment compounded according to the art of the
> perfumer. It shall be a holy anointing oil. <u>With it you
> shall anoint the tabernacle of meeting</u> and the ark of the
> Testimony; the table and all its utensils, the lampstand
> and its utensils, and the altar of incense; the altar of
> burnt offering with all its utensils, and the laver and its
> base. You shall consecrate them, that they may be most
> holy; whatever touches them must be holy. - Exo 30:25-
> 39

This oil was apparently only used once for the initial dedication
of a temple and its furnishings, though it also had other uses, like
for anointing the priests. But in regard to its use for anointing the
holy place it was only to be used for temple <u>dedications.</u>

Interestingly there is a belief in rabbinic Judaism that the original
oil that was used to dedicate the tabernacle would still be around
when it came time to anoint the future as yet un-built temple
described by Ezekiel. Whether this is true or not is unimportant,

but it does show you that there was an understanding that a new temple needed to be anointed.

In the passage we read, after the dedication of the first temple by Solomon, God says that he will cut off the people and the temple if they disobeyed Him. In that same verse God said that he *consecrated* the temple *Himself.*

> then I will cut off Israel from the land which I have given them; and this house which I have consecrated for My name I will cast out of My sight. - 1Ki 9:7

The word he used there is the word *Quedesh.* That is a word used to describe what happened to the temple after it was anointed, in Exodus 30:29:

> You shall consecrate them [the tabernacle and the altar etc.] that they may be most holy; whatever touches them must be holy. - Exo 30:29

So if this is correct this verse would read almost exactly as the ESV does without the word "one" since the idea of it being a person is not conveyed in the original as we have seen. So it would read:

> And after the sixty-two weeks, the anointing shall be cut off and shall have nothing. - Dan 9:26

It you translated it as LXX has it, it would read:

> [after the sixty-two weeks] the anointing shall be cut off and judgment is no longer in it. - Dan 9:26 (LXX)

It's interesting to note that the LXX says "and judgment is no longer in it." In other words not only did the scholars behind the LXX think that the anointing was a thing, not a person; they thought it was a place, a place where judgment apparently at one point could be found.

I am going to suggest to you that what this verse is referring to is the temple being cut off or destroyed, exactly what God told

Solomon would happen if the people broke the covenant. This of course fits the context like a glove too.

If this is true then how do we explain the next phrase which says:

And shall have nothing

So after the sixty-two weeks the anointing shall be cut off and have nothing?

The phrase here in the ESV is translated "and shall have nothing," while the KJV translators translate this phrase "but not for himself" obviously to bolster the case that this anointed one is Christ and this is speaking of His death.

The NET Bible in a footnote says of this:

> "The KJV rendering "but not for himself," apparently suggesting a vicarious death, cannot be defended."[25]

Stephen Miller says of it:

> "The KJV's translation would signify that Christ's death was for others, which is certainly a scriptural truth. But the phrase is in Hebrew an idiom for "not have" (cf. Gen 11:30; Isa 27:4)."[26]

In light of this, most people these days who are trying to explain this as being about Christ's death say things like: "When Christ died He didn't have anything. Remember how he said "Why have you forsaken me?" on the cross?" Or as Miller says:

> "Thus when Christ died, his earthly ministry seemed to have been in vain. His disciples had deserted him, and from all appearances he had not accomplished what he had set out to do."[27]

Commentators are trying to force the theological idea that Christ **had nothing** at the time of His death in order to make their presupposition about this verse make sense. There is certainly no explicit teaching that would suggest that Christ had nothing at the time of His death. This is perhaps why the KJV rendered it "not for Himself" even though it wasn't accurate, that is to avoid the theological trouble of saying Christ had nothing at His death.

A few pre-cross verses seem to suggest that Christ had quite a lot:

> The Father loveth the Son, and <u>hath given all things into his hand.</u> - Joh 3:35

> <u>Jesus, knowing that the Father had given all things into His hands,</u> and that He had come from God and was going to God, rose from supper and laid aside His garments, took a towel and girded Himself. - Joh 13:3-4

In addition I don't think that Peter's denying Christ or the disciples hiding after the crucifixion can be seen as them no longer being Christ's at the time of His death, especially in light of John 18: 7-9 where the soldiers came to take Christ away, which says:

> Then He asked them again, "Whom are you seeking?" And they said, "Jesus of Nazareth." Jesus answered, "I have told you that I am *He.* Therefore, if you seek Me, let these go their way," that the saying might be fulfilled which He spoke, "<u>Of those whom You gave Me I have lost none.</u>" - Joh 18:7-9

The underlying Hebrew for this term "have nothing" is not very specific. It basically is just a word that means "nothing" or "not exist" or "non-entity" none of which have to do with Jesus and hence all the odd theology from people convinced this must be about Jesus. Charles Cooper renders this phrase:

> "After the sixty-two weeks, the anointed place shall be cut off and there will be <u>nothing left of it.</u>"

This is speaking of the temple, and based on the timeline we are about to see it makes perfect sense to be speaking of the destruction of the temple as that is exactly what happened after the 62 weeks.

This would also make the words of Christ concerning this event all the more meaningful:

> Then Jesus went out and departed from the temple, and His disciples came up to show Him the buildings of the temple. And Jesus said to them, "Do you not see all these things? Assuredly, I say to you, not *one* stone shall be left here upon another, that shall not be thrown down." - Mat 24:1-2

Just a recap on the way I and folks like Charles Cooper believe the verses we have been studying so far should read:

> Know therefore and understand that from the going out of the word to restore and build Jerusalem to the coming of an anointed one, a prince, there shall be seven weeks (49 years). Then for sixth-two weeks (434 years) it shall be built again with squares and moat, but in a troubled time. After the sixty-two weeks, the anointed place shall be cut off and there will be nothing left of it.

The people of the prince who is to come shall destroy the city and the sanctuary.

This part of the verse fits perfectly with the context and it is giving us more information about it, namely *who* will destroy the city and the sanctuary. It tells us: "**The people of the prince who is to come**" will destroy Jerusalem and the Temple.

This phrase is often taken to be speaking of the Antichrist. In other words it would be saying something like: "There is a prince to come way in the future, but he won't be around at the time of the destruction of the temple; only his people will, and they will destroy the temple."

This then is often taken as a way to determine the nationality of the Antichrist. Therefore most people who hold to this view see

222

the Antichrist as Roman, since the Romans destroyed the temple in 70 AD. However it should be noted that Joel Richardson and other proponents of a Middle Eastern Antichrist site Josephus and others that attest that the Roman armies that laid siege to Jerusalem were mostly Arab mercenaries.

Both of those views are missing the point by a mile in my opinion.

It should also be remembered that if indeed Daniel 2 or Daniel 7 isn't speaking of a so-called revived Roman Empire, which I firmly believe they are not as noted in the commentaries of those chapters, then this verse would constitute the only verse in the Bible that suggests a Roman nationality for the Antichrist. And even if I thought this verse was saying the Antichrist would be Roman or Arab, it would not be a good idea to build doctrine on this one verse alone.

That being said I don't think this verse is talking about the nationality of Antichrist or anyone else's nationality, for that matter, though it should be noted that I do think the Antichrist is in view in the next verse. And therefore my opposition to the normal futurist interpretation is not because I am not a futurist - I certainly am - but it is only because I think there is a much more logical explanation for this verse.

When it says the people of the prince who is to come shall destroy the city and the sanctuary, I believe it is trying to convey what actually happened in 70 AD.

Titus' people, that is the people under his command, destroyed the city and the temple, not Titus. In almost any other sacking of any other city by the Romans, there would be no need to make this distinction. After all, if Titus or any other general ordered this to happen, he is responsible for it, and scripture would be right to put the blame on him. But the events of that day made it necessary for scripture to describe the destruction of the temple and city as not being by Titus, but instead by his people.

According to Josephus, who was literally present and part of the court of Titus at the destruction, Titus did not order the temple destroyed. He had wanted to turn it into a temple for the Roman gods. But the people destroyed it anyway. It would be one thing if this were only briefly mentioned by Josephus, but instead Josephus describes in many ways the mob-like destruction of the temple and city despite Titus' repeated orders for it to be stopped.

I will quote a few excerpts:

First Josephus quotes Titus in a meeting with his generals about what to do with the temple. This was because the Jews were using the temple as a citadel for a kind of last stand. Josephus says:

> But Titus said, that "although the Jews should get upon that holy house, and fight us thence, yet ought we not to revenge ourselves on things that are inanimate, instead of the men themselves;" and that he was not in any case for burning down so vast a work as that was, because this would be a mischief to the Romans themselves, as it would be an ornament to their government while it continued.

Then after Titus was informed that despite his orders the soldiers set fire to the temple, Josephus describes the following scene:

> And now a certain person came running to Titus, and told him of this fire, as he was resting himself in his tent after the last battle; whereupon he rose up in great haste, and, as he was, ran to the holy house, in order to have a stop put to the fire…. Then did Caesar, both by calling to the soldiers that were fighting, with a loud voice, and by giving a signal to them with his right hand, order them to quench the fire. But they did not hear what he said, though he spake so loud, having their ears already dimmed by a greater noise another way; nor did they attend to the signal he made with his hand neither, as still some of them were distracted with fighting, and others with passion. But as for the legions that came running thither, neither any persuasions nor any threatenings

could restrain their violence, but each one's own
passion was his commander at this time;

And more still

> But as the flame had not as yet reached to its inward
> parts, but was still consuming the rooms that were
> about the holy house, and Titus supposing what the
> fact was, that the house itself might yet he saved, he
> came in haste and endeavored to persuade the
> soldiers to quench the fire, and gave order to Liber-
> alius the centurion, and one of those spearmen that
> were about him, to beat the soldiers that were
> refractory with their staves, and to restrain them; yet
> were their passions too hard for the regards they had
> for Caesar, and the dread they had of him who
> forbade them, as was their hatred of the Jews, and a
> certain vehement inclination to fight them, too hard
> for them also.

> Moreover, the hope of plunder induced many to go
> on, as having this opinion, that all the places within
> were full of money, and as seeing that all round about
> it was made of gold... And thus was the holy house
> burnt down, without Caesar's approbation.

So I think if the scripture had said that the prince, that is Titus,
destroyed the temple it would have been a factually inaccurate
statement, but instead it said the people of the prince destroyed
it, which I think you can now see why that would be an
important distinction to make.

The "to come," as in **the people of the prince is to come,** is
therefore from Daniel's perspective, as this event was almost 500
years in the future at the time he wrote, but for us looking back
that prince to come has already come and gone.

One more note on this idea of a "prince". Though the word can
mean general, leader, or king, or indeed a literal prince as in son
of a king, it is interesting to note that at the time of the
destruction of Jerusalem, Titus' father Vespasian was the

emperor, making Titus a literal prince who would soon become emperor himself, as well as a general of an army. This means that Titus would fulfill every possible meaning for that word "prince."

The end of it *shall be* with a flood, And till the end of the war desolations are determined.

The "it" here as in **the end of it** is referring to the sanctuary. This is not just my opinion but the opinion of many commentators and translators such as the KJV/NKJV.

Shall be **with a flood**

The NET Bible I think captures the idea of this when it says:

> "will come speedily like a flood."

The speed in which Jerusalem and the temple went from just fine to a heap of ashes was very quick. This was in part because of the fury of the Roman soldiers once they finally breeched the walls of the city.

So when did the destruction of Jerusalem happen? Was it 434 years after Nehemiah finished his walls? Remembering that is says:

> **After** the sixty-two weeks, the anointed place shall
> be cut off and there will be nothing left of it.

According to Charles Cooper's very detailed calculations, which I will talk more about in a minute, the 434 years, marking the end of the 69th week ended, and then less than <u>two months after</u> that, the Roman armies surrounded the city.

The important thing is that the destruction of the city and temple had to occur <u>after</u> the 434 years was up, and it did. By August there was nothing left of either the city or the temple. It should be noted that at the time the clock ran out on the 69th week the Romans were already in Israel and had been for two years or so, and they had already killed thousands of Jews and destroyed

226

many towns, but they had not yet destroyed Jerusalem or the temple. But after the 69th week ran out - which again it was required to be <u>after</u>, not during - they finally surrounded Jerusalem itself.

Dan 9:27 "Then he shall confirm a covenant with many for one week; But in the middle of the week He shall bring an end to sacrifice and offering. And on the wing of abominations shall be one who makes desolate, Even until the consummation, which is determined, Is poured out on the desolate."

Then he shall confirm a covenant with many for one week;

Who is this "**he**"? Scholars often debate this very interesting question.

There are really only two good possibilities from a grammatical perspective about what the antecedent for the "he" in verse 27 is, though you will never hear either of them in a commentary on this passage.

The only possibilities you will hear from commentaries will be first that the best antecedent for the "he" here is the "prince to come" of verse 26. This will be told to you by the average futurist, and though I don't agree with them about the grammar here, it should be noted that I **do** agree with the reason they are trying to make this claim, that is because they think that this last verse is a yet future event and the person who we are about to read about is who we call the Antichrist.

The other possibility you will hear is that the antecedent for the "he" in verse 27 is the "anointed one" of verse 26. This is usually put forth by preterists, and despite it being nearly impossible from a grammatical perspective, they put this forth because they believe that verse 27 is not future, which puts them in a precarious position by having to defend why Jesus would do the things that the next few verses say that this person does.

If one were to just consider this verse from a grammatical perspective, not a theological perspective, one would have to conclude that the "people" as in the "people of the prince to come" are the antecedent for this "he" in verse 27. I will quote from a study of this passage that brings out this point:

> "With regards to the above passage the subject noun is 'People' (the ones destroying) and the parsed Hebrew word יַשְׁחִית 7843 (ishchith - shachath) 'He shall destroy' is used as a Hebrew hiphil, verb, imperfect, 3rd person, masculine, singular and, is completely acceptable in Hebrew with the use of the singular subject noun 'People', whereas the translated word 'People' in the above Passage is implied to be acting as a single unit – therefore a singular noun and, NOT a plural noun, receiving a 3ms verb.
>
> In addition, the Hebrew word 'shachath' MUST also be translated as 'He shall destroy' and NOT just simply as 'shall destroy' unless the 'HE' is either implied or articulated – written or verbally spoken BECAUSE, the Hebrew word 'shachath' is used in this Passage as a Hebrew hiphil, verb, imperfect, 3rd person, masculine, singular.
>
> Dan. 9:26 …and the people of the prince that shall come (He) shall destroy the city and the sanctuary…
>
> Therefore, if the subject noun in the above KJV, et. al., Passage is the singular 'People' (and it indeed is) and it receives the corresponding 3rd ms verb 'He shall destroy' then by legitimate Hebrew and English grammatical standards who MUST the 'HE' of Dan. 9:27 be (and He shall confirm...)?
>
> Does consistent contiguous grammatical standards dictate that the 'HE' of Dan. 9:27 be the SAME preceding antecedent singular subject noun 'People' (the ones destroying) or can we just simply arbitrarily choose to substitute a different subject noun in the place of 'people' – in this case the 'a coming prince'"

They conclude this way:

"Once again, any attempt then to 'substitute' an alternate and arbitrary subject noun (*a coming prince*) for the *HE* of Dan. 9:27, even if we assume a theoretical GAP, other than the clearly grammatically defined antecedent *'People'*, the *HE* of Dan. 9:26, is to simply IGNORE ALL Hebrew and English grammatical rules merely to fit a theory.

If we are going to go down that slippery slope where we ignore grammatical rules and standards simply to fit our theories then there is LITTLE hope of ever arriving at the TRUTH of scripture."[28]

In other words IF the "he" of verse 27 is supposed to look back at anything, it must look back to the "people" but the problem is that that makes no sense, not grammatically, contextually, or anything else.

This brings us to the last good possibility for the antecedent for the "he" of Daniel 9:27…

There is none.

I wrote Charles Cooper about this when trying to figure it all out and this was his response:

"This is what I am convinced the text is actually intending. The "he" of verse 27 does not have an antecedent which drives scholars mad. They force the Hebrew to say something I don't believe it intended. The he of verse 27 does not look backwards, it points forward to a character not identified in the previous verses. This has caused much problem. It will continue."

I believe that the "he" of verse 27 does speak of the Antichrist, so I have no reason to argue this point other than the fact that it is wrong to say that the "prince to come" in verse 26 is also referring to the Antichrist.

The "he" in verse 27 just comes out of nowhere, and as I will demonstrate we are given all the tools we will ever need to determine who the "he" is because literally every aspect of the "he" here is described by Daniel in at least triplicate in other places in his writings.

Many people have come to the conclusion that there is a gap of 2000 plus years between the 69th and 70th weeks. I think this is the only way to read the text. Many who do not believe that such a gap exists, are told that people believe in a gap between the 69th and 70th weeks for silly reasons, but as I hope to demonstrate to you there is no other option but to see the 69th week ending at the second temple destruction and the last week beginning after another temple is built, an event that as of Nov. 2013 has not occurred yet.

If this is true then it also would explain the out of nowhere nature of the "he" at the beginning of verse 27. That is it comes out of nowhere because the context of this verse would be far removed from the previous verse chronologically speaking. It is not as if the "he" would be unrecognized though, as Daniel seems almost fixated on him in Daniel 7, 11 and 12, describing in detail his actions so we are not left to guess as to who the "he" is in this verse.

The preterist sees the "he" as Jesus here and I will discuss this view at length later on.

Then he shall confirm a covenant with many for one week;

So verse 27 starts out by saying that there will be a covenant which this "he" will be involved with that will be for one week. This would mean seven years, remembering the word for week here basically means seven.

Many people say that this is speaking of the Antichrist making a seven-year peace agreement with Israel which would allow them to build the temple again.

I would say that this is a possibility, but I think it is worth looking at this idea in depth because if this is supposed to be something we are to watch for, we should be informed about the specifics of it.

Confirm a covenant

This is a strange term. The word "confirm" in the Hebrew basically means to overcome, or prevail against, but it can also mean to strengthen. This is the only time the word is translated as "confirm" in the Bible.

Some translations, noting that it has this connotation of prevailing, say that it should be translated as "he shall make a strong covenant" such as the ESV has it. The fact that we are given a time reference for this covenant, that is for seven years, in addition to the next part of the verse which discusses what will happen in the middle of the week, leads me to believe that this is probably saying that the Antichrist will either strengthen an already existing contract, or perhaps make a very strong contract which will ultimately be for seven years.

Though it should be noted that the text does not make it clear that the Antichrist will say that the agreement is a seven-year one, only that it will last that long. In other words he may say that it will be an eternal covenant, but scripture, looking forward, tells us the duration. That being said it could just as easily be advertised as a seven-year agreement.

This covenant I think maybe an attempt of the Antichrist to fulfill messianic expectations of the jews regarding a new covenant. We as Christians take for granted that the New Covenant has already been instituted with Christ. Jews however still await for the many prophecies of a "new covenant" to be instituted by their awaited messiah.

Here is a small sampling of verses in the OT that refer to the New Covenant:

> Behold, the days come, saith the LORD, that I will make a new covenant with the house of Israel, and with the house of Judah. - Jer 31:31

231

> Moreover I will make a covenant of peace with them; it
> shall be an everlasting covenant with them: and I will
> place them, and multiply them, and will set my
> sanctuary in the midst of them for evermore. - Eze 34:25

This "covenant of peace" also mentioned in Isa 54:10 both refer
to the millennium, or "Kingdom age" as the Jew would say. As I
described in detail in my book *Mystery Babylon When Jerusalem
Embraces the Antichrist*, I think that the Antichrist will try very
hard to make it seem as if this time has begun, and if he does try
to do that, it would be imperative for him to make a "new
covenant" with the Jews in order to seem to legitimately be
fulfilling the prophecies of the messiah. (See also: Isa 55:3, Jer
32:40, Eze 16:60, 62, Hsa 2:18)

But the idea could be referring to a military agreement made
with the Antichrist. This would have support if one were willing
to see the verses before Daniel 11:36 as also referring to the
Antichrist instead of just to Antiochus when it says:

> And after the <u>league *is made* with him</u> he shall act
> deceitfully, for he shall come up and become strong
> with a small *number of* people. He shall enter
> <u>peaceably</u>, even into the richest places of the
> province; and he shall do *what* his fathers have not
> done, nor his forefathers: he shall disperse among
> them the plunder, spoil, and riches; and he shall
> devise his plans against the strongholds, but *only* for
> a time. - Dan 11:23-24

Covenant with many

Some make the case, like John Walvord, that the word for **many**
has to mean Israel. Though I do not find that argument very
compelling, I don't see this as being a point of contention either.

If the agreement *is* with Israel, but is also a peace agreement as
Walvord says, it would also need to be with its neighbors too, if
it were to be about peace. After all, a peace treaty with only one
nation at the negotiation table won't do much good.

But in the middle of the week He shall bring an end to sacrifice and offering. And on the wing of abominations shall be one who makes desolate, Even until the consummation, which is determined, Is poured out on the desolate.

So here we find that in the **middle of the week** he shall bring an **end to sacrifice and offerings**.

If this happens in the middle of the week then it happens 3.5 years after the covenant is made. This is a very interesting time reference as 3.5 years is spoken of all throughout scripture as the time frame that will begin the last and most terrible part of the Antichrist's career. In fact this 3.5-year period is by far the most spoken about time frame in all of Bible prophecy. Here are a few examples:

> And he was given a mouth speaking great things and blasphemies, and he was given authority to continue for <u>forty-two months.</u> - Rev 13:5

> Then the woman fled into the wilderness, where she has a place prepared by God, that they should feed her there <u>one thousand two hundred and sixty days.</u> - Rev 12:6

> But the woman was given two wings of a great eagle, that she might fly into the wilderness to her place, where she is nourished for <u>a time and times and half a time,</u> from the presence of the serpent. - Rev 12:14

> But leave out the court which is outside the temple, and do not measure it, for it has been given to the Gentiles. And they will tread the holy city underfoot for <u>forty-two months.</u> - Rev 11:2

What's very interesting about this is the fact that Daniel in another place refers to the 3.5-year time period associated with the same event, that is the **taking away of the daily sacrifice** and the **abomination of desolation**:

> "And from the time that the daily sacrifice is taken away, and the abomination of desolation is set up, there shall be one thousand two hundred and ninety days." - Dan 12:11

This is part of the death knell to the preterist interpretation of this verse.

They say verse 27 is talking about Jesus and He confirms a covenant (which they say refers to His atoning death). They basically disregard the seven-year part of the prophecy saying that it isn't to be taken literally, as obviously the new covenant didn't just last seven years. They then say that when it says that after 3.5 years he takes away sacrifice and offering, it means that after Jesus' death it effectively ended the need for sacrifices. They again say the 3.5 year part is irrelevant.

The reason that Daniel mentioning this event three times is such a devastating problem for the preterist should be obvious if we compare the verses:

> "And from the time that <u>the daily sacrifice is taken away</u>, and the <u>abomination of desolation</u> is set up, there shall be <u>one thousand two hundred and ninety days.</u> - Dan 12:11

> And forces shall be mustered by him, and they shall <u>defile the sanctuary</u> fortress; <u>then they shall take away the daily sacrifices, and place there the abomination of desolation.</u> - Dan 11:31

> Then he shall confirm a covenant with many for one week; But in the <u>middle of the week</u> He shall bring an <u>end to sacrifice and offering.</u> And on the <u>wing of abominations shall be one who makes desolate,</u> Even until the consummation, which is determined, Is poured out on the desolate." - Dan 9:27

It should be clear from reading these that Daniel is talking about the same event in all three verses - the 3.5 years is mentioned in two of them, and all three mention that the taking away of the

234

sacrifice was associated with an abomination. Daniel 11:31 says that the taking away of the sacrifices defiled the temple. Are preterists really sure they want to associate Jesus with this event?

When we consider that we know what Antiochus did when he set up an alter to Zeus and sacrificed a pig which then caused the sacrifices to be taken away because of this abomination, we must say that this was in no way a prefiguration of the atoning death of Jesus Christ.

All of that to say that Daniel obviously intends the taking away of the sacrifices to be a horrible thing that defiles the temple; this is not speaking of the atoning death of Christ.

Further the mention of the 3.5 years or the "middle of the week" link this event to the Antichrist in The Revelation conclusively. Consider that the preterist, because of their supposition that there will be no Antichrist, is forced to disregard the references to the 3.5 years as irrelevant and say that this obviously horrific event by the Antichrist mentioned at least two other times by Daniel is in fact speaking of Jesus. That is a dangerous position to take if I have ever heard one

Before I go any further I will quote Jesus and Paul in the New Testament about this event:

> "Therefore when you see the 'ABOMINATION OF DESOLATION,' spoken of by Daniel the prophet, standing in the holy place" (whoever reads, let him understand) - Mat 24:15
>
> Let no one deceive you by any means; for that Day will not come unless the falling away comes first, and the man of sin is revealed, the son of perdition who opposes and exalts himself above all that is called God or that is worshiped, so that he sits as God in the temple of God, showing himself that he is God. - 2Th 2:3-4

Because of phrases like "standing in the holy place" used by Jesus and "sits as God in the temple of God, showing himself that he is God," we have great confidence, confirmed here in the New Testament, that the abomination of desolation will be an event that happens in the temple when a man declares himself to be God at the 3.5-year mark after he confirms a covenant with many. This event will cause the sacrifices in this future temple to stop.

This also is right in line with the context of this entire prophecy. Since the previous verse (26) ended with the destruction of the second temple, verse 27 is essentially saying there will be another temple after that one. In other words since the sacrifices will be stopped at the midpoint (remember that both Paul and Jesus confirm that this event will happen in a temple, that is it is not a metaphorical thing) then we can be sure that a temple must be rebuilt in the future for this to occur.

In context then this prophecy of the 70 weeks predicts three things happening regarding the future of the temple system.

A temple would be built after Daniel had the vision (keeping in mind there was no temple standing at the time the prophecy was made, this was fulfilled, and is what we know of as the second temple).

Then it prophesied that the second temple would also be destroyed, which was fulfilled by Titus.

And finally it says a third temple will be built. This is the one the Antichrist will defile and then, as we will see, it also is destroyed.

I would even suggest that since verse 24 says that 70 weeks are determined until the anointing of the most holy place referring to Ezekiel's millennial temple, that this prophecy is the story of three future temples, two of which will be built and destroyed and one that will be, for all intents and purposes, eternal.

And on the wing of abominations shall be one who makes desolate

This is a difficult phrase which quite honestly makes no sense in most translations. What does **on the wing of abominations** mean? I used to guess the phrase meant that there was a metaphorical bird of abominations which had more abominations riding on its wing so it brought wave after wave of abominations...or something like that. As I said, I didn't really know. I found out that I was trying to make sense of a phrase that really doesn't make any sense at all.

The word for **wing** here, simply means wing. It can mean a bird's wing or a wing of a palace, an extremity, edge, border or corner.

The Septuagint says that the word means temple and it basically is saying the same thing here as all the other passages in Daniel. In other words "and upon the temple shall be the abomination of desolation."

Probably one of the best technical treatments of this from a Hebrew scholar comes from the Pulpit Commentary on Daniel 9.[29]

But to make a long story short, many translations now translate this verse either as setting up an abomination in the temple or on the wing (an outer part) of the temple. Here are a few examples of modern translations that follow the Septuagint's lead on this:

> … And the abomination of desolation will be on a wing of the temple until the decreed destruction is poured out on the desolator."(HCSB)

> .. And at the temple he will set up an abomination that causes desolation, until the end that is decreed is poured out on him." (NIV)

> .. and there shall be in the temple the abomination of desolation: and the desolation shall continue even to the consummation, and to the end. (DRB)

Even until the consummation, which is determined, Is poured out on the desolate.

You will notice in this last phrase that the last word **desolate** is here not desolator as some of the previous examples have it. Again it depends on the context. The word itself does not tell us whether the end which will be **poured out** will be on the desolator or the desolate.

I would suggest that if we consider the meaning of the phrase "abomination of desolation" we can see that the abomination causes the temple to be desolate, in other words to be abandoned, with no sacrifices occurring in it. If this is correct, then it would follow that the **consummation** would here be the destruction of the temple that Antichrist uses. I believe that this destruction would be in view in Revelation 18 (see my book on the destruction of Mystery Babylon).

Calendar Issues

Before I close this chapter I would like to talk in a general sense about the methodology used to calculate the years of this prophecy to arrive at the dates that we did. The calculations are very in depth and it would require a lot more time to explain it all here. But I think it is very important to do if one wants to be sure they have arrived at the right date.

For all the specific details I will refer you to Charles Cooper's book: *God's Elect and the Great Tribulation: An Exposition of Matthew 24:1-31 and Daniel 9.*

Just as in Sir Robert Anderson's *The Coming Prince,* the 360-day year was used in the calculations of this timeline. This was done not only because the Jewish calendar has 360-day years (minus the intercalary months added by the high priests), it also seems clear from several passages that the Bible considers a 360-day year to be the ideal year, which we see by comparing Genesis 7:11 and 24 which refer to Noah after the flood. If one were to take these passages literally, then years were exactly 360 days back in Noah's day with no intercalary months.

This along with the fact that when referring to future prophecy, particularly the abomination of desolation and other events
238

surrounding the 3.5-year period, because of the many different ways this time is referred to - i.e., 42 months, 1260 days , middle of the week etc. - we know that a 360-day year was intended to be used.

There are a number of reasons that we can speculate why prophecy is expected to be counted using 360-day years, one of which being that because the Hebrew calendar was already 360 days long but required an active high priest to calculate the intercalary months, something that would have been impossible after 70 AD and the destruction of the temple, that the intercalary month system was stopped as well.

I tend to look at the 360-day year as a perfect year, 12 30-day months would mean that the earth makes a perfect circle around the sun which is not implausible to assume that it used to be that way. Chuck Missler cites the fact that all ancient calendars used a 360-day year:

> "All early calendars appear to be based on a 360-day calendar: the Assyrians, Chaldeans, Egyptians, Hebrews, Persians, Greeks, Phoenicians, Chinese, Mayans, Hindus, Carthaginians, Etruscans, and Teutons all had calendars based on a 360-day year; typically, twelve 30-day months."[30]

He then says that at about the same time in history (701 BC) they all changed, trying to adjust their calendars in various ways to make up for the fact that they no longer were accurate.

He attributes this to a near pass of Mars with Earth in 701 BC. He cites studies which suggest that the two planets used to have orbital resonance with one another which was disturbed after the event resulting in the slight change in the length of time it takes the earth to revolve around the sun thereby forcing everyone to change their calendars to keep up with the seasons.

Cooper on the other hand calls the 360-day system the "modified Egyptian calendar" and has his own reasons about why it was used by scripture, reasons which are also very compelling, and the two ideas are not mutually exclusive.

Another item that is important about the calculation of this time
is that there is a major problem with secular history's version of
the length of the Persian Empire. This and a few other issues are
explained in detail by Mr. Cooper in his book, and are important
reading if one wants to look under the hood of the theory I
presented here in order to check and see if it is indeed accurate.

Chapter 10

An Angel Appears to Daniel

Dan 10:1 In the third year of Cyrus king of Persia a message was revealed to Daniel, whose name was called Belteshazzar. The message *was* true, but the appointed time *was* long; and he understood the message, and had understanding of the vision.

In the third year of Cyrus king of Persia

Daniel was still in Babylon two years after the decree of Cyrus which let the Jews return to Israel. Some speculate this failure to return to Israel had to do with his advanced age and the difficulty of such a journey for an aged man. Others speculate that Daniel, as a high ranking member of the Persian government, decided to stay in office where he could do more for the returning Jews in a political sense, than he could if he went with them, though this latter view has problems because it seems that based on Daniel 1:21 that Daniel only continued his political career until the first year of Cyrus, so Daniel may have been retired by this point.

The fact that Daniel seems to be near 85 years old at this point is probably a sufficient reason to explain his lack of return, but there are a number of scenarios that could explain this as well. The fact is that the text does not say clearly.

A message was revealed to Daniel, whose name was called Belteshazzar.

Daniel calls himself by the name given to him by the Babylonians. One commentator suggests this is to make it clear that this is the same Daniel who wrote during the Babylonian times that is writing this present letter.

The message *was* true, but the appointed time *was* long

The truthfulness of the vision is described as the reason the vision should be preserved in the earlier vision of Chapter 8.

> "And the vision of the evenings and mornings Which was told is true; <u>Therefore</u> seal up the vision, For *it refers* to many days *in the future.*" - Dan 8:26

The last part of this phrase **but the appointed time *was* long** is often translated in certain Bible versions as being about **conflict or war** as opposed to it being a long time away.

The idea of being **long** here according to some Hebrew scholars was that it was long in the sense of being about a great conflict; therefore, many translations translate this passage similar to the NET bible which says:

This message was true and concerned a great war.

Since understanding this depends on understanding a lot about the Hebrew language and how it developed, which I do not, I will take a pass on explaining this, and only note that regardless of how you take it, it is true. The following three chapters, which constitute the message Daniel is going to receive, do have to do with great wars, but they also are not appointed for a long time.

And he understood the message, and had understanding of the vision.
This is interesting how Daniel makes it known that he understood the vision. This is perhaps in contrast to the other two visions he had seen, the first in Chapter 7 and then in Chapter 8, where he seems to simply record the visions but not have a good understanding of them.

He seems to explicitly say this at the end of the vision of Chapter 8 when he says:

I was astonished by the vision, but no one
understood it. - Dan 8:27

In the vision in Chapter 9, the 70 weeks vision, there Daniel is
given the ability to understand the vision (9:22) and is
commanded to understand it (9:25).

At the end of this vision in Chapter 10 which concludes in
Chapter 12, Daniel says he doesn't understand what the angel
says about the timing of the end of the vision, but it would
appear that Daniel does claim to understand the main points of
the vision, and in particular how the vision relates to his concern
for the Jewish people whom we will see he is praying for before
this vision is given and whom the angel says this vision is about.

**Dan 10:2 In those days I, Daniel, was mourning three full
weeks.**
**Dan 10:3 I ate no pleasant food, no meat or wine came
into my mouth, nor did I anoint myself at all, till three
whole weeks were fulfilled.**

I, Daniel, was mourning

Why was Daniel mourning? In one sense he had gotten the very
thing he prayed for in Daniel 9. The Jews were set free, they
were back in the land and they had been given the authority to
rebuild the city and the temple. But things were not going well
with the rebuilding process back in Jerusalem. I think the cause
of Daniel's mourning can be found in Ezra 4:4, 5 which
describes a big problem with the rebuilding process which was
so near and dear to Daniel:

> Then the people of the land tried to discourage the
> people of Judah. They troubled them in building, and
> hired counselors against them to frustrate their
> purpose all the days of Cyrus king of Persia, even
> until the reign of Darius king of Persia. - Ezr 4:4-5

The people back in Israel were so frustrated by the tactics
employed by these people that the building process would stall

altogether until God sent the prophets Haggai and Zechariah to get the Jews back on track and building again.

In other words, based on Daniel saying he was in the third year of Cyrus in Verse 1, and based on Ezra 3:8, which says that the laying of the foundation which sparked the opposition to the building occurred in the second month of the second year of their coming, it's safe to assume that Daniel had recently been given word of the stalled work on the temple.

This in my opinion is the reason that Daniel was mourning — he could see that because of the fear of man and the craftiness of their opposition, the great work of rebuilding the city and the temple, that he had prayed for so earnestly, was dead in its tracks.

I ate no pleasant food, no meat or wine came into my mouth, nor did I anoint myself at all, till three whole weeks were fulfilled.

Daniel here was doing a type of fast which was characterized by self-denial. It wasn't an abstaining from food altogether, only "choice food" nor "meat" nor "wine."

The refraining from anointing mentioned here probably refers to oils that would be put on the skin in hot and dry climates to help the skin in such conditions. This then was indeed a form of self-denial.

Stephen Miller in the New American Commentary says of fasting:

> "Fasting is a personal matter between the individual and God. It is voluntary. However, if giants of the faith like Moses, David, Esther, Daniel, Paul, and Jesus himself felt the need to fast, it would seem reasonable that modern saints should be willing to deny themselves in order to pray more earnestly for the furtherance of the kingdom of God in a world that lies in deep spiritual darkness."[31]

244

Dan 10:4 Now on the twenty-fourth day of the first month, as I was by the side of the great river, that *is*, the Tigris,
Dan 10:5 I lifted my eyes and looked, and behold, a certain man clothed in linen, whose waist *was* girded with gold of Uphaz!
Dan 10:6 His body *was* like beryl, his face like the appearance of lightning, his eyes like torches of fire, his arms and feet like burnished bronze in color, and the sound of his words like the voice of a multitude.

During this three week fast, Daniel was by the Tigris River when he sees this great messenger.

It is often pointed out that the description of this being given to us by Daniel is similar to the description that the Apostle John gives to us of the risen and glorified Jesus in Revelation Chapter 1.

For example in Revelation 1 the following characteristics of Jesus are mentioned that could be considered matches:

- He is girded about the chest with a golden band.
- His eyes are like a flame of fire.
- His feet were like fine brass, as if refined in a furnace,
- His voice as the sound of many waters.
- His countenance was like the sun shining in its strength.
- He is also clothed with a garment down to the feet though I would submit that this is not a match since "linen" is not mentioned. It may seem like a minor point, but considering the very particular use of linen in scripture, and the fact that linen is mentioned being worn by the **angels** in the same chapter of Revelation, I don't think it should be assumed that the fabric that Jesus was wearing was linen, though it is possible and even likely.

A few other characteristics are mentioned of Jesus such as his hair being white that are not mentioned by Daniel.

Before we investigate who this being is that appears to Daniel at the Tigris River, we must also realize that very similar characteristics are also applied to several angels in the Book of Revelation like the so-called "strong angels" that appear three times in the book (Rev: 5:2, 10:1, 18:21).

Also in Chapter 15, the seven angels with the seven vials also appear to have similar characteristics.

- Are clothed in pure bright linen.
- Have their chests girded with golden bands.
- Have faces like the sun.
- And feet like pillars of fire.
- Have a loud voice "as when a lion roars."

If we stopped right there it would be a tie. But I think there is another data point found in Revelation 10 when one of the "strong angels" is being referred to.

In that passage we read the following:

> The angel whom I saw standing on the sea and on the land raised up his hand to heaven and swore by Him who lives forever and ever, who created heaven and the things that are in it, the earth and the things that are in it, and the sea and the things that are in it, that there should be delay no longer - Rev 10:5-6

The reason this is interesting is because back in Daniel, if you fast forward to the end of the interaction between Daniel and these beings you find an almost identical verse:

> And *one* said to the man clothed in linen, who *was* above the waters of the river, "How long shall the fulfillment of these wonders *be?*" Then I heard the man clothed in linen, who *was* above the waters of the river, when he held up his right hand and his left hand to heaven, and swore by Him who lives forever, that *it shall be* for a time, times, and half *a time;* and when the power of the holy people has been

> completely shattered, all these *things* shall be
> finished. - Dan 12:6-7

So here we have the same thing. A being, standing above some waters, holding up hands, swearing in a way that is only seen in these two passages in scripture. It certainly is not a coincidence that they both are wearing linen and a gold belt and all the rest of it.

The difference is that in Revelation 10 the amazingly similar being is called an "angel" several times, and it is unlikely that John would make such a mistake considering he was given a lesson in not comparing angels with Jesus in Revelation 19:10, and that in the places where John is explicitly referring to Jesus he never calls him an angel or anything like it.

In addition, the strong angel in Revelation 10 is contextually angelic. For example, in Revelation 10:8 the "Voice from heaven" which is obviously divine speaks to the angel, severely limiting the possibility that the strong angel is Jesus, as contextually Jesus is on the throne in heaven at this time.

In addition, the strong angel makes appeals to God for the end to come at the sounding of the final trumpet, again making the context support the idea of an angelic identity.

The reason that people suggest that Daniel is visited by none other than Jesus Himself in Daniel 10 is based solely on the five or so characteristics that are a match with the description of the risen Christ in Revelation 1, which certainly does contain many exact and very interesting matches with the being that Daniel describes.

They hold this even though such characteristics can also been seen of particularly high ranking angels in the same book.

I believe there is a reason that Jesus shares some characteristics with angels, which I will discuss in a moment, but we must first look at some arguments against the idea that the being in Daniel 10 is an Old Testament appearance of Jesus.

The primary problem arises because of Verse 13 of Daniel 10:

> But the prince of the kingdom of Persia withstood me twenty-one days; and behold, Michael, one of the chief princes, came to help me, for I had been left alone there with the kings of Persia. - Dan 10:13

The idea that Jesus could be withstood in such a way by man or angel as to need help from Michael the archangel is not a theology we find anywhere in scripture, though we do find that Michael is often matched against Satan, another angelic being of a similar rank in Jude and Revelation 12.

Theologians paint themselves into a theological corner when they argue that this being is Jesus because they have to find some explanation as to why Jesus, that is God himself, is unable to defeat one of his creatures, namely the Prince of Persia.

I heard one commentator suggest that being helped by Michel to defeat the Prince of Persia was similar to when Jesus was ministered to by angels during His temptation in the wilderness, but that explanation is no good. In that instance the temptation Jesus was given by Satan was to make bread for Himself during a time of critical hunger, in other words to use His divine power to manifest bread instead of trusting His father for provisions in a situation where there was no earthly possibility to obtain food.

This temptation was only a part of our Lord's brief earthy sojourn and He was tempted and tried as we are in all ways, but that time of self-imposed weakness is over for Him, neither can it be said that such a weakness existed in Him in His pre-incarnate state.

Other commentators attempting to have their cake and eat it too will view Verse 10 as shifting from talking about Jesus to a run-of-the-mill angel. I will quote a verse before the verse in question so you can get the context. Look for the phrase "suddenly a hand touched me." That phrase is supposed to signify the change in characters:

> Yet I heard the sound of his words; and while I heard
> the sound of his words I was in a deep sleep on my
> face, with my face to the ground. Suddenly, a hand
> touched me, which made me tremble on my knees
> and *on* the palms of my hands. - Dan 10:9-10

So in this reading Daniel has a vision of Jesus, but then an angels takes over the conversation from there.

This is an improvement from the previous interpretation but it is unnecessary as the only reason people think they have to make this being be Jesus is because of the physical description, a description that can be shown to have at least 20% more to do with angels than with Jesus.

So we can let these angels be angels in my opinion. But it does bring up the question: Why does Jesus in His glorified state look so much like angels? I mean shouldn't He look much more awesome than they are?

The reason is that Jesus was the firstfruits of the coming resurrection (1 Cor 15: 20-23), that is to say that Jesus is currently enthroned in heaven in a glorified body, a body that we too will wear once we are resurrected.

> Beloved, now we are children of God; and it has not
> yet been revealed what we shall be, but we know that
> when He is revealed, we shall be like Him, for we
> shall see Him as He is. - 1Jn 3:2

So in some sense Jesus is still a man on the throne, even though He is in a glorified body.

The next point is that this glorified body is very similar to what angels have.

> And the angels who did not keep their proper
> domain, but left their own abode, He has reserved in
> everlasting chains under darkness for the judgment of
> the great day - Jud 1:6

When Jude refers to the abode or habitation that the angels left in order to come down and have sex with human women, he is using a very rare Greek word, used only twice in the Bible, once here in Jude and the other time it's referring to the glorified body that believers in Christ will have upon the resurrection. The verse is found in 2 Corinthians 5:2 and the word is translated there as "habitation:"

> For we know that if our earthly house, *this* tent, is destroyed, we have a building from God, a house not made with hands, eternal in the heavens. For in this we groan, earnestly desiring to be clothed with our habitation which is from heaven - 2Co 5:1-2

So we can see here that upon the resurrection we will obtain the type of body that the angels had before falling, a body type that Christ, as the firstfruit of the resurrection, has right now.

This seems to be explicitly taught by the Lord himself:

> For in the resurrection they neither marry nor are given in marriage, but are like angels of God in heaven. - Mat 22:30

So in conclusion on this point, there is no need to see the angel that is speaking with Daniel as Jesus, as the exact same physical characteristics are spoken of in regard to angels and the description seems to be pretty standard for most heavenly beings regardless of rank.

Jesus certainly outranks any man, though we will probably look similar to Jesus in our glorified state. By the same token, having angels described similarly to the Lord in His resurrected body is expected based on the points made above.

Dan 10:7 And I, Daniel, alone saw the vision, for the men who were with me did not see the vision; but a great terror fell upon them, so that they fled to hide themselves.

A similar event to this happened with Saul on the road to Damascus in the book of Acts when Jesus appeared to him. It would seem that there is was unmistakable presence that could be felt by onlookers. In the case of Saul of Tarsus the people could see a light (Acts 9:7) and hear a voice (Acts 22:9) but they could not make out any particulars about them. It also caused them to be afraid.

Some people believe this is another reason that Jesus is the being in Daniel 10, but again we remember that the Book of Acts was post-resurrection, as was the Book of Revelation; therefore, all the previous points about Jesus being in a sense like angels because of the nature of His glorified body apply to the Road to Damascus incident as well.

It should be noted that fear because of the overwhelming presence **of angels** is common in other places in Daniel, as well as the Book of Revelation, and It is not uncommon in those passages for the angel to say things like "Fear not." In other words the idea of the presence of angels causing fear is well documented in scripture.

Dan 10:8 Therefore I was left alone when I saw this great vision, and no strength remained in me; for my vigor was turned to frailty in me, and I retained no strength.
Dan 10:9 Yet I heard the sound of his words; and while I heard the sound of his words I was in a deep sleep on my face, with my face to the ground.
Dan 10:10 Suddenly, a hand touched me, which made me tremble on my knees and *on* the palms of my hands.

This exact same thing happened in a previous vision of Daniel's recorded in Daniel 8, though in that case the angel that caused this sleepiness was named explicitly as Gabriel:

> And I heard a man's voice between *the banks of* the Ulai, who called, and said, "Gabriel, make this *man* understand the vision." So he came near where I stood, and when he came I was afraid and fell on my face; but he said to me, "Understand, son of man, that the vision *refers* to the time of the end." Now, as he was speaking with me, I was in a deep sleep with my

251

face to the ground; but he touched me, and stood me upright. - Dan 8:16-18

It is for this reason that many scholars believe the angel in Daniel 10 is the same one in Daniel 8, that is Gabriel. While I would say we can't be100% certain of that, it is certainly possible, even probable.

Dan 10:11 And he said to me, "O Daniel, man greatly beloved, understand the words that I speak to you, and stand upright, for I have now been sent to you." While he was speaking this word to me, I stood trembling.

O Daniel, man greatly beloved

Daniel will be told this by the angel one more time in this chapter, and he was also told the same thing in the previous vision. It appears based on the next usage of the term that the angel is using God's love for him as a kind of title for Daniel:

> And he said, "O man greatly beloved, fear not! - Dan 10:19

This makes the comparison with the Apostle John even more interesting as John too had a similar title "the disciple whom Jesus loved," and as previously mentioned both of these men were given these great apocalyptic visions by God's messengers.

It should also be said more generally here that God wants us to know we are loved. His word declares this to us in many ways, often very directly (Rom 5:8-9, John 3:16).

Dan 10:12 Then he said to me, "Do not fear, Daniel, for from the first day that you set your heart to understand, and to humble yourself before your God, your words were heard; and I have come because of your words.

What a great encouragement for us to pray this verse is. Daniel had a divine messenger dispatched "**because of [his] words.**" Jesus tells us that mountains can be moved in prayer if we have faith. scripture tells us time and time again in various ways that prayer is the catalyst for God to act in our lives.

Dan 10:13 But the prince of the kingdom of Persia withstood me twenty-one days; and behold, Michael, one of the chief princes, came to help me, for I had been left alone there with the kings of Persia.

In discussing this verse I will also read two verses from the end of the chapter before we begin.

> Then he said, "Do you know why I have come to
> you? And now I must return to fight with the prince
> of Persia; and when I have gone forth, indeed the
> prince of Greece will come. But I will tell you what
> is noted in the Scripture of Truth. (No one upholds
> me against these, except Michael your prince. - Dan
> 10:20-21

So here we have this Prince of Persia withstanding this angel for 21 days, apparently preventing him from reaching Daniel with this message about the future of the world and the Antichrist.

There have been a lot of proposals as to the nature of this Prince of Persia, so we will take a few of them and see if they can be defended.

Some commentators say that the Prince of Persia is a human prince such as the son of Cyrus at the time Cambyses II; some will even say it was Cyrus himself. This view is attractive to those who lean toward an anti-supernatural view, but it has many difficulties:

1) Two times the angel contrasts the Prince of Persia with Michael who is also a Prince, suggesting that they are of the same quality, and we know that in the case of Michael "prince" means angel.
2) The context suggests an angelic being here because this **Prince of Persia** seems to be an even match for the angel that is speaking

(probably Gabriel) and the Prince of Persia is
only overcome with the addition of another
angel to the fight, that is Michael. It is very
difficult to think of an earthly king or son of a
king being described this way for any reason
whatsoever.

Some will say that the Prince of Persia is Satan himself. They do
this citing Matthew 4:8-9 in which Satan suggests that all the
nations of the world are his, without contradiction from Jesus.

This would be supported by the idea that at least twice we see
Michael engaged with fighting Satan, in Jude over the body of
Moses, and Revelation 12 just before the midpoint of the 70th
week of Daniel.

The problem for this view shows up in Verse 20 where it says:

**Then he said, "Do you know why I have come to you? And
now I must return to fight with the prince of Persia; and
when I have gone forth, indeed the prince of Greece will
come.**
If the Satan theory is correct, then the Prince of Greece must also
be Satan, but in this verse the Prince of Persia and Greece are
contrasted making the satanic view difficult, if not impossible.

I think that the Prince of Persia as well as the Prince of Greece
are similar in nature to Michael and Gabriel; that is to say they
are angels. However in their case they are angels that have fallen
and aligned with Satan and his purposes, which of course would
include preventing Daniel from being given such vital
information concerning his plan.

I recommend the paper in the Journal Bibliotheca Sacra by
David E. Stevens called "*Daniel 10 and the Notion of Territorial
Spirits*" in which Mr. Stevens protests the idea that these angels
are "territorial spirits" and instead calls them "Empire Spirits."

In other words, he says that it is wrong to use Daniel 10 as a
proof that there are fallen angels assigned to every geographical
territory. He points out that the actions of the Prince of Persia are
254

generally opposing the plan of God, and not necessarily concerned with their territory per se.

But his strongest point, in my opinion, is in regard to the mentioning of the Prince of Greece as coming afterwards and about the nature of Michael being a prince of Daniel's "people," not of the land itself.

Persia was the empire that ruled the world at the time of this vision. The empire that would come next, which would defeat the Persian Empire, was Greece. This was explained quite explicitly to Daniel in Chapter 8, probably by the very same angel. So Daniel could be expected to understand the reference to the Prince of Greece coming afterwards.

The alternative is difficult to imagine. It would mean that the angel here is telling Daniel that the territorial angel over Persia was fighting him, and he was going to go back to continue this fight and he somehow also knew that another territorial angel, that is over Greece, is going to come and join the fight which was presumably not happening on its territory. The idea is possible, but it seems to be a stretch, especially considering there is such a strong case that Daniel knew that the Grecian Empire would follow the Persian Empire.

Although it must be said that we cannot really know the exact nature of these spiritual wars, the idea of these beings being associated with whatever world power is on the scene could be a likely scenario, as Stevens suggests. I might even go so far as to say that the angels could be assigned to more than one place at a given time, but the idea of territorial spirits being over every nation is not defendable from this passage, in my opinion.

Dan 10:14 Now I have come to make you understand what will happen to your people in the latter days, for the vision *refers* to *many* days yet *to come.*"

Here we are told that the focus of the vision will concern Daniel's **people,** that is the Jewish people. Though it can be said that since the end of the prophecy concerning Israel will draw in the whole world, this can also be said to be a detailed prophecy about the future of the world in the end times.

Dan 10:15 When he had spoken such words to me, I turned my face toward the ground and became speechless. Dan 10:16 And suddenly, *one* **having the likeness of the sons of men touched my lips; then I opened my mouth and spoke, saying to him who stood before me, "My lord, because of the vision my sorrows have overwhelmed me, and I have retained no strength. Dan 10:17 For how can this servant of my lord talk with you, my lord? As for me, no strength remains in me now, nor is any breath left in me." Dan 10:18 Then again,** *the one* **having the likeness of a man touched me and strengthened me. Dan 10:19 And he said, "O man greatly beloved, fear not! Peace** *be* **to you; be strong, yes, be strong!" So when he spoke to me I was strengthened, and said, "Let my lord speak, for you have strengthened me."**

So Daniel is made weak by the presence of the angel, but the angel strengthens him with a touch. Again, a similar instance happened last time Daniel met Gabriel in Daniel 8:18.

Dan 10:20 Then he said, "Do you know why I have come to you? And now I must return to fight with the prince of Persia; and when I have gone forth, indeed the prince of Greece will come. Dan 10:21 But I will tell you what is noted in the Scripture of Truth. (No one upholds me against these, except Michael your prince.

See discussion on verse 13.

Chapter 11

Dan 11:1 "Also in the first year of Darius the Mede, I, *even* I, stood up to confirm and strengthen him.)

This verse seems to belong to the end of the previous chapter; the chapter division was probably incorrectly put here because it has a phrase that usually appears at the beginning of chapters:

In the first year of Darius the Mede

So the end of the previous chapter should read:

> But I will shew thee that which is noted in the scripture of truth: and *there is* none that holdeth with me in these things, but Michael your prince. [Chapter break]"Also in the first year of Darius the Mede, I, *even* I, stood up to confirm and strengthen him. - Dan 10:21-11:1

Therefore, this should be taken as Gabriel strengthening Michael as opposed to Darius.

Stephen Miller, in the New American Commentary, says of this:

> "In 10:13, 21 it is revealed that Michael had helped the interpreting angel; now in 11:1 Gabriel related that he had supported and protected Michael. The first year of Darius42 the Mede was ca. 538 B.C., two years before this vision. Gabriel's awesome power is evidenced by the fact that he was called on to "support" Michael"[32]

The Angel Gives a Message to Daniel

Dan 11:2 And now I will tell you the truth: Behold, three more kings will arise in Persia, and the fourth shall be far richer than *them* all; by his strength, through his riches, he shall stir up all against the realm of Greece.

Three more kings will arise in Persia

Three more kings did arise in Persia, but as discussed in the commentary on Daniel 9:1, there were also co-ruling Median kings who account for the discrepancies in some kings lists by historians. Failing to understand that there were often two kings at a given time ruling over the Medo-Persian Empire has caused a number of problems for bible commentators as well as secular historians, but these problems are perfectly reconciled when this is understood.

The fourth shall be far richer than *them* all; by his strength, through his riches, he shall stir up all against the realm of Greece.

The fourth king mentioned here is clearly Xerxes I, and this is a very accurate way for the angel to describe him in advance.

By his strength and riches, he raised an army so big that the number of soldiers that Herodotus gave for it is questioned by modern scholars because of how high it is. He used this army to advance on Greece. This began with the famous battle of Thermopylae, portrayed often in movies where 300 Spartan soldiers put up a good fight, though ultimately losing to the massive Persian army.

I think it's fascinating the way that scripture describes the main thing that Xerxes did: he simply **stirred up Greece**. The reason this is interesting is first, because that's all he really did to the Greeks. He ultimately did not conquer them at all. But second, it was the stirring up of Greece that gave rise to Alexander the Great. It is very unlikely that Alexander would have done what he did when he did if Xerxes had not **stirred up** Greece.

After the battle of Thermopylae, Xerxes entered the deserted city of Athens and burned it, an act that outraged the Greeks, as that was considered a war crime of sorts in those conditions. Some say that Xerxes did it in a fit of rage and realized his mistake and tried to rebuild it the next day, but whatever happened, it certainly became a huge part of the anti-Persian sentiment in Greece after that.

Xerxes had all kinds of problems with storms and other factors, which eventually resulted in his retreat, but the hatred of the Persians by the Greeks after this war was at a consistent fever pitch.

And as soon as Alexander the Great took power in Greece, his hatred of Persia led him to immediately march toward Persia in a military campaign that would literally change the course of human history.

So when scripture tells us that the main act of Xerxes was that he stirred up Greece, it is no small matter.

As we move to the next verse, we will see that this idea is validated, as the next prophecy that the angel gives is of Alexander the Great.

Dan 11:3 Then a mighty king shall arise, who shall rule with great dominion, and do according to his will.
Dan 11:4 And when he has arisen, his kingdom shall be broken up and divided toward the four winds of heaven, but not among his posterity nor according to his dominion with which he ruled; for his kingdom shall be uprooted, even for others besides these.

This **mighty king** who arose is universally agreed upon to be Alexander the Great, who defeated the Persian Empire and began the Greek Empire. One of the reasons that we can be so sure that this is speaking of him is because of the details given in verse 4, which states that his kingdom will not be given to his descendants, as was the custom, but divided up among four non-descendants.

This of course happened because Alexander died at age 33, and though he had two sons, they were too young to rule, and were later assassinated anyway.

Alexander did not name a successor on his deathbed, instead only saying to "give it to the strong". This led to a 22-year war among his generals, which eventually ended with a peace treaty dividing the empire between **four** of them.

1. Lysimachus - Thrace and Bithynia (and much of Asia Minor)
2. Cassander - Macedonia and Greece
3. Seleucus - Syria, Babylonia, and the lands to the east
4. Ptolemy - Egypt, Palestine, and parts of Arabia

Note: Seleucus = Seleucus I Nicator (r. 312-280 BC), Ptolemy = Ptolemy I Soter (r. 323-282 BC)[33]

Verse 4 also notes that this dividing would not be **according to his dominion with which he ruled.** In other words, it wouldn't look exactly like the kingdom Alexander had left, and that was true as well. After the 22 years of war, there developed many changes in the boundaries of the Greek Empire. For example, the vast area that Alexander controlled to the east of Syria had almost all been lost.

Dan 11:5 "Also the king of the South shall become strong, as well as *one* of his princes; and he shall gain power over him and have dominion. His dominion *shall be* a great dominion.

The king of the South is a reference to one of Alexander's four generals: Ptolemy I Soter. He was one of Alexander's greatest generals, and when the dust settled after the wars, he controlled the prized territory of Egypt and the surrounding lands, which, from here on out, I will refer to as either the king of the South or by the technical name of the kingdom which derives from his name, that is the Ptolemaic Empire.

***One* of his princes; and he shall gain power over him and
have dominion. His dominion *shall be* a great dominion.**

This is a reference to Seleucus I Nicator, another of the original
generals of the four divisions of the Greek Empire mentioned
earlier . We also call his division by his proper name today, that
is the Seleucid Empire.

It says in verse 5 that Selucus was one of Ptolemy's princes or
commanders before getting his own kingdom, and this is true.

During the turbulent years of the wars between these generals,
before it was at all clear who would rule what, Selucus, a lesser
former general of Alexander's, was put over the city of Babylon
as a satrap, kind of like a mayor or governor.

But, as was so often the case during these 22 years of war,
Antingonus, another one of Alexander's generals, seized
Babylon. Selucus, the satrap, fled toward Egypt after this
takeover and became one of the king of the South's (Ptolemy's)
princes or commanders.

About four years later, Ptolomy, with the help of Selucus, went
back to Babylon and defeated Antigonus, who by that time had
built up the northern kingdom pretty well. So when Ptolemy
gave Selucus back the northern lands, he was giving him a good-
sized kingdom. Selucus then enlarged it even more, eventually
making it, as it says in verse 5, a larger dominion than
Ptolemy's.

The two kingdoms lived in peace for some time, but eventually
Selucus to the north claimed dominion over the hotly contested
lands of Israel and the surrounding lands which lay between the
two empires. This sparked hostilities between the two nations,
which would eventually result in 130 years of war between these
two divisions of the Greek empire.

The next 15 or so verses in Daniel detail the wars between them.
Israel would always be controlled by the empire which had the
most power at the time.

Dan 11:6 And at the end of *some* years they shall join forces, for the daughter of the king of the South shall go to the king of the North to make an agreement; but she shall not retain the power of her authority, and neither he nor his authority shall stand; but she shall be given up, with those who brought her, and with him who begot her, and with him who strengthened her in *those* times.

The two kings, Ptolemy I and Selucus I, died, and their sons basically started some wars which were based on their fathers' dispute over control of the lands surrounding Israel, in what is known as the first and second Syrian wars.

And at the end of *some* years they shall join forces

After the second Syrian war, they **joined forces** by coming to terms in a peace treaty which stipulated that Berenice, **the daughter of the king of the South**, was to marry the king of the North, who at this time was Ptolemy I's grandson Antiochus II Theos.

The problem was that Antiochus II already had a wife named Laodice. Antiochus II, however, exiled her to Ephesus and transferred the right to succeed him to the sons of his new wife as per the peace treaty.

She shall not retain the power of her authority, and neither he nor his authority shall stand; but she shall be given up, with those who brought her, and with him who begot her,

Berenice did not **retain the power of her authority** because after her father back home in Egypt died, her new husband put her away and took Laodice back.

Laodice, however, perhaps not liking that she had been exiled in the first place, when she was back in the palace poisoned her husband and told everyone that his last words were to have her son be the next ruler.

Berenice contested this and said her son should be the ruler, but Laodice had both Berenice and her infant son killed.

This killing of her son is what may be meant by the phrase "**and with him who begot her**" which the NET bible translates as "her child", a translation which has support in the Greek versions of the Old Testament.

Dan 11:7 But from a branch of her roots *one* shall arise in his place, who shall come with an army, enter the fortress of the king of the North, and deal with them and prevail. Dan 11:8 And he shall also carry their gods captive to Egypt, with their princes *and* their precious articles of silver and gold; and he shall continue *more* years than the king of the North.

From a branch of her roots *one* shall arise in his place

This came to pass when Berenice's brother back in Egypt, Ptolemy III, rose to power after the death of his father.

Who shall come with an army, enter the fortress of the king of the North, and deal with them and prevail.

Ptolemy III raised a great army and attacked the king of the North to avenge his sister's murder by Laodice. Laodice was effectively now ruling the North, though technically it was her son, Seleucus II Callinicus, who was officially on the throne.

Ptolemy's Egyptian army crushed the Syrian armies and even captured Antioch, the capital city, and killed Laeodice. This is what is known as the third Syrian war.

And he shall also carry their gods captive to Egypt, with their princes *and* their precious articles of silver and gold;

Ptolemy spent a lot of time plundering the east after the war, bringing back treasures of all kinds. He made it at far as Babylon on his plundering trips, even taking things back to Egypt that were said to originally have been the property of Cambyses

(Cyrus's son). He brought so much wealth back to Egypt that they gave him the title of Euergetes, which means "Benefactor."

The war ended with a peace treaty which awarded Ptolomy III of Egypt even more wealth. The text says **he shall continue *more* years than the king of the North.** He did. In fact, he enjoyed a 24 year reign, a very long time for the period.

Dan 11:9 "Also *the king of the North* shall come to the kingdom of the king of the South, but shall return to his own land.

There is some confusion as to what this verse is actually saying. Basically it's hard to tell if this is saying that king of the North will try to invade Egypt, but return quickly, or if it is simply summing up the previous discussion by saying the king of the South will return home.

The Pulpit commentary sums the problem up nicely:

> "The Septuagint Version differs less than usual from the Massoretic, "The King of Egypt shall enter into (his) kingdom certain days and return to his land." Theodotion renders, "And he shall enter into the kingdom of the king of the south, and return into his land." The Peshitta differs more, "The king of the south shall enter in strength, and turn to his own land." The Vulgate does not differ from the others. This verse, assuming the king of the south, Ptolemy Euergetes, to be the subject of the verb, merely completes the statements of the previous verse, and seems to describe the triumphant return of Euergetes into Egypt. If we take - which, however, is not so natural - the king of the north as the subject, then the reference may be to the unsuccessful attempts made by Seleucus Callinicus to invade Egypt. " - The Pulpit Commentary

I don't have an informed position on this, but will only say that the verse is describing a very mundane thing any way you look at it (either a return trip home, or a planned invasion by the king of the North that ends in retreat, which the next verse seems to suggest is the case), but since either way it brings us to the same place, I will take a pass on taking a stand on it.

Dan 11:10 However his sons shall stir up strife, and assemble a multitude of great forces; and *one* shall certainly come and overwhelm and pass through; then he shall return to his fortress and stir up strife.

The king of the North had two **sons.** The eldest only ruled for a few years and was assassinated by his army while on campaign. The younger son was named Antiochus III the Great. Both of these sons [**stirred up strife, and assembled a multitude of great forces**].

***One* shall certainly come and overwhelm and pass through; then he shall return to his fortress and stir up strife.**

This is a reference to Antiochus III (the younger son) campaigning in Lebanon, lands that were claimed by the king of the South at the time. Though he had to **return to his fortress** because his attempt to take Lebanon was unsuccessful, he definitely **stirred up strife** when he began to plan another attack on the hotly contested region, which was claimed by the South. His actions in Lebanon sparked the reactions of the king of the South in the next verse.

Dan 11:11 "And the king of the South shall be moved with rage, and go out and fight with him, with the king of the North, who shall muster a great multitude; but the multitude shall be given into the hand of his *enemy*.

The king of the South, who by now was Ptolemy IV, went out to defeat the king of the North (Antiochus III), who did indeed **muster a great multitude,** including not just his regular forces but also 10,000 Nabateans and Arab forces. This, however, wasn't enough because, as it says in verse 11, **the multitude shall be given into the hand of his *enemy*.** In other words, the king of the North (Antiochus III) was defeated at this great battle in 217 BC, sometimes called the battle of Raphia (southwest of modern Gaza).

Dan 11:12 When he has taken away the multitude, his heart will be lifted up; and he will cast down tens of thousands, but he will not prevail.

Though the Hebrew here is difficult, it seems this is talking about how this complete victory at Raphia made the Egyptian king proud. The Pulpit commentary suggests that the last part of this verse, speaking of him **not prevailing** even though he was the victor, is talking about his refusal to follow up the victory by pursuing those that fled and destroying them, which, as we will see, will ultimately be a terrible mistake.

J Paul Tanner suggests that the latter part of this verse is referring to the defeated Antiochus III, who, though responsible for the deaths of tens of thousands, survived the battle and spent the next 14 years putting down revolts.

This would seem to make the most sense historically considering that Antiochus III is again in view in the next verse.

Dan 11:13 For the king of the North will return and muster a multitude greater than the former, and shall certainly come at the end of some years with a great army and much equipment.

About 15 years after the previous verse, the defeated Syrian King Antiochus III was not so weak anymore, He would return to fight the Egyptians with a much greater force, also with **great equipment.** This would mark the beginning of the fifth Syrian war.

In fact, this verse marks the end of general Egyptian dominance as well; after this point, the Syrian kingdom would be consistently the stronger of the two nations.

Dan 11:14 "Now in those times many shall rise up against the king of the South. Also, violent men of your people shall

exalt themselves in fulfillment of the vision, but they shall fall.

When Antiochus III went to attack the Ptolemaic strongholds around Israel, he found some allies in certain Jewish men. The bible calls them here **violent men of your people.** This phrase is mostly used for thieves and murderers in the Old Testament, and it appears that only these types of men joined Antiochus III.

However, the *general* discontentment with the Egyptians who were ruling Judah at this time was great, and the Jews were living very difficult lives as a result of Ptolemaic rule, so it not surprising that certain Jewish men would jump at the chance to join a strong army and revolt against their oppressors.

It says that these Jewish soldiers fighting with Antiochus **shall exalt themselves in fulfillment of the vision, but they shall fall.**

Clark says that the vision these men were trying to fulfill is in Isaiah 30. He says:

> "Shall exalt themselves to establish the vision - That is, to build a temple like that of Jerusalem, in Egypt, hoping thereby to fulfill a prediction of Isaiah, Isaiah 30:18-25, which seemed to intimate that the Jews and the Egyptians should be one people. They now revolted from Ptolemy, and joined Antiochus; and this was the means of contributing greatly to the accomplishment of prophecies that foretold the calamities that should fall upon the Jews."[34]

It says that **they shall fall.** This is an interesting lesson here, because this is the one time that Israel bet on the right horse, so to speak, yet they still wound up **falling**.

Usually, despite all God's warnings not to trust their neighbors for security, Israel chose someone to protect them, and then that nation would end up being defeated by the nation that they wanted to be protected from, and Israel would be punished severely for their rebellion, in other words they would be in worse shape than if they had not chosen a side in the first place.

But in this case they did make the right decision in one sense: Antiochus III was a great power, and he would end up defeating their oppressors. But the battles were not won quickly or easily, and in fact, Antiochus suffered an early defeat at the hands of an Anatolian general named Scopas who, even though he would only hold out a little longer against Antiochus, used his brief victory to punish these men for their rebellion, thus causing them to **fall.** Though I should submit that there is very little history I could find about the details of this last event, and I am relying primarily on Clark's commentary, so I would be open to a different interpretation at this point.

Dan 11:15 So the king of the North shall come and build a siege mound, and take a fortified city; and the forces of the South shall not withstand *him.* Even his choice troops *shall have* no strength to resist.

In 200 BC, Antiochus launched a 2nd attempt to defeat Scopas. This time, he was successful. Scopas retreated to **a fortified city** (Sidon) on the coast to try to escape the pursuit of Antiochus. However, as it says here, **the forces of the South shall not withstand *him.* Even his choice troops *shall have* no strength to resist.** The forces gave in at Sidon and surrendered to Antiochus III. This would mark the end of Ptolemaic rule of Judah.

Dan 11:16 But he who comes against him shall do according to his own will, and no one shall stand against him. He shall stand in the Glorious Land with destruction in his power.

J. Paul Tanner says of this verse (a reference to the victorious Antiochus III):

> "The important port-city of Sidon had now fallen to Seleucid control, an event that enabled the Seleucids to maintain control over the interior lands. Since Egypt was too weak to mount another offensive, Antiochus III

could essentially do as he pleased. Antiochus III (with power to destroy) spent the first half of 198 BC extending his control over the rest of the former province of Coele-Syria, including Judea and Jerusalem, the Beautiful Land. Antiochus now completely dominated Coele-Syria, the prize that the Seleucid kings had long sought for (and felt was their rightful possession) since the Battle of Ipsus in 301 BC."[35]

Dan 11:17 "He shall also set his face to enter with the strength of his whole kingdom, and upright ones with him; thus shall he do. And he shall give him the daughter of women to destroy it; but she shall not stand *with him,* or be for him.

Antiochus III then began to extend his empire to the lands to the east of Syria and had great success. However, this great success came to the attention of Rome, which was beginning to become the great power in the region.

Rome essentially forced Antiochus to make a peace agreement with Egypt. Antiochus gave his daughter to the King of Egypt, which was a customary peace arrangement. However he did this hoping that, when the time was right, she would turn on her husband, and essentially be an agent for his plan to defeat the Egyptians. This is what is meant by **he shall give him the daughter of women to destroy it.**

This plan, however, did not work. When the time came, she sided with her new Egyptian family. This is what is meant by **but she shall not stand *with him,* or be for him.**

Dan 11:18 After this he shall turn his face to the coastlands, and shall take many. But a ruler shall bring the reproach against them to an end; and with the reproach removed, he shall turn back on him.

These next verses predict the downfall of the great Antiochus III.

After he made the peace agreement with the Egyptians by giving his daughter to them, he once again turned his attention to conquering more land, this time the **coastlands.**

The ESV translates this verse this way:

> (ESV) Afterward he shall turn his face to the coastlands and shall capture many of them, but a commander shall put an end to his insolence. Indeed, he shall turn his insolence back upon him.

The conquering of the coastlands of Asia Minor by Antiochus once again angered the Romans, who had many interests in the area, so they organized campaigns to destroy him. The **commander** that is referenced is Scipio Asiaticus, who defeated Antiochus in the Battle of Magnesia.

Antiochus was not killed in battle, and instead was forced to sign the Treaty of Apameia, in which he abandoned all lands east of the Tarsus Mountains, which Rome then distributed.

Dan 11:19 Then he shall turn his face toward the fortress of his own land; but he shall stumble and fall, and not be found.

After the signing of this treaty, Antiochus went to the eastern provinces of **his own land** to deal with rebellion. He was killed by an angry mob when, in need of money, he plundered the temple of Zeus in that city. The mob, outraged at this, killed him and those who were with him.

Dan 11:20 "There shall arise in his place one who imposes taxes *on* the glorious kingdom; but within a few days he shall be destroyed, but not in anger or in battle.

Antiochus III was succeeded by his son, Seleucus IV Philopator, Seleucus inherited a huge financial burden because of the taxes Rome had forced on his kingdom after their defeat and the subsequent Treaty of Apameia.

Again the ESV helps us to get a better sense of this verse:

270

"Then shall arise in his place one who shall send an exactor of tribute for the glory of the kingdom. But within a few days he shall be broken, neither in anger nor in battle. (ESV)

The **exactor of tribute** who was sent out by Seleucus was named Heliodorus. He was basically a tax collector and was hated by many. He was also sent to Jerusalem to collect taxes from the temple, but a Jewish legend says that a vision of an angel stopped him from doing so. In any case, it was this Heliodorus who would fulfill the next part of this verse, namely that King Seleucus would not be killed in **anger or in battle**. Heliodorus poisoned the king in hopes of taking his place.

Dan 11:21 And in his place shall arise a vile person, to whom they will not give the honor of royalty; but he shall come in peaceably, and seize the kingdom by intrigue.

And now we come to the most infamous Antiochus: Antiochus IV or Antiochus Epiphanies. He is the **vile person** being referred to in this verse, mostly because of his persecution of the Jews, which we will detail later.

They will not give the honor of royalty; but he shall come in peaceably, and seize the kingdom by intrigue.

Antiochus did not come to power by the usual way, either by conquest or by being the rightful heir to the throne. He was also a son of Antiochus III, just like his brother Seleucus, whom we just talked about.

However, after Heliodorus the tax collector killed his brother, the rightful heir to the throne was Seleucus' son, who was in Rome at the time, though Heliodorus took the throne after he killed the king anyway.

Antiochus had Heliodorus the usurper killed, and he took the throne himself. He was only able to get away with this because he declared that he would be co-ruling with the rightful heir (his

271

nephew) who was still in Rome. However, he later had his nephew killed, and thus took the kingdom **by intrigue.**

Dan 11:22 With the force of a flood they shall be swept away from before him and be broken, and also the prince of the covenant.

There is some disagreement on this passage, which I think derives in part because of some difficulties with the Hebrew at this point.

After Antiochus took power, he heard that the Egyptians were planning a war to retake the area around Israel (Coele-Syria). So he preemptively attacked the Egyptian armies and **swept away** and **broke** all the armies he encountered. In fact, he conquered almost all of Egypt, with the exception of Alexandria.

During this first campaign, he also took captive the prince Ptolemy VI, who could be the referent for the **prince of the covenant**, though some make a good case for this being a reference to Onias III, the high priest in Jerusalem, who was ousted by an arrangement with pro-Hellenist elements within the Jewish nobility with the backing of Antiochus.

After his capture, Ptolemy VI made a covenant to become an ally of Antiochus if the Syrians would help him regain his throne in Egypt, which had been taken by his younger brother, Ptolemy VII. Antiochus was delighted to make such a pact, for he felt that it would give him a foothold in Egypt.[36]

Dan 11:23 And after the league *is made* with him he shall act deceitfully, for he shall come up and become strong with a small *number of* people.

After Antiochus and Ptolemy made this pact, Ptolemy would end up breaking the terms of the agreement. Instead of being a pro-Syrian puppet, as Antiochus had hoped, Ptolomy would join forces with his brother, which was **a small *number of* people** which would **become strong.** They would eventually ally with the Romans as well and defeat Antiochus.

But in the meantime, after Antiochus' initial victory over all but Alexandria, he would have a time of great prosperity.

Dan 11:24 He shall enter peaceably, even into the richest places of the province; and he shall do *what* his fathers have not done, nor his forefathers: he shall disperse among them the plunder, spoil, and riches; and he shall devise his plans against the strongholds, but *only* for a time.

This verse is referring to the time just after Antiochus defeated all but Alexandria. He was able to basically loot all of Egypt, which was incredibly wealthy. It says **he shall do *what* his fathers have not done, nor his forefathers: he shall disperse among them the plunder, spoil, and riches**
This is a reference to what Antiochus did with the wealth he obtained during this period. A book written about his life in 2006 by Peter Franz Mittag is kind of a revisionist history trying to paint him in a good light, yet nevertheless it offers never-before-heard information about Antiochus and his career.

In it, there is a section that seems to validate this verse, where it describes the various ways that Antiochus used the spoils of this particular war to please the people.

He shall devise his plans against the strongholds, but *only* for a time.

During this time, Antiochus had high hopes about what he could accomplish if he could only finish the job and attack the **stronghold** of Alexandria. He plotted and planned, but this time of high hopes was not to last. It was indeed *only* **for a time.**

Dan 11:25 "He shall stir up his power and his courage against the king of the South with a great army. And the king of the South shall be stirred up to battle with a very great and mighty army; but he shall not stand, for they shall devise plans against him.

Dan 11:26 Yes, those who eat of the portion of his delicacies shall destroy him; his army shall be swept away, and many shall fall down slain.

Starting here and ending at verse 28, the text goes into more detail about the 1st campaign of Antiochus. In other words, it kind of rehashes the same information that appears in verses 22-24 about the first and only successful campaign of Antiochus. This is also the view of Miller.[37]

This time, however, it seems to focus more on the deceptive nature of Ptolemy's advisors, and the role they played in the initial downfall of Egypt in the first part of the war.

He shall stir up his power and his courage against the king of the South with a great army.

This is a reference to Antiochus conquering nearly all of Egypt, which was discussed earlier.

But he shall not stand, for they shall devise plans against him.

The reason that Ptolomy was defeated by Antiochus is because **they shall devise plans against him.**
The "**they**" is clarified in the next verse when it says **Yes, those who eat of the portion of his delicacies shall destroy him.**

This is referring to the counselors of Ptolomy (who was only a boy king of 16). The counselors were in the pay of Antiochus and seemed to sabotage the whole affair. Some suggest that because they forced Ptolemy to declare war on Antiochus, it gave him the moral high ground to "preemptively strike".

It seems that there was an attempt already to oust Ptolomy in favor of his brother and his niece Cleopatra. This deception by his counselors may have been the ends to those means.

Dan 11:27 Both these kings' hearts *shall be* bent on evil, and they shall speak lies at the same table; but it shall not prosper, for the end *will* still *be* at the appointed time.

This is again a reference to the deal between Antiochus and his now prisoner, Ptolomy, to work together to put Ptolomy back on the throne in exchange for him becoming a puppet of Antiochus. This verse indicates that neither Antiochus nor Ptolomy had any intention of following through with this plan.

Dan 11:28 While returning to his land with great riches, his heart shall be *moved* against the holy covenant; so he shall do *damage* and return to his own land.

It is tempting to see this verse as the famous incident of Antiochus going to Israel in a rage after his defeat by the Romans, but that will come later. This verse is speaking of his first victorious return from Eqypt to his **own land** (Syria). Of course, to get there, he had to pass through Israel, during which he went into the temple and stole the treasures therein. He did not at this time commit the abominations that are so famous.

This looting the temple on his way back to Antioch is mentioned in I Maccabees 1:20-24; this is the *damage* he will do before he returns **to his own land.**

Dan 11:29 "At the appointed time he shall return and go toward the south; but it shall not be like the former or the latter.

Now we get to Antiochus' second attempt to take the kingdom of Egypt. One of the reasons that his invasion would **not be like the former or the latter** was because, during his absence from Egypt, his puppet king reconciled with his brother and joined forces. When Antiochus heard of this betrayal, he made haste to attack them both. However, the new Egyptian coalition had another trick up its sleeve: the Romans.

The Egyptians had written to Rome and told them about how Antiochus was behaving in violation of the Treaty of Apameia signed by Antiochus' father. In fact, the only reason that Antiochus had success in his first campaign against Egypt was probably because at the time Rome was tied up in the third Macedonian war and didn't have the resources to enforce the treaty.

But by Antiochus' 2nd attempt to take Egypt, Rome had finished its war, and had both the time and the resources to deal with the situation. It sent help to the Egyptians.

Dan 11:30 For ships from Cyprus shall come against him; therefore he shall be grieved, and return in rage against the holy covenant, and do *damage.* **"So he shall return and show regard for those who forsake the holy covenant.**

For ships from Cyprus shall come against him

The literal phrase is not Cyprus, but rather Kittim, which in Jewish literature (such as the Dead Sea Scrolls) was used specifically for Rome, but it was also generally used for the region of the Mediterranean including Cyprus. Since the following event occurred in Cyprus, it would seem that, either way, this is a match.

What happened is that Rome, hearing that the Ptolomaic kingdom was about to be destroyed, and having just concluded its war against Macedon, sent ships to Cyprus to attack Antiochus.

After they defeated Antiochus, the general Gaius Popillius Laenas did something from which we get the phrase "line in the sand". He demanded the defeated Antiochus immediately end the war and completely withdrawal from Egypt. Antiochus basically said he needed to think about it, but Gaius Popillius Laenas drew a circle around him in the sand and told him that he needed to give an answer before he stepped out of the circle. Antiochus, totally humiliated, then agreed to all the Roman terms.

Therefore he shall be grieved, and return in rage against the holy covenant, and do *damage.*

Antiochus was **enraged** for a number of reasons at this point as he headed back to Israel.
The first is obvious: he had lost a battle in a humiliating way, a battle that he spent his whole political career planning for, and had come very close to winning.

The second reason was that a revolt had broken out in Judea, partially because a false report said that Antiochus had died, which then caused the Jewish people to oust the puppet high priest whom Antiochus had put in to rule them. But when Antiochus arrived and it was obvious that he hadn't died, he reinstated his high priest and began a number of atrocities which are in view in the following verses.

He shall return and show regard for those who forsake the holy covenant

This verse states pretty much the same thing as verse 32, which says:

> "Those who do wickedly against the covenant he shall corrupt with flattery"

At this point in Jewish history, there were a number of factions in Israel, one of which was radically pro-Greek or pro-Hellenist. Antiochus had a policy of acting favorably to those Jews willing to turn from the biblical faith and embrace Hellenization.

This paints an interesting picture of Antiochus who is usually described at this point as a madman, but there seems to have been a method to his madness, even in this time of humiliation and defeat. His main goal seems to have been the stabilization and consolidation of what parts of his empire he had left. This would necessarily include (as he saw it) making an example of the Jews who did not embrace Hellenism, and who were a part of the recent rebellion against his Hellenist puppet.

The fact that he is twice referred to as being kind to those who got with the program is evidence that he was not acting in blind rage, but with a sense of political savvy.

This also perhaps gives up some insight into the Antichrist, who also will cause a great apostasy, not just by deception, but also by providing incentives to apostatize. In the case of the Antichrist, the ones who leave their faith will have their lives spared, but they will also be able to buy and sell again. This is a deal that is hard to refuse, and will require steadfast faith on the part of the saints to do so.

Though it will not be until verse 36, five verses later, that the future Antichrist will be in view, I do think that about here we start to see the beginnings of the "fade effect", where certain elements apply to one or both Antiochus and the Antichrist.

There will be more on why conservative scholars are in agreement that the future Antichrist is in view when we get to verse 36.

Dan 11:31 And forces shall be mustered by him, and they shall defile the sanctuary fortress; then they shall take away the daily *sacrifices*, and place *there* the abomination of desolation.

Antiochus's **forces** carried out a wide range of policies and acts that **defile the sanctuary fortress.**

Here is a list of these acts and policies from J. Paul Tanner:

> (a) A special emissary was sent to Judea to force the Jews to transgress the
> laws of their religion.
> (b) Jewish ritual was prohibited (1 Macc 1:45-6).
> (c) The sacred precincts were formally given over to the worship of Zeus
> Olympias (1 Macc 1:54; 2 Macc 6:2).
> (d) Copies of the Torah were burned.
> (e) Sabbath keeping and circumcision were forbidden.

(f) Jews were forced to celebrate the king's birthday every month and to
participate in the festal procession of Dionysus.
(g) High places and altars on which swine and other animals were to be
sacrificed were erected throughout Judea. Inspectors were appointed to
enforce this.[38]

Then they shall take away the daily *sacrifices,* and place *there* the abomination of desolation.

The worst of all the atrocities was the **abomination of desolation.** Having taken away **the daily *sacrifices,*** as they were a part of Jewish rituals which Antiochus saw as a threat to Greek rule, in their place, he put some kind of pagan altar. Its exact nature is disputed somewhat, though according to 2 Macc 6:2, the sanctuary was to be renamed "the temple of Olympian Zeus."[39]

Dan 11:32 Those who do wickedly against the covenant he shall corrupt with flattery; but the people who know their God shall be strong, and carry out *great exploits.*

The first part of this verse was covered in the discussion of verse 30.

But the people who know their God shall be strong, and carry out *great exploits.*

Miller explains this reference to those who opposed Antiochus's attempt to outlaw Judaism:

> "Yet even in this dark period there were true believers ("the people who know their God") among the Jews who remained faithful to their God... Foremost among those who resisted the oppressive measures of Antiochus were the Maccabees.

> A certain priest named Mattathias ...refused to forsake
> his God (cf. 1 Macc 2:1–14). He had five sons, three of
> whom ... became known as the Maccabees...
>
> The Maccabees successfully overthrew the Syrian yoke
> through a series of brilliant military victories (apparently
> predicted in Zech 9:13–17) against Antio-chus's military
> commanders... as a result the temple was rededicated
> (Hanukkah) to Yahweh on 25 Chislev (December 14)
> 164 B.C. (1 Macc 4:52)."[40]

**Dan 11:33 And those of the people who understand shall
instruct many; yet *for many* days they shall fall by sword and
flame, by captivity and plundering.**
**Dan 11:34 Now when they fall, they shall be aided with a
little help; but many shall join with them by intrigue.**
**Dan 11:35 And *some* of those of understanding shall fall, to
refine them, purify *them,* and make *them* white, *until* the time
of the end; because *it is* still for the appointed time.**

These verses describe the actions of those involved in the
Maccabean revolt on the one hand, describing their martyrdom
in their fight to restore their right to practice Judaism.

However, because the next verse after this begins the
unambiguous shift from Antiochus to the Antichrist, and
considering that the abomination of desolation spoken of in verse
31 is supposed to in part refer to the future abomination of the
Antichrist (see Dan 12:11), I think I am on firm footing here
when I see these verses as partially, if not mostly to do with the
saints persecuted by the Antichrist in the future, as well as
referring in part to the Maccabean rebellion.

If the fade-in, fade-out example I used earlier is true, then this
would be the point in the fade where you can see more details
from the picture that you were fading to at this point rather than
the picture you were fading from, and by the next verse (36), I
don't think you will be able to see the Antiochus picture
anymore at all, which is precisely the reason the next section is
so interesting.

If these three verses apply to the future persecuted church by the Antichrist after the "abomination of desolation", then it is an accurate picture of that time, since we see a few key elements that are repeated in the New Testament of that persecution.

For example, the reason for allowing the martyrdom is **to refine them, purify** *them,* **and make** *them* **white,** *until* **the time of the end.**

This is also the reason why God grants the Antichrist the power to kill the saints (1 Peter 4:12-19, Rev 6:9-11).

Also the next line *until* **the time of the end; because** *it is* **still for the appointed time**

It seems to be a parallel to Matthew 24 when the Lord talks at length about the time of the Antichrist's persecution. He says:

> And ye shall hear of wars and rumours of wars: see that ye be not troubled: for all *these things* must come to pass, but the end is not yet. - Mat 24:6

The "end" will come after the persecution of the saints, which Jesus clarifies a few verses later:

> Then shall they deliver you up to be afflicted, and shall kill you: and ye shall be hated of all nations for my name's sake. And then shall many be offended, and shall betray one another, and shall hate one another. And many false prophets shall rise, and shall deceive many. And because iniquity shall abound, the love of many shall wax cold. But he that shall endure unto the end, the same shall be saved. And this gospel of the kingdom shall be preached in all the world for a witness unto all nations; and then shall the end come. - Mat 24:9-14

Dan 11:36 "Then the king shall do according to his own will: he shall exalt and magnify himself above every god, shall speak blasphemies against the God of gods, and shall prosper

till the wrath has been accomplished; for what has been determined shall be done.

Up to this point in Daniel chapter 11, we have been dealing with a succession of kings from the Seleucid and Ptolemaic Empires, concluding in verses 21-35 with the "vile" King Antiochus IV Epiphanies.

In this verse, however, we have the beginning of a transition to someone other than Antiochus.

Stephen Miller says on this point:

> "Exegetical necessity requires that 11:36–45 be applied to someone other than Antiochus IV."[41]

Miller is expressing the majority view of conservatives about this section of scripture. That is, by the time we get to verse 36 of Daniel 11, there are certain clues in the text that demand the reader see the king spoken of there as someone other than Antiochus.

Most of these conservative scholars would say that this new king is referring to the Antichrist of the last days, for reasons we will detail later.

First of all, we should note that such a transition has precedent within this very chapter.
Very often in chapter 11: 1-36, the actual king who is in view will change from one verse to the next, while still calling him the "King of the North" or the "King of the South."

The reader, by this point in the chapter, has become accustomed to looking for a new historical character from one verse to the next, even though he is referred to by the same general title, i.e. "King of the North" or "South".

Even the significant leap forward in time from one character to the next, which would be required in the Antichrist interpretation, has precedent in the chapter.

J. Paul Tanner expresses the point this way:

> "A sudden leap forward in time from Dan 11:35 to 11:36 is consistent with other leaps in time throughout the chapter (e.g. 11:2–3)."[42]

The following are some of the points that scholars have cited as their reasons for seeing a shift from Antiochus to someone else at this point:

1.) In verse 40, we are told that the temporal context of this king is during the "time of the end". There is a further defining of what that phrase means in 12:1, which starts out with the phrase "at that time", i.e. during the time of this "time of the end" king.

It goes on to say that "at that time" will begin "a time of trouble, such as never was since there was a nation, Even to that time," an obvious reference to the so-called "Great Tribulation" which begins at the midpoint of Daniel's 70th week.

If that wasn't enough to place this king in an eschatological context, he then goes on to say that "at that time" also includes the resurrection of the dead (12:2).

2.) The previous section about Antiochus was accurate to the last detail, yet from verse 36 on, we find descriptions of this king that are impossible to apply to Antiochus. These same details, in many cases, can be found in other places in scripture as descriptions of the Antichrist.

> "For example, Antiochus did not exalt himself above every god (vv. 36–37), reject "the gods of his fathers," or worship "a god unknown to his fathers" (v. 38); on the contrary, he worshiped the Greek pantheon, even building an altar and offering sacrifices to Zeus in the Jerusalem

temple precincts. Daniel also predicted that this king "will come to his end" in Palestine (v. 45), but it is a matter of historical record that Antiochus IV died at Tabae in Persia."[43]

As we go through this study, we will find many other points of divergence between Antiochus and this new king.

3.) J. Paul Tanner notes "Verse 35 still anticipates the "end time," whereas v. 40 reflects that the "end time" has finally come."[44]

4.) Tanner makes another very important point that we will defend at length later on when he says:

> "In vv. 21–35 Antiochus IV served in the role of the "King of the North," as did the other Seleucid kings before him. In v. 40, however, "the king" is apparently in contention with both the "King of the North" and the "King of the South."[45]

5.) Finally, it should be noted that the king in verse 36 is simply called "the king" not the "King of the North" or the "King of the South," as has been the very consistent pattern previously.

This is especially important when you take into account all the other kinds of shifts that happen at verse 36. In other words, if there was ever a time to reestablish which king you are talking about, it would be verse 36, yet the text simply calls this person "the king."

For these, as well as many other reasons that I am about to explain, I will be writing this commentary with the assumption that the Antichrist is in view in verses 36-45, a view which I share with nearly every conservative expositor.

"Then the king shall do according to his own will:

It is certainly possible that this reference to the king doing **his own will** could simply be a reference to his not taking orders from anyone else, especially in contrast to Christ, who consistently did his "Father's will" (John 5:30).

I think it's also possible that this phrase could have something to do with his military might, as the phrase is used by Daniel to refer to earthly kings like Alexander the Great (8:4) and Antiochus I the Great (11:16). In that context, "doing their own will" is speaking of them conquering in a military sense. Both views are possible and not mutually exclusive.

> I saw the ram (Alexander) pushing westward, northward, and southward, so that no animal could withstand him; nor was there any that could deliver from his hand, <u>but he did according to his will</u> and became great. - Dan 8:4

He shall exalt and magnify himself above every god, shall speak blasphemies against the God of gods

We are given similar information about the Antichrist in Daniel 7:26:

> "He shall speak pompous words against the Most High"

We are told that he will **magnify himself above every god.** This particular idea that the man of sin will not just be a blasphemer, but will declare himself greater than all gods, including Yahweh, is quoted by Paul in 2 Thessalonians 2:4 when he says of the Antichrist:

> Who opposes and exalts himself above all that is called God or that is worshiped, so that he sits as God in the temple of God, showing himself that he is God.

It would appear that the so-called "revealing" of the Antichrist occurs here at the midpoint when he sits in the temple and makes this blasphemous declaration. It is not at all clear to me if this was his public theology for the first 3.5 years; I suspect not. It is my guess that the abomination of desolation occurs at some point after his apparent resurrection from the dead, and this is possibly when this theology about being higher than every god develops.

And shall prosper till the wrath has been accomplished; for what has been determined shall be done.

This is a reference to the Antichrist being given power to **prosper** for a short time.

> It was granted to him to make war with the saints and to overcome them. And authority was given him over every tribe, tongue, and nation. - Rev 13:7

He will only prosper **till the wrath has been accomplished.** This is a reference to God's wrath, a wrath that must come as a part of the eschatological end of the age. This is referenced by Daniel in other places. For example, in Daniel 8:19 he calls it there the "latter time of the indignation." When God's wrath has been accomplished, the man of sin will be imprisoned in the Abyss with the false prophet and eventually be destroyed (Rev 20: 2-10).

Dan 11:37 He shall regard neither the God of his fathers nor the desire of women, nor regard any god; for he shall exalt himself above them all.

He shall regard neither the God of his fathers

This verse is often twisted and tweaked to suit a particular commentator's presuppositions about the Antichrist. Even certain Bible translations make the "G" in god lowercase and add an "s" (making it gods and not God) to make it seem as if Yahweh is definitely not in view here. I have even heard commentators say that, "in the Hebrew, "Elohim" is plural in this case," but such a statement is either ignorant or dishonest.

Take Arnold Fruchtenbaum, for example, who writes:

> "Any student of Hebrew would see from the original Hebrew text that

the correct translation should be 'the gods of his fathers' and not the 'God of his fathers'"[46]

First of all, this statement is simply not true. Dr. Michael Hesier is more than "any student" of Hebrew, having a PhD in Hebrew Bible and Semitic languages. He points out the fallacy of Fruchtenbaum's statement when he says:

"Elohim can be either singular or plural depending on context."[47]

Hesier goes on to give an example of how to determine if Elohim is singular or plural. He says the word Elohim or "God" in Hebrew is a lot like the word "sheep" or "deer" in English; they can be singular or plural, depending on the context. For example, in the sentence "The sheep are lost", we know that the usage is plural, but in the sentence "The sheep is lost", we know that it is singular.

Dr J. Paul Tanner, also a Hebrew expert, agrees with Hesier, and adds another point in favor of this being a reference to Yahweh in his class notes on Dan 11:

"The Hebrew term Elohim can be translated as "God" or "gods."
Elaboration: While either translation is grammatically correct, we should observe that the
expression "the God of his fathers" is a commonly used phrase in the OT to refer to Israel's
covenant God, Yahweh, who had long associated Himself by covenant with the "fathers" of the
nation.

He goes on to reference a number of instances when this Hebrew phrase is used:
Ex 3:16, 1 Chr 28:9, 2 Kg 21:22, Gen 31:29, Gen 46:1,3, Jer 19:4, Dan 2:23.

Think of how damaging that point is to Fruchtenbaum's argument. He says that "any student" of Hebrew would know that Elohim is plural here, yet in other instances in scripture, the exact same phrase is translated as <u>singular</u>, where it is quite clear that Yawheh is in view, not pagan gods, while conversely the phrase is never used to refer to pagan gods.

The significance of this verse is that it would be strong evidence that the Antichrist will be of Jewish origin. This would seem to make sense if he is to pass himself off as the Messiah, as there would be little hope of a man being accepted as the Messiah to the Jews unless he was in fact Jewish. Although this doctrine is difficult to be dogmatic about, there are other passages that seem to suggest this too, such as Ezekiel 28:10.

Joel Richardson, author of *The Mideast Beast* and a proponent of the Islamic Antichrist theory, somewhat ironically agrees with the idea that this phrase is speaking about Yahweh and not pagan gods, though he makes the case that when it says that the Antichrist will not regard the "God of his fathers," it is a reference to how an Islamic person's lineage ultimately would go back to Abraham through Ishmael.

This too would have problems.

1.) It is unprecedented. There is no indication of any usage of the phrase "God of his fathers" to refer to anyone except Jews in the Bible.
2.) The "fathers" are a very district group of people when used in this context. Often they are even named as Abraham, Isaac, and Jacob. The very idea that multiple "fathers" plural are in view in this phrase is an argument against this because, in Richardson's view, there is only one father who could be said to be part of Ishmael's lineage, and that is Abraham. Abraham's son Jacob, later re-named Israel, is where the patriarchal covenant line starts. It is highly doubtful then that scripture would use this phrase "God of His fathers" to refer to someone outside the covenant line of Abraham, Isaac, and Jacob, which Ishmael certainly would be.

Nor the desire of women

288

There are two main views about this passage:

1.) That the Antichrist will be a homosexual, or at least unconcerned with women.
2.) This phrase is a way of speaking of Jesus, that is that the Antichrist will have no regard for the true Messiah, who is desired of women in the sense that Jewish women desire to give birth to the Messiah.

I would suggest a third option before discussing each one, and that is that this could simply be referring to childbirth itself, not necessarily messianic childbirth, in other words, that the Antichrist will not care about the desire of women, which is having children in general, a common biblical theme. This could be referring to 1 Timothy 4:3, which says that in the "latter times," marriage will be prohibited, which could be extended to mean there will be an end-times ban on childbirth as well.

I think that all three interpretations are possible based on the grammar. However, I tend to lean toward the view that this is talking about Jesus because of the context.

Let's look at this verse again to see why I say that.

> "He shall regard neither the God of his fathers **nor the desire of women**, nor regard any god; for he shall exalt himself above them all."

There are three ideas expressed here, the first that he won't regard the God of his fathers, the second idea is the one in question, and the third is about him exalting himself above any god.

It would seem to me that the second idea about the desire of women would most likely be associated with the theme of his blasphemous acts, which the first and third ideas are. If it were talking about him being a homosexual or abolishing childbirth, it would seem to be contextually out of place, sandwiched between two ideas of the same nature. However, if it were talking about

Chapter 11   Daniel

the Messiah, then it would make great sense. It would read something like this:

> "He will not regard God or the Messiah but will exalt himself above them both."

Many commenters take this position, and though I have not seen clear evidence myself of the historical or cultural desire of Jewish women being to give birth to the Messiah, there is some indication of this found in the Gospel of Luke, in which Mary says:

> "My soul magnifies the Lord, and my spirit has rejoiced in God my Savior. For He has regarded the lowly state of His maidservant; for behold, henceforth all generations will call me blessed" (Luke 1:46–48).

It may be that Daniel used this (desire of women) idea to refer to the Messiah's prophesized human birth. We see in Genesis 3:15 that the Messiah would come thorough childbirth, that is through Eve. One could also see his references to the "son of man" in Daniel 7:13-14 as a precursor to this language in Daniel which he used to refer to the Messiah.

Dan 11:38 But in their place he shall honor a god of fortresses; and a god which his fathers did not know he shall honor with gold and silver, with precious stones and pleasant things.

But in their place he shall honor a god of fortresses;

The Antichrist seems to honor a god other that the true God and his son. This is also paradoxical. On the one hand, we are just told he honors no gods but himself, and on the other, we are told that he does honor a god. In order to try to figure this out, we need to read the entire section and get as much information about this **god of fortresses** as we can.

> But in their place he shall honor a god of fortresses; and a god which his fathers did not know he shall honor with gold and silver, with precious stones and pleasant things. Thus he shall act against the strongest fortresses with a foreign god, which he shall acknowledge, and advance its glory; and he shall cause them to rule over many, and divide the land for gain. - Dan 11:38-39

It appears that this worshipping of the god of fortresses is not simply for show, but in fact real homage is paid and genuine reward for that homage is given, rewards such as him being able to successfully conquer lands and causing him to rule over many, both of which are attributed to this god that he worships.

If one considers these details, then the identity of this **god of forces** or fortresses can be surmised, because we know by what power the Antichrist conquers the nations and rules over many:

> Now the beast which I saw was like a leopard, his feet were like the feet of a bear, and his mouth like the mouth of a lion. <u>The dragon gave him his power, his throne, and great authority.</u> - Rev 13:2

The dragon is an unambiguous reference to Satan in Revelation 13.
Another example of this idea that the Antichrist derives his power from Satan is in 2 Thessalonians 2:

> The coming of the lawless one <u>is according to the working of Satan, with all power, signs, and lying wonders.</u> - 2Th 2:9

It is admittedly difficult in this reading to understand the phrase **a god which his fathers did not know**, because in one sense Satan was known even by Adam. Perhaps it could be a reference to a more intimate "knowing", like in this case worshipping. There is no clear picture of anyone knowingly worshipping Satan in the Bible that I am aware of.

He shall honor with gold and silver, with precious stones and pleasant things.

There is only one other place that this phrase "gold and silver, with precious stones can be found in the Bible. That is in Revelation 18:12, in reference to the items that are brought to Mystery Babylon.

In my book *Mystery Babylon When Jerusalem Embraces the Antichrist*, I go through every item that the merchants bring to the city of Jerusalem and show that, in each case, there is a connection to the rebuilding of the temple, the reinstitution of the sacrificial system, as well as a massive worldwide pilgrimage system which I'm sure the Antichrist intends to make look like the institution of the millennial reign.

I believe that this sacrifice of Gold and silver to Satan is fulfilled with the image of the beast.

> And he [false prophet] deceives those who dwell on the earth—by those signs which he was granted to do in the sight of the beast, telling those who dwell on the earth to make an image to the beast who was wounded by the sword and lived.
> He was granted power to give breath to the image of the beast, that the image of the beast should both speak and cause as many as would not worship the image of the beast to be killed. - Rev 13:14-15

The image of the beast seems to be placed in the temple after the abomination of desolation for the purpose of receiving the worship of humanity. Paul tells us that spiritual beings can essentially receive the worship that people direct toward idols (1 Cor 10:20). It would seem probable that Satan is receiving the worship directed to the image of the beast.

Revelation 13:4 seems to make this point clear:

> So they worshiped the dragon who gave authority to the beast; and they worshiped the beast, saying, "Who is like

the beast? Who is able to make war with him?" - Rev
13:4

Here we are told that the dragon (Satan) is worshipped, and also
the beast (the Antichrist). This dual worship could be explained
by the scenario I outlined here.

I suggest that the image of the beast is an image of the Antichrist
put in the temple to be worshipped. This is done because the
Antichrist cannot stay in the temple, as he has wars to make.
This must be done however in order to seem to fulfill the
prophecies of the Messiah sitting in the temple and receiving
gifts from the world pilgrimage continually.

It may even be that the materials used in the image of the beast's
construction are "**gold, silver, and precious things.**" I say this
because the false prophet tells *those who dwell on the earth* to
make an image to the beast, and it may be, that it is just like in
Exodus when the people used their gold jewelry to make the
image of the calf. That is they used their **gold, silver, and
precious things** to make the image of the beast But this point is
unclear.

**Dan 11:39 Thus he shall act against the strongest fortresses
with a foreign god, which he shall acknowledge, and advance
its glory; and he shall cause them to rule over many, and
divide the land for gain.**

**Thus he shall act against the strongest fortresses with a
foreign god**

This is referring to the wars of the Antichrist, which are detailed
in verses 40-45. Satan, as we have seen, is the power behind this
conquering of **fortresses** by the Antichrist.

Acknowledge, and advance its glory;

It is difficult to reconcile the idea of the Antichrist exalting
himself above every god as well as **acknowledging** and
advancing this **foreign god,** though I think the answer can be

found in Revelation 13:4, where people are worshipping Satan, who gave the beast his power as well as the beast himself.

While this verse seems to suggest an **acknowledging** of Satan by the Antichrist in some way, it is not clear to me if this acknowledging of Satan will be obvious to the people who may interpret this god of the Antichrist in a different way.

Which he shall acknowledge, and advance its glory; and he shall cause them to rule over many, and divide the land for gain.

This phrase is a little hard to understand in the NKJV, so I will quote from the NET to give a better Idea of its meaning:

> "To those who recognize him he will grant considerable honor. He will place them in authority over many people, and he will parcel out land for a price."

This is a similar tactic to that employed by Antiochus IV, where in Daniel 11:30,32, we see that he gave rewards to those who forsook God and followed him. It seems that the people in view here are rulers of nations and that they go over to his banner when he offers them these rewards.

So we should expect that in addition to wars, the Antichrist uses generous diplomatic tactics to help conquer much of the world.

And he shall cause them to rule over many, and divide the land for gain.

It would appear that the Antichrist's wars, detailed in the following verses, suggest that the world will be remade in such a way that he is able to decide who rules what. There might be more information about who these people are in Daniel 7, as well as in the following verses:

Dan 11:40 "At the time of the end the King of the South shall attack him; and the King of the North shall come against him like a whirlwind, with chariots, horsemen, and

with many ships; and he shall enter the countries, overwhelm them, and pass through.

At the time of the end

Here we have an explicit indication of this being eschatological, especially when combined with 12:1, which refers to the Great Tribulation and the resurrection of the dead.

The King of the South shall attack him

We learn that the Antichrist will be attacked by the King of the South. Most scholars see this southern king as being the King of Egypt, as that was the identity of the King of the South in the earlier parts of this chapter. It would seem that verse 43 validates this idea, as there we are told specifically that Egypt will be conquered by the Antichrist. I would suggest that this phrase King of the South in the end times could include more countries than Egypt but it must also include Egypt.

And the King of the North shall come against him like a whirlwind, with chariots, horsemen, and with many ships;

Because the grammar is not quite clear as to whom "him" is referring to here, there has arisen a division on how to interpret this verse.

Two main theories have been developed; they are sometimes called the "three king theory" and the "two king theory."

On the one hand, you have the three king theory, which sees there being three subjects in verse 40: the Antichrist, the King of the North, and the King of the South. Using brackets to explain the pronoun referents, it would read as follows:

> And at the end time the King of the South will collide with him [the Antichrist], and the King of the North will storm against him [the Antichrist]…and he [the Antichrist] will enter countries, overflow them, and pass through.[48]

So, in this reading, the King of the South attacks the Antichrist, then the King of the North attacks him as well, but the Antichrist defeats them both.

The two king theory has only two subjects in view. This is because they see the King of the North as the Antichrist, so it would read like this:

> And at the end time the King of the South will collide with him [the King of the North = the Antichrist], and the King of the North [the Antichrist] will storm against him [the King of the South]…and he [the King of the North = the Antichrist] will enter countries, overflow them, and pass through.[49]

In this reading, it would be saying that the King of the South attacks the King of the North, who is also the Antichrist, but the King of the North / Antichrist attacks the King of the South as well, and the Antichrist will be victorious.

One way to explain the difference is to say that, after the introduction of the Antichrist in verse 36, all pronouns "him" or "his" are referring to the Antichrist, whereas the two king view has the references going back and forth.

It may not seem like it, but this is a crucial point if the church hopes to derive the geopolitical rise of the Antichrist from this chapter, and in the correct way.

Depending on your view, you could be looking for a very different set of events for the rise of the Antichrist on the world scene.

J. Paul Tanner has demonstrated that the Hebrew grammar is not much help for either view, and that both readings are technically possible.[50] So we will have to rely on other factors if we hope fully understand this most critical verse.

Tanner defends the three king theory in his paper *Daniel's "King of the North": Do We Owe Russia An Apology?* And I would direct anyone interested in this to read that paper, as he also interacts with the leading arguments against his theory.

I propose that the three king theory is the correct way to understand this passage, and I will sum up a few points about why I think so. Then I will interact with some criticism made recently about this view by Joel Richardson.

First, I think that the usage of "him" here to refer to different kings back and forth without clarification is unprecedented in this chapter, and it would constitute an entirely new way to express who is fighting whom. Tanner sums it up this way:

> "In Dan 11:40, the pronouns on the prepositions marking the recipient of the verbal action (עָלָיו
> and עָלָיו) are quite *out of keeping* with the way the hostilities between the two kings were previously described in the chapter. What I mean to say is that elsewhere in the chapter, whenever an assault by one of the kings against the other was mentioned, the one who was the object is specified by his full title (not merely by a pronoun)…In light of this characteristic writing style of the author, the "him" is more likely the same referent in this verse, namely, "the king" of the preceding paragraph, i.e., the Antichrist. This favors the three-king theory."[51]

Tanner also notes that when referencing this king in verse 36, it simply calls him "the king," not using either "of the North" or "of the South," a particularly important point considering that it would mark the only time in this chapter when this occurs (save verse 27, when it is referencing both kings).

I suggest that the three king theory is the most natural reading of the text, and that is why it is the majority view. Basically, after the Antichrist is introduced by the angel in verse 36, it quickly becomes obvious that the angel is again describing the same guy who has dominated Daniel's attention through the entire book, like in Daniel 7, where Daniel specifically asks the angel to tell him more about the Antichrist, or in Daniel 8, when after hearing about the Antichrist, Daniel is sick for many days. And so when it becomes clear that that same guy, who has now been the main subject of three separate visions of Daniel, is again in view, it is only natural that from then on, the word "him" refers back to that dominating character, You can see the same basic pattern of pronouns in any of the other visions concerning the Antichrist in the book of Daniel.

Joel Richardson, a proponent of the two king theory, argues that in the three king view, the King of the North and the King of the South have become allies, a point that he strongly disagrees with.

> "… the kings of the North and South, who are enemies throughout the historical portion of the prophecy, are suddenly cast as allies together against the Antichrist."[52]

I have two things to say about this point; the first is that this is not a necessary conclusion of the three king theory at all. Richardson quotes Tim Lahaye, who theorizes that since the King of the North attacks the Antichrist, and the King of the South attacks him, that this is coordinated attack of allies against their common enemy (the Antichrist).

That view is assumed by Lahaye, but the text certainly does not say that they are coordinated, joint attacks against the Antichrist or that these two kings are allies in any way. In addition, we are not given the chronology of these attacks. How far apart is the attack of the King of the North from the attack of the King of the South? We are not told. It could be years between these attacks. It could simply be that the Antichrist is attempting to gain control over the entire region, and these are isolated attempts of these countries at protecting themselves from the Antichrist.

The second point I would like to make is that even IF these countries make an alliance here against the Antichrist, it is not damaging to the three king theory at all. In fact, contrary to what Richardson said, such a thing has precedence in the historical portion of Daniel 11. For example, an alliance was formed in verse 6 between the King of the North and the King of the South. There is no biblical reason that these kings would not find it advantageous to form an end-times alliance in light of a mutual enemy of the magnitude of the Antichrist.

Another criticism of the three king view that Richardson makes is the following:

> "The three king view turns Antiochus into both a type of the Antichrist (throughout all of Daniel chapter 8 as well as Daniel 11:21-35) and a type of the Antichrist's greatest enemy [He says this because the antichrist will defeat the King of the North which Antiochus was obviously a part of when that title referred to the Seleucid Empire]."[53]

Richardson first assumes that Antiochus is in view after verse 36, which almost every conservative scholar would disagree with. Antiochus cannot be said to have fulfilled anything past verse 36.

By this point (v. 36), a transition has been made that now describes someone wholly different and unconnected with Antiochus.

This particular genre of a "type" that we see with Antiochus IV and the Antichrist, where there is a complete divergence from the first individual, can also be seen in Ezekiel 28, where the first part of the chapter seems to be talking of an earthly king, the King of Tyre.

Then there is a point where the actions of both the King of Tyre and Satan seem to overlap for a moment, and by the time we get to verse 12 of Ezekiel 28, it becomes clear that Satan is only individual in view, and the King of Tyre has absolutely nothing to do with what follows.

For example, the King of Tyre was not in the "Garden of Eden", nor was he a "covering cherub" in the "mountain of God." A change was made and the inspiration for that change is dismissed, never to be returned to. A similar pattern for this kind of type can be seen in Isaiah 14 about the King and Prince of Babylon.

In the Ezekiel example, we wouldn't expect the fact that the King of Tyre was the inspiration for the section about Satan to mean that Satan really was the King of Tyre and that he lived in Lebanon, or that Satan or the Antichrist would be from Tyre in Lebanon. It would be applying this type in a way that scripture never intended.

In Richardson's view, since Antiochus was from the Seleucid Empire, the Antichrist must also be, because that was the historical person that the type grew out of in this chapter. But what would prevent a person then from saying that the Antichrist is from all the places that the various biblical types of the Antichrist are from? Surely we wouldn't do that, as we would have several contradictory origins of the Antichrist.

Richardson believes that his two king view fits the theory that the Antichrist will be a Muslim, but even if we assumed the two king view, then we still have to deal with the fact of the Antichrist conquering Egypt, a decidedly Muslim country, as well as chasing after, and clearly intending to destroy all the Muslim communities surrounding Israel (v.41), as well as Libya. In Richardson's book, it was not explained why his Muslim Antichrist will be so hostile to the Muslim world. Either the two or three king views would seem to me to be an incompatible belief with the idea of a Muslim Antichrist.

I will sum up by saying that although I, like a majority of evangelical expositors, hold to the three king view and will continue this exposition with that in mind, I will say that both views are technically possible based on the grammar, and it is difficult to be too dogmatic about this for that reason.

The main difference in terms of what to watch for on the geopolitical stage would boil down to the following:

If the two king theory is true, we are looking for a war where Egypt and its allies attack a northern coalition of Arab states, including Syria, and Syria and its allies absolutely destroy Egypt and take all of its wealth and power, as well as the countries to Egypt's west and south, like the Sudan and Libya.

If the three king theory is true, not only will the Antichrist attack Egypt and its neighbors after first being attacked by them, he will, in addition, also conquer a coalition of northern Arab countries, including Syria after first being attacked by them.

It appears that the first wars of the Antichrist are defensive in nature. I suspect they have been provoked by the Antichrist in some way so that he can make himself look like the deliverer of Israel from their enemies, an attempt to look like the Biblical Messiah. Whatever the case, it is clear that during these two conflicts, the Antichrist does not strike first.

Like a whirlwind, with chariots, horsemen, and with many ships; and he shall enter the countries, overwhelm them, and pass through.

These attacks from his enemies will be repelled by the Antichrist and he will use tremendous force and superior materials to overwhelm them.

Dan 11:41 He shall also enter the Glorious Land, and many countries shall be overthrown; but these shall escape from his hand: Edom, Moab, and the prominent people of Ammon.

Here we see that the Antichrist will enter Israel (the **Glorious Land**) and **many countries shall be overthrown**. It is interesting to note here that there is no direct language that allows us to assume that the Antichrist intends to destroy or attack the Jewish people here. In fact, I would submit that the only groups that we can be sure he is attacking once he reaches Israel are Israel's Arab neighbors.

One possible scenario is that he wants to appear to Israel as a deliverer of their enemies. Though this is not at all clear and it can also be seen as the moment just before the eschatological sacking of Israel (Rev: 17:16, Luke 21:20), perhaps there is even room for both of them to be true.

But these shall escape from his hand: Edom, Moab, and the prominent people of Ammon.

Notice that it says "but these shall **escape** from his hand". This means that the Antichrist will not want to let these nations go, but in his attempt to **overthrow** countries in this region, these three will escape his grasp.

This is interesting because these three nations now constitute modern-day Jordan, Israel's Arab neighbor to the southeast. I emphasize this point because so often commentators assume that these countries will somehow be allied with the Antichrist. This is especially promulgated by those who think the Antichrist will be a Muslim. But we can see that these countries will run from a pursuing Antichrist, certainly not the actions of allies.

Based on the text so far, it is a very possible scenario that the Antichrist will enter Israel looking to destroy only Arab nations. I say this not as a dogmatic statement, because it could be true that he will also seek to destroy Jewish cities, but I say it because the text only mentions that he will destroy Muslim nations and cities.

Dan 11:42 He shall stretch out his hand against the countries, and the land of Egypt shall not escape.

He shall stretch out his hand against the countries

This word for "the countries" is very general and could mean the land or the earth. It seems that, on a very general level, we are to know that after the Antichrist enters Israel, he will have more victories. It singles out **Egypt** as one country that **will not escape** his grasp.

Dan 11:43 He shall have power over the treasures of gold and silver, and over all the precious things of Egypt; also the Libyans and Ethiopians shall follow at his heels.

The **power over the treasures of gold and silver, and over all the precious things** seems to be referring to Egypt's wealth particularly. This presumably happens after his conquest of them.

The Libyans and Ethiopians shall follow at his heels.

These two countries have represented Egypt's southern allies in other places in scripture (Eze 30:5; Nah 3:9).

Follow at his heels

The NET Bible translates this "will submit to him."

Dan 11:44 But news from the east and the north shall trouble him; therefore he shall go out with great fury to destroy and annihilate many.

It is difficult to make any assertions about the specific locations being referred to by the terms **east** and **north** here.

It seems reasonably certain that these are two new locations that have not yet played any role in the back-and-forth saga of chapter 11. The mention of the "east" is an entirely new idea in this chapter.
Though many expositors assume these two new threats to the Antichrist are countries that are some distance away (such a Russian and China), it should be noted that the text could just as easily be referring to a very near threat to his location (Israel) which just happens to be to his east and north.

One thing that seems certain is that whatever news **troubles** him will cause him to go attack and overcome these new threats.

This then is a pattern of the Antichrist's conquests in this chapter. He seems to be an enemy to the region. Many nations will plot against him. In the case of the kings of the North and the South, they will both attack him first, and then he will destroy them. In this case, though we are not told what the news from the north and east is, it can be assumed to a degree that this news is of a military threat to him of some sort.

We must conclude that the Antichrist will be quite hated before the midpoint by at least some groups. If this chapter is any indication, then those groups will be Muslim, This is true whether one holds to the two or three king theory.

Dan 11:45 And he shall plant the tents of his palace between the seas and the glorious holy mountain; yet he shall come to his end, and no one will help him.

Tents of his palace

This is an odd word for palace used only here in scripture. The NET has "royal tents".

Between the seas and the glorious holy mountain

This seems to be a reference to Jerusalem, as we know that the glorious holy mountain is Mt Zion, and the seas refer to the Mediterranean Sea. This would also make sense in context because we see in the next verse (though it is separated by an artificial chapter break) that this is when the Antichrist sits in the temple of Jerusalem, declaring himself to be God.

Yet he shall come to his end, and no one will help him.

Because this phrase, which forecasts the Antichrist's destruction, is placed at the end of this chapter, it tempts the reader to think that the Antichrist will come to his end just as he reaches Jerusalem. This conjures up images of Gog and Magog in many people's minds, the Antichrist attempting to take Jerusalem, but miraculously being defeated by God.

Such an interpretation of this verse would be wrong. This can easily be demonstrated by reading the next verse (12:1):

> At that time Michael shall stand up, The great prince
> who stands watch over the sons of your people; And
> there shall be a time of trouble, Such as never was since
> there was a nation, Even to that time… - Dan 12:1

The time spoken of is unambiguously talking of the Antichrist
setting up his royal tents in Jerusalem. This is significant because
it then uses the same language that Jesus uses in Matthew 24 to
refer to the time just after the abomination of desolation called
The Great Tribulation. In other words, there are at least 3.5 more
years of the Antichrist after he sets up his royal tents.

The mentioning of his **end** coming is not unlike other occasions
where the Antichrist is mentioned, while adding a declaration of
his ultimate destruction.

Take for example 2: Thessalonians 2:8. When Paul introduces
the Antichrist, he does so in this way:

> And then the lawless one will be revealed, whom the
> Lord will consume with the breath of His mouth and
> destroy with the brightness of His coming. - 2Th 2:8

Paul goes onto talk at length about the lawless one, but his
introduction here also includes a reference to his end, much like
Daniel does in 11:45.

Another possibility is that this could mean that when the
Antichrist "comes to his end" that his "end" in 11:45 could be a
reference to his being killed and seemingly resurrected (Rev 13:
3, 12,14), which would fit nicely in the chronology if the next
event is the abomination of desolation.

In other words, the Antichrist's apparent resurrection may come
in Jerusalem just before he declares himself to be God in the
temple and thus begins the Great Tribulation, just after he fights
the wars detailed in 40-45.

Chapter 12

Dan 12:1 "At that time Michael shall stand up, The great prince who stands watch over the sons of your people; And there shall be a time of trouble, Such as never was since there was a nation, Even to that time. And at that time your people shall be delivered, Every one who is found written in the book.

At that time

This phrase connects us back to the events of the previous chapter. Namely a time when the Antichrist is making war on Egypt and the king of the North, as well as his arrival in Jerusalem. It may even be said that the following event occurs just after those events. Based on some other factors which we will soon see, it appears that "that time" might specifically refer to the mid-point of Daniel's 70th week. The time of the "abomination of desolation" spoken of by Jesus in Matthew 24:15, and Paul in 2 Thessalonians 2:4.

Michael shall stand up, The great prince who stands watch over the sons of your people

Michael the archangel, as he is called in Jude 9, seems to be in view here. God has apparently assigned Michael to **watch over** Israel.

Michael is an angel with great power In fact, he seems to be put opposite of Satan in a fight in a number of instances in scripture, at least one of which he obviously wins (Jude 1:9, Revelation 12:7-9).

David Guzik makes the remark that some think that God and Satan are opposites, but a much more theologically correct view would be saying that Michael the archangel and Satan are opposites.

So what does Michael "**standing up**" have to do with the Great Tribulation?

Many see this verse as a reference to Michael standing up, in the sense of getting ready to defend Israel during the "**time of trouble**" that immediately follows this phrase. But this is a problematic interpretation. One reason is because if that is his mission, to protect them, then he fails at it.

This time is linked to the same period described by Jesus in Matthew 24: 15-22. If this is the case, then the very moment that Michael tries to protect them, he loses more of them than ever before in history. Such a conclusion is unlikely to be true.

Contextually, it would appear more likely that Michael's "standing up" is what allows the "time of trouble" to begin.

Colin Nicholl, in his paper *Michael, The Restrainer Removed*, points out that the term used here for "standing up" was understood by Jewish commentators like Rashi to mean to "stand still" or to move aside to allow the time of trouble to happen to the Jewish people. Nicholl points out that Hebrew term for stand is very often used in scripture to refer to inaction, in direct contrast to action, (i.e. to stand still) (Josh. 10:13; Hab. 3:11; 1 Sam. 9:27; 2 Sam. 2:28; Nah. 2:9 and 2 Kgs. 4:6) or to refer to inactivity (2 Chr. 20:17), or to describe the cessation of an action (2 Kgs. 13:18; cf. Gen. 29:35; 30:9; Josh. 1:15) or to mean 'stand silent' (Job 32:16).

He also points out that the term, by the time of the Apostle Paul, was frequently used in a figurative sense, meaning 'to disappear' or 'to pass away'.

These and a great many other things he details in his paper lead him to the view that Michael is the restrainer of 2 Thessalonians 2.

This would of course make a huge amount of sense, as in that passage we see that the abomination of desolation is being held back only by the restrainer ceasing to restrain, which is exactly what we would have here. The Great Tribulation, which begins at the abomination of desolation, is here said to be contingent upon the inaction of Michael. It is an almost certain conclusion that this passage is where Paul gets this idea, after of course being directed by the Lord to study the same passage in Matthew 24:15.

For our purposes, it is only important to note his conclusion about our verse in Daniel 12a, namely that the "standing" that Michael does represents a ceasing to protect Israel at the midpoint, thus allowing the Antichrist to commit the abomination of desolation and begin the "time of trouble" that follows it.

And there shall be a time of trouble, Such as never was since there was a nation, Even to that time. And at that time your people shall be delivered, Every one who is found written in the book.

Jesus makes reference to this **time or trouble,** which will be unparalleled in the history in Matthew 24: 15-22. Even the word "tribulation" in Greek that Jesus uses in Matthew 24:21 (thilipsis) is the same word that was used in the LXX to render the Hebrew "trouble" in Daniel 12:1.

In addition, the Lord brings up this point of the Great Tribulation in Matthew 24:21 in an effort to answer the disciple's question (24:3) about when the resurrection or parousia would occur. It is therefore no surprise that this is the section in Daniel that Jesus points his hearers to in Matthew 24:15, as it's the one in which Daniel gives us the clearest depiction of the Rapture in the Old Testament, which we will cover in the next two verses.

Dan 12:2 And many of those who sleep in the dust of the earth shall awake, Some to everlasting life, Some to shame and everlasting contempt.

Here we see a picture of the resurrection of the dead. We know it as the Rapture. This is when the dead in Christ will rise first, and those who are alive and remain on the earth at that time will be caught up to heaven to be with Jesus just before the wrath of God begins on the ungodly (1 Thes 4:15-17).

Daniel tells us that there is another kind of resurrection as well. He tells us that there will be a resurrection of the unjust or wicked dead in addition to the righteous dead. We are given more information about the resurrection of the unjust in Revelation 20, in which we find out that this resurrection happens at the close of the millennial reign (Rev 20: 7-15).

They are judged and sentenced according to their works to the lake of fire.

It seems that everyone will be resurrected. The only question is if that resurrection will be to **everlasting life** or **to shame and everlasting contempt.**

Dan 12:3 Those who are wise shall shine Like the brightness of the firmament, And those who turn many to righteousness Like the stars forever and ever.

Here the reward of the righteous dead is depicted as a shining.

Jesus perhaps had this verse in mind when he said:

> "the righteous will shine like the sun in the kingdom of their Father" (Matt 13:43).

Forever and ever

Though the reward here (shining) is probably partly or totally allegorical, this idea of an everlasting or eternal state is a consistent theme. Heaven is an eternal state.

310

Dan 12:4 "But you, Daniel, shut up the words, and seal the book until the time of the end; many shall run to and fro, and knowledge shall increase."

This verse marks an end to the vision. Now the angel will give some final instructions to Daniel, as well as a few additional details about it.

Shut up the words, and seal the book until the time of the end

Steven Miller argues against the widely held belief that this idea of "sealing" the book does not mean to make them unable to be understood until the time of the end, but rather that he is telling him to properly store them so that they would be preserved for future generations.

I think that there are good arguments for and against this view.

I would argue that there would be very little that Daniel himself could do in order to make his writings unable to be understood until the time of the end, unless he knew of a way to encode them in such a way that only could be deciphered by the last generation, an idea that seems farfetched. This is because the things that he described were things he saw and heard Therefore, the visions had to have been already "sealed" divinely before they were conveyed to Daniel, an idea that we will see later has merit.

This then would make the angel's charge to him to **seal up the book until the time of the end** more of a rhetorical device, as that would be an act for a divine being to do.

The arguments for this being about a "sealing up" that renders the meaning wholly or partially un-decipherable can be found in the consistent way that the angel speaks of this "sealing" in relationship to the content of the message being understood.

For example, in this verse, he goes on to connect the idea that **knowledge shall increase** to the "sealing" up of the book, suggesting perhaps that in the last times, there would be sufficient knowledge to understand it. Later, in verses 8 and 9, we see something that gives the idea more credibility.

> <u>Although I heard, I did not understand.</u> Then I said, "My lord, what shall be the end of these things?" And he said, "Go your way, Daniel, <u>for the words are closed up and sealed till the time of the end.</u> - Dan 12:8-9

Daniel, after hearing a kind of angelic conversation about an interpretation of the vision he just saw, said he heard it, but could not understand it. The angel's response to Daniel seems to be reiterating that the vision can't be understood because it has been sealed until the time of the end.

This not only connects the sealing to a lack of understanding once again, but it also shows that even at this time, the vision was sealed, that is, before Daniel had obviously written anything down about it or had a chance to encode or store it, as the other two options would have it.

This makes a very strong case that the angel asking Daniel to seal it was unnecessary, as the vision itself was delivered already spiritually sealed, if you will.

Many shall run to and fro, and knowledge shall increase.

It seems possible that this is a reference to Amos 8:12, which says:

> They shall wander from sea to sea, And from north to east; <u>They shall run to and fro, seeking the word of the LORD,</u> But shall not find it.

In context, this is speaking of a time of spiritual famine in Israel, when there would be a desire to have revelation from God through the prophets, but they did not find it, and though in the case of this verse they were unsuccessful, the text in Daniel seems to imply that the running **to and fro** in the last days, seeking the Word of the Lord, will in fact be successful.

It should be noted that the last days referred to here could be said to have begun during the first century (Acts 2:16-17) and that Jesus's revelation in the NT about this prophecy in Daniel, and well as many other prophecies in the OT, could be the key to understanding them.

In other words, Daniel needed to wait for the revelation of Jesus Christ in order for his messages to be understood, but it's technically possible for his messages to be understood by anyone today, as we are beneficiaries of the writings in the NT. This view then would be opposed to the idea that we are still waiting for the ability to properly understand these verses, though that could be argued as well.

Dan 12:5 Then I, Daniel, looked; and there stood two others, one on this riverbank and the other on that riverbank.
Dan 12:6 And one said to the man clothed in linen, who was above the waters of the river, "How long shall the fulfillment of these wonders be?"

Daniel then heard two angels calling to one another, one on each bank of the river.

There is a lot of discussion and belief that angel in **linen** is Christ. However, I remain unconvinced, as there is no reason I can see to distinguish any of the angels here from a so-called "strong angel", which seems to be a certain class of angels who, among other things, wear linen, which I discussed at length in the section on Daniel 10: 4-6.

Dan 12:7 Then I heard the man clothed in linen, who was above the waters of the river, when he held up his right hand and his left hand to heaven, and swore by Him who lives forever, that it shall be for a time, times, and half a time; and when the power of the holy people has been completely shattered, all these things shall be finished.

The man clothed in linen

As in other occasions, such as Daniel 10, the angel is referred to as a man because it appears in human form. See the discussion on Daniel 10, and how Gabriel is referred to as a man, and later as an angel.

Who was above the waters of the river, when he held up his right hand and his left hand to heaven, and swore by Him who lives forever

This oath on the water is almost identical to an oath taken by an angel in the book of Revelation. There it is clearly called an angel.

> The angel whom I saw standing on the sea and on the land raised up his hand to heaven and swore by Him who lives forever and ever, who created heaven and the things that are in it, the earth and the things that are in it, and the sea and the things that are in it, that there should be delay no longer - Rev 10:5-6

For a time, times, and half a time

This is a reference to the three-and-a-half-year period which begins after the abomination of desolation. This period begins at the midpoint of Daniel's 70th week.

Although the idea of 3.5 years is expressed many ways in Daniel and the book of Revelation, one such verse (Revelation 12:14) actually uses the same phrase: "time, times and a half of time." There we can confirm that it is a reference to 3.5 years because in the same chapter (Rev 12:6), the time period is given as 1260 days, i.e. 3.5 years.

When the power of the holy people has been completely shattered, all these things shall be finished.

Many Bible versions give the impression that the **finishing** of **all these things** is contingent on **the power of the holy people being completely shattered**, but this conclusion would be wrong.

314

The NET Bible renders the phrase this way:

> "It is for a time, times, and half a time. Then, when the power of the one who shatters the holy people has been exhausted, all these things will be finished."

This seems to reverse the meaning. It is saying that the 3.5 years is based on the exhausting of the power of the Antichrist, not the power of the people he "shatters."

While the NET makes this case based on a linguistic argument,[54] it also enjoys some scriptural support.

> And he [Antichrist] was given a mouth speaking great things and blasphemies, and he was given authority [power] to continue for forty-two months. - Rev 13:5

Here we are told that the Antichrist is given "authority" for 42 months or 3.5 years.
We can see that the 3.5 years will come to a conclusion, not because of anything that the people or the Antichrist do, but rather because that is the time allotted to him by God. When that authority is exhausted, God will **finish** him.

So that is the meaning of the phrase "when the power of the one who shatters the holy people has been exhausted, all these things will be finished.""

Dan 12:8 Although I heard, I did not understand. Then I said, "My lord, what shall be the end of these things?"
Dan 12:9 And he said, "Go your way, Daniel, for the words are closed up and sealed till the time of the end.

As mentioned in the discussion on verse 9, this is an argument in favor of the **sealing** having to do with making the prophecy difficult, if not impossible, to understand until the time of the end, though that time could potentially be seen as any time after the 1st century.

Dan 12:10 Many shall be purified, made white, and refined, but the wicked shall do wickedly; and none of the wicked shall understand, but the wise shall understand.

Here we see what this persecution of the saints is for, that is spiritual purification. This is why the so-called 5th seal martyrs in Revelation 6 were told by God to be patient regarding God beginning his vengeance on the persecutors of the Great Tribulation, because God intended more of them to be killed, as their persecution was a prerequisite to His judgment.

The idea of the Great Tribulation having purification as one of its functions is mentioned in several places (Rev 7:13-14, Dan 11:35, and others).

It is true that Christians in a salvific sense are already purified because they are 100 percent righteous in Christ. However, this purification is twofold. On one hand, it is a purification of the Jews (Zec_13:9) in a time that Jeremiah calls the "time of Jacob's trouble."

The other purification will likely come about in the sense that the Antichrist's ultimatum to worship him or be killed will separate the true believers from those who are not truly saved.

Dan 12:11 "And from the time that the daily sacrifice is taken away, and the abomination of desolation is set up, there shall be one thousand two hundred and ninety days. Dan 12:12 Blessed is he who waits, and comes to the one thousand three hundred and thirty-five days.

The angel tells us that the "end of these things" mentioned in verse 8 will be 3.5 years after the mid-point of Daniel's 70th week plus 30 days. He then tells us that blessed is he who waits 45 more days after that.

We find that there are two additional and distinct periods of time after the seven-year-long "70th week" ends. They are a 30 day period and a 45 day period.

Dr. Elbert Charpie has a great study of these two periods on his website[55], and his view is virtually the same as Robert Van Kampen's and Marvin Rosenthal's on this point. Charpie states:

> "The 30 day portion can be classified as The Reclamation Period, and the 45 day portion can be called The Restoration Period. These names are chosen to clarify the things that will happen during each specific period."

I will give a list of some of the things we can know about what happens in the first 30 day period, but again if you want to know the details of why we know this I suggest you visit his website, prewrathministries.com, and look for the section on the 30 and 45 day periods.

- Two witnesses killed (Rev 11:7-8)
- All Israel saved (Rom 11:25-26, Rev 10:7, Hosea 6:1-3, Micah 2:12-13)
- The Journey to from Edom and Bozra to Jerusalem by Christ with the wilderness Jews (Isaiah 63:1-4, Hosea 11:10-11, Isaiah 14:1, Zec 12:10, Rev 11:10-11, Exodus 19:10-11, Obadiah 1:21, Rev 11:15, Rev 14:7, Rev 14:19-20, Rev 15:1, Zechariah 14:4-5, Isaiah 26:20-21, Rev 16:1)
- The Seventh Trumpet and the Bowl Judgments (Revelation 16:1-21)

This means that Armageddon takes place not at the last day of the 70th week, but on the last day of this 30 day reclamation period.

The 30 day period ends up looking like this:

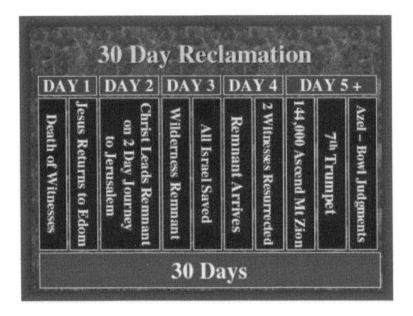

After the last bowl, there will be a need for restoration. Dr. Charpie notes:

> "The seventh bowl symbolizes total devastation. The earth will suffer a catastrophe as never before. It is described as an earthquake more severe than has ever happened before. The cities of the nation's collapse and mountains and islands can no longer be found."

There will be a 45 day period as well. The things that happen during this time all have the sense of a preparation for the millennial kingdom. This is why it has been dubbed the Restoration period.

Here are some things that are said to happen during this time:

- The Restoration of Mt. Zion (Zechariah 14:10, Isaiah 2:2, Ezekiel 20:40)
- The Restoration of Israel (Jeremiah 31:10-12, Isaiah 10:20-22, Isaiah 43:5-7, Micah 7:7-9, Isaiah 56:6-8)

- The Restoration of the Temple (Ezekiel 43:6-7, Zechariah 6:12-13)
- Christ to rule over the earth (Daniel 7:11,13-14)

Here is an image from Dr. Charpie's website that will help to make sense of this timeline:

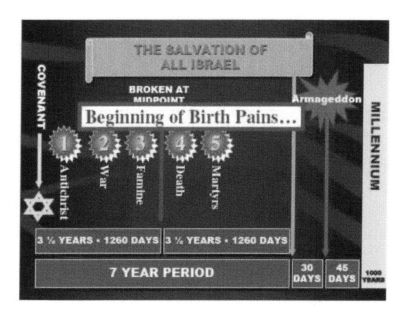

It is interesting to note that these 30 day and 45 day periods have a very interesting connection to the fall feasts which have yet to be fulfilled. But that subject is out of the scope of this commentary.

Dan 12:13 "But you, go your way till the end; for you shall rest, and will arise to your inheritance at the end of the days.

What a wonderful end to this book. This could be a "life verse" for someone. Despite all that is coming, we should go our way, looking for our heavenly inheritance, in the end of days. We will all see this time, whether we, like Daniel, will be resurrected at the Rapture, or if we are alive and remain, having gone through the difficult times that precede it.

This sentiment is mirrored precisely by Paul in a statement that we should all strive to be able to say when it is our time to die:

> For I am already being poured out as a drink offering, and the time of my departure is at hand. I have fought the good fight, I have finished the race, I have kept the faith. Finally, there is laid up for me the crown of righteousness, which the Lord, the righteous Judge, will give to me on that Day, and not to me only but also to all who have loved His appearing. - 2Ti 4:6-8

---

[1] Miller, Stephen B. (1994-08-31). The New American Commentary Volume 18 - Daniel (p. 74). B&H Publishing. Kindle Edition.

[2] Miller, (p. 81). B&H.

[3] The KJV Old Testament Hebrew Lexicon

[4] Driver proposes that the image was in the likeness of Nebuchadnezzar himself and was a monument to his achievements,25 but worship of a deity is clearly involved in this command to bow before the statue (cf. 3:28). In some ancient cultures the king was considered divine, but this was not the case in the Babylonian Empire.26 More plausible is Wiseman's proposal that the image was in the likeness of one of Babylon's gods, probably the principal god, Marduk.27 - Miller, Stephen B. (1994-08-31). The New American Commentary Volume 18 - Daniel (p. 112). B&H Publishing. Kindle Edition.

[5] http://en.wikipedia.org/wiki/Backdraft

[6] 5W. H. Shea, "Daniel 3: Extra-Biblical Texts and the Convocation of the Plain of Dura," AUSS 20 (1982): 37–50. A. L. Oppenheim's English translation of the Babylonian text may be found in ANET, 307–8.

[7] 52G. A. Larue, Babylon and the Bible (Grand Rapids: Eerdmans, 1969), 57–58. Cf. Wiseman, "Babylon," ZPEB.
Miller, Stephen B. (1994-08-31). The New American Commentary Volume 18 - Daniel (p. 170). B&H Publishing. Kindle Edition.

[8] This queen was not Belshazzar's wife, for as Young observes: "The text explicitly states that the wives of the king were already present."[67] Yet she must have been a highly prestigious individual to enter the banquet hall uninvited, and when she arrived, she seemed to take charge. For these reasons most commentators since the time of Josephus[68] (first century A.D.) have identified her as the queen-mother, either the wife of Nebuchadnezzar or the wife of Nabonidus.[69] If the

wife of Nebuchadnezzar,[70] she probably was the grandmother of Belshazzar,[71] unless Leupold is correct in suggesting that Nabonidus married a widow of Nebuchadnezzar with a child (Belshazzar) by the former king whom Nabonidus adopted as his own.[72] In this case Nebuchadnezzar's widow (and Nabonidus' wife) would have been Belshazzar's mother. Most likely she was the wife of Nabonidus, and a daughter, not a widow, of Nebuchadnezzar. If so, she may have been the famous Nitocris.[73] At any rate, this woman displayed firsthand information concerning the affairs of Nebuchadnezzar that would not have been known by a younger wife of Belshazzar, and she seems to have observed Daniel's ministry in Nebuchadnezzar's court. (Miller, 1994-08-31, pp. 159-160)

[9] Miller, (pp. 185-186).

[10] Miller, (p. 186).

[11] Miller, (p. 195).

[12] http://christiananswers.net/dictionary/eagle.html

[13] Miller, (p. 206).

[14] Miller, (p. 222).

[15] Miller (p. 198)

[16] Jamieson, R., Fausset, A. R., & Brown, D. (1997). *Commentary Critical and Explanatory on the Whole Bible* (Da 8:4). Oak Harbor, WA: Logos Research Systems, Inc.

[17] Cited quote as per media (documentary piece) titled "Engineering an Empire – The Persians". *History Channel*. Release date: December 4, 2006. Media available for viewing online via history.com or via Google Video. Host: Peter Weller. Production: United States.

[18] Miller, (p. 236)

[19] Miller, (p. 291).

[20] Miller, (pp. 250-251).

[21] http://www.ligonier.org/learn/devotionals/atoning-iniquity/

[22] http://www.pickle-publishing.com/papers/harold-hoehner-70-weeks.htm#4imp

[23] Nehemiah 6:15 indicates that he finished the work on the 25th day of Elul, it also indicates it took 52 days to complete. Which means it began 3rd day of the month of AV. Nehemiah reports he was in Jerusalem 3 days Then he "arose in the night" [Neh 2:11] Nehemiah must have arose on the night before the third day of the month of AV. And if the month of AV has 30 days then he arrived in Jerusalem on the 28th day of Tammuz. – Charles Cooper

[24] Biblical Studies Press. (2006). *The NET Bible First Edition; Bible. English. NET Bible.; The NET Bible*. Biblical Studies Press.

[25] Ibid.

[26] Miller, (p. 267).

[27] Ibid.

[28] http://www.shalach.org/Antichrist/DAN-HE.htm

[29] http://pulpit.biblecommenter.com/daniel/9.htm

[30] http://www.khouse.org/articles/2003/479/

[31] Miller, (p. 279).

[32] Miller, (p. 289).

[33] Dr. J. Paul Tanner, *Historical Developments in Daniel 11*, Pg 2

[34] http://bibleapps.com/clarke/daniel/11.htm

[35] http://paultanner.org/English%20Docs/Daniel/Outline%20Notes/Dan%2011_Bib%20Text%20and%20Notes_J%20P%20Tanner_1st%20ed.pdf

[36] Miller, (p. 299).

[37] Miller, (pp. 299-300).

[38]

http://paultanner.org/English%20Docs/Daniel/Commentary/Dan%20Comm%20for%20BEE%20-%20Ver%201.4.pdf

[39] Miller, (p. 328).

[40] Miller, (p. 302).

[41] Miller, (p. 305).

[42] . Vol. 35: Journal of the Evangelical Theological Society (JETS) Volume 35. 1992 (3) (317). Lynchburg, VA: The Evangelical Theological Society.

[43] Miller, Daniel (p. 305)

[44] . Vol. 35: Journal of the Evangelical Theological Society Volume 35. 1992 (3) (317). Lynchburg, VA: The Evangelical Theological Society. . Vol. 35: Journal of the Evangelical Theological Society Volume 35. 1992 (3) (317). Lynchburg, VA: The Evangelical Theological Society.

[46]

http://www.raptureready.com/featured/ice/TheEthnicityofTheAntichrist.html

[47] http://www.sitchiniswrong.com/dc101elohim.pdf

[48] *Vol. 35*: *Journal of the Evangelical Theological Society Volume 35*. 1992 (3) (319). Lynchburg, VA: The Evangelical Theological Society.

[49] *Vol. 35*: *Journal of the Evangelical Theological Society Volume 35*. 1992 (3) (319). Lynchburg, VA: The Evangelical Theological Society.

[50] Vol. 35: Journal of the Evangelical Theological Society Volume 35. 1992 (3) (317). Lynchburg, VA: The Evangelical Theological Society.

[51] Observations on Daniel 11:40 - Two Kings or Three? - Dr. J. Paul Tanner

[52] Richardson, Joel (2012-06-08). Mideast Beast: The Scriptural Case for an Islamic Antichrist (p. 121). Joel Richardson. Kindle Edition.

[53] http://www.joelstrumpet.com/?p=4645

[54] **tc** The present translation reads יַד־נֹפֵץ (*yad-nofets*, "hand of one who shatters") rather than the MT נַפֵּץ־יַד (*nappets-yad*, "to shatter the hand").[54]

[55] http://prewrathministries.com

Manufactured by Amazon.ca
Bolton, ON

12323085R00179